William Tryon
and the
Course of Empire

William Tryon, by J. Wollaston. This oil portrait, inscribed on the back, "Govr. Wm. Tryon of No. Carolina—J. Wollaston, pinxt. New York—Anno D. 1767," hangs in Tryon Palace, New Bern, North Carolina. There is some doubt about the identity of the portrait's subject. If the portrait is of Tryon, it is the only known likeness of him. (Courtesy of the North Carolina Division of Archives and History)

PAUL DAVID NELSON

William Tryon
and the
Course of Empire

A Life in British Imperial Service

The University of North Carolina Press

Chapel Hill and London

Publication of this work was assisted by a grant from the
Kellenberger Historical Foundation.

The paper in this book meets the guidelines for permanence and
durability of the Committee on Production Guidelines for
Book Longevity of the Council on Library Resources.

Design by April Leidig-Higgins

94 93 92 91 90   5 4 3 2 1

Library of Congress Cataloging-in-Publication Data

Nelson, Paul David, 1941—
  William Tryon and the course of empire : a life in British
imperial service / by Paul David Nelson.
    p. cm.
  Includes bibliographical references.
  ISBN 0-8078-1917-4 (alk. paper)
    1. Tryon, William, 1729–1788. 2. North Carolina—Governors—
Biography. 3. New York (State)—Governors—Biography. 4. Colonial
administrators—Great Britain—Biography. 5. North Carolina—
History—Colonial period, ca. 1600–1775. 6. New York (State)—
History—Colonial period, ca. 1600–1775. 7. North Carolina—
History—Regulator Insurrection, 1766–1771. I. Title.
F257.T79N45 1990
975.6'02'092—dc20
[B]   90-11998
                                                            CIP

For my students,
past and present

Contents

viii   *Contents*

Illustrations

Preface

William Tryon, British army officer and royal governor of North Carolina and New York in the years preceding the American Revolution, was an important participant in the events leading to England's loss of her thirteen mainland colonies to republican revolutionaries. His life history is interesting in and of itself, but it also highlights larger scholarly issues that have engaged many historians of the Revolutionary era in recent years. First, his career as a faithful and talented supporter of Crown prerogatives during the 1760s and 1770s is a useful case study of British administrative ineptitude that supplements other works covering the same topic. Although Tryon shrewdly warned officials in London that it was impossible for Britain to maintain peaceful control over America if ministers and monarch refused to make timely concessions on questions of direct taxation, his admonitions went unheeded. Second, his activities as a major general in the British army during the American war speak to the importance of the work of insightful military historians, members of a growing group of Revolutionary War scholars who divide British officers, in their prosecution of the war against the rebels, into hard-liners (like Tryon) and conciliators. Third, his fellow feeling with Loyalists, who like him supported the lost cause of empire, places his life's story in the body of literature that deals with those unhappy people.

Given Tryon's importance, it is rather surprising that there has been no full-scale analysis of his career prior to this one. Certainly a biography is badly needed. But if historians have not looked at his life as a whole, they have shown interest in different aspects of it. Considerable attention has been paid to Tryon's years as governor of North Carolina, beginning with Marshall DeLancey Haywood's *Governor William Tryon and His Administration in the Province of North Carolina, 1765–1771*, published in

1903. Over the years, Haywood's work has been supplemented, and sometimes supplanted, by a number of books and masters theses (plus articles in the *North Carolina Historical Review*) on topics as diverse as currency and ecclesiastical reform, the Stamp Act crisis, and the Regulator movement. In 1955 Alonzo T. Dill published *Governor Tryon and His Palace*, a readable and scholarly book that discusses Tryon, Tryon Palace, New Bern, and Craven County during the colonial and Revolutionary periods. William S. Powell's introductory essay on Tryon in the first of his two volumes of *The Correspondence of William Tryon* (1980–81) is excellent though necessarily brief. Tryon's gubernatorial administration in New York has received less attention. A Ph.D. dissertation, Solomon Henner's "The Career of William Tryon as Governor of the Province of New York, 1771–1780," completed in 1968, has had to suffice. As for Tryon's military career under Generals William Howe and Henry Clinton, it has received no complete assessment prior to this biography.

The source materials for this book are located in a large number of repositories in Great Britain, Canada, and the United States. Most of the materials consist of official correspondence between Tryon and government officials in London because Tryon's personal letters unfortunately have been lost. A large number were destroyed by a fire in New York in December 1773, and the remainder have disappeared in ways unknown. Although lack of a large collection of private papers necessarily hampers a biographer of Tryon, the man could be extraordinarily revealing in his public letters and has left many clues to his interior life. Moreover, persons near him, especially Councillor William Smith of New York, observed him perspicaciously over a number of years and wrote penetrating assessments of his character, highlighting the inner man. I hope, therefore, that I have been able to present a well-rounded assessment of Tryon's personality.

I want to take this opportunity to thank all the curators and librarians of the numerous archives containing materials on Tryon's life. My debt to them is incalculable. Although a complete listing of these repositories is found in the bibliography, I especially want to express my gratitude to the officers and staffs of those with the largest and most valuable collections of Tryon materials: the British Public Record Office; the William L. Clements Library, University of Michigan; the Houghton Library, Harvard University; and the British Library. Crown-copyright on documents in the Public Record Office is vested in the controller of Her Majesty's Stationery Office. Also, I acknowledge my enormous obligation to William S. Powell, editor of *The Correspondence of William Tryon*, for his contributions to my research. Not only did his two massive volumes of documents on Tryon's career guide me to collections on two continents, but also his careful attention to publishing all relevant papers held by the North Carolina Collection at the University of North Carolina and the North Carolina Division of Archives and History in Raleigh relieved me from having to do research in those important repositories. The value of his collection for me is revealed by the numerous references to it in the notes of my book.

I am particularly grateful to Berea College for its generous financial support for this project. Both Alfred Perkins, academic vice president and dean of the college, and the Professional Growth Committee of the College Faculty, assisted me with the wherewithal to pursue my historical inquiries. Without their financial aid, I would have been unable to make two extremely valuable research trips to Great Britain to examine Tryon papers in the Public Record Office and the British Library. I also appreciate the assistance of the National Endowment for the Humanities, which provided me with a Travel to Collections grant.

Finally, I want to thank John R. Alden for suggesting many years ago that I undertake this project, and Gerald F. Roberts, special collections librarian, and Edith L. Hansen, reference librarian, of Hutchins Library, Berea College, for special assistance in my research. As always, I am indebted to my wife, Rebecca P. Nelson, for her assistance in, and support of, my unconventional life as a historian.

William Tryon
and the
Course of Empire

CHAPTER ONE

English Origins

I n late 1780, Major General William Tryon, formerly British royal governor of North Carolina and New York and at that time an officer in the army of His Majesty, King George III, boarded ship at New York City and sailed for home. After devoting sixteen years of his life to Crown service in America, Tryon had little to show for his tenure—neither personal reward nor enhanced authority for his sovereign. It was true, of course, that he still commanded the respect of many friends and colleagues, and in this he could take comfort. Thomas Jones, a New York Loyalist, still maintained that Tryon was "a gentleman of activity, whose honesty, honor, sincerity, and probity" were beyond suspicion, that his "word was sacred and as binding as his obligation," and that he "was beloved, esteemed . . . kind, charitable, humane, and benevolent." Also, the Reverend Charles Inglis, rector of Trinity Church in New York, continued to believe, as he had in 1771, that Tryon was "a Gentleman of excellent Sense," who lived a life "most exemplary" and who was "a warm Friend to Religion."[1]

Yet the controversial Tryon had many detractors, both within the rebel ranks and among the king's friends. An American, Lewis Morris, Jr., denounced him as a "fawning, treacherous Courtier." A Loyalist minister, the Reverend John Vardill, asserted with equal spleen that Tryon, "tho a Gentleman of Integrity & Fortitude," was "made by his *Vanity* a dupe to every flattering Imposter."[2] Tryon's own assessment of his service was that he had done his best under almost impossible circumstances. Now, in 1780, tired and sick, he anxiously anticipated reunion with his family and friends and the approbation of the monarch he had served with such unstinting devotion. In these expectations he was not to be disappointed, and as he was a man of essentially optimistic outlook, once he was home he did not, like many other British officials and Loyalists in similar circumstances, waste much time in bitter retrospection or in torturing himself with might-have-beens. Instead he spent his hours happily with his wife and compatriots, reflecting upon his long, active, often productive, sometimes exciting career, living in ease on income derived from a fortune that his wife had brought to their marriage.

William Tryon was born on June 8, 1729, at his family's seat, Norbury Park, in Surrey, England. His ancestry was distinguished. Although members of the Tryon family had lived in England since the Norman invasion, he was quite likely a descendant of Peter Tryon (or Trieon), a wealthy Flemish refugee who in 1562 had fled the persecution of the duke of Alba with a fortune of £60,000 sterling. In any case, throughout his life William Tryon used as his own the arms and crest that had been granted to Peter Tryon in 1610. The first documented ancestor of William Tryon was Abraham Tryon, who appears in the historical record in 1620 as purchaser of Bulwick Hall, Northampton. In subsequent years Abraham Tryon would be the first of many in his family to maintain a close association with the Church of Bulwick, where various records of the Tryon family are found. The church's annals for October 1679, for instance, note the birth and baptism of Charles Tryon, "Sonne and Heir to James Tryon Esq." This Charles Tryon, the grandfather of William Tryon, later inherited a new Bulwick Hall that had been constructed in 1679, married Jane Savile, and died prematurely at the age of twenty-seven in November 1705.[3]

Before Charles Tryon's death, he and Jane Savile Tryon produced a family heir, Charles, in September 1702. This Charles Tryon, the father of William Tryon, married Lady Mary Shirley on July 3, 1722, in the Bishop of London's Chapel at Fulham. William Tryon's mother, Lady Mary Tryon, was the daughter of Robert Shirley, Earl Ferrers. Through her, William Tryon was descended from Robert Devereux, earl of Essex, a sometime favorite of Elizabeth I, and the royal house of Plantagenet. He was related as well to other prominent Tryons in various parts of England, including Moses Tryon, son of the Huguenot Peter Tryon, a high sheriff of County Harrington in 1624, and William and Thomas Tryon, both West India merchantmen who died in the 1740s. His family records clearly reveal that William Tryon was well born and in an excellent position to use highly placed relatives for advancement. Indeed, during his tenure as a servant of the Crown, he would capitalize upon these advantages to advance professionally and to receive other kinds of highly useful preferment.[4]

Charles Tryon, father of William Tryon, artist unknown. This portrait hangs in the master bedroom of Tryon Palace, New Bern. Charles Tryon was descended from family members dating back to 1066. His wife, William Tryon's mother, was Lady Mary Shirley, daughter of Robert Shirley, Earl Ferrers. (Courtesy of the North Carolina Division of Archives and History)

Before William Tryon was born, his father and mother had departed Bulwick Hall in Northampton and moved to Norbury Park in Surrey. They had already produced three sons, Charles, Robert, and James. After William, their fourth child, was born, they also had three daughters, Mary, Sophia, and Ann. Excepting James, who died in 1733, all of these children lived to adulthood; thus William was surrounded by siblings as he grew to maturity. In later life only two of his brothers and sisters achieved any distinction, and neither achieved as much as he did for his service in America. Robert, the second-born, became rector of the Church of Seaton, in County Rutland, and Mary, the eldest daughter, served for thirty-five years as Queen Charlotte's maid of honor at the Court of St. James's (where she was privy to much court gossip, which she passed on to brother William). Ann Tryon, the youngest member of the family, never married, and while her brother William was governor of North Carolina, she was his guest for a time in that colony. The Tryon women outlived their brothers, usually by a wide margin. Both Charles and Robert Tryon died in their mid-forties, and William reached only the age of fifty-eight. Mary, however, was sixty-four at the time of her death, and Sophia and Ann, the two youngest sisters, were in their seventies before they departed this world.[5]

Surrounded by the splendors of Norbury Park (which he later affectionately called his "Hobby Horse"), Tryon grew to adulthood. His education was not neglected, for by the time he reached maturity he was polished in both intellect and the social graces. Although Councillor William Smith of New York asserted in 1773 that Tryon "had not even a Grammar School Education," nevertheless the man's letters show a well-developed wit, elegance, and ability to produce subtle innuendo, or even "at times a well-turned impertinence." Certainly his parents never intended to mold Tryon into a scholar, but still they put him through a rigorous program of reading in English, French, and Latin classical literature, as well as mathematics, history, science, and philosophy. At an early age he began a lifelong habit of acquiring books, and by the time he reached his forties he had built a collection of 370 titles, containing a total of 800 volumes. Judging from these books, he cultivated interests in poetry, English and French literature, law, military history and theory, engineering, geography, mathematics, ancient and modern history, morality, religion, theology, politics, agriculture, philosophy, navigation, natural science, and chess—to name only the most prominent subjects in his library catalog. He was particularly learned in French, and many of his volumes, especially those on literature, history, and military science, were written in this language. He could also compose in French but overmodestly declared that he possessed no more than an ability to "blunder on" in a language that he knew "imperfectly." Tryon's education, in sum, had equipped him with a wide range of skills, interests, and accomplishments. He was, in the best eighteenth-century sense of the term, a "man of parts."[6]

Whereas Tryon's library reveals much about his education and academic interests, the influences that helped to form Tryon's personality and character remain obscure. No records of his youth survive—his personal papers were destroyed by fire in 1773—and all his subsequent private correspondence has also disappeared. Therefore it is possible to examine his traits of personality only as they appeared in adulthood. Certainly his father, mother, brothers, and sisters were important to him, for whenever he was able, he brought them into his home for visits. Almost everyone who knew Tryon agreed that he was an intelligent and able man with an orderly and sensitive mind. In his dual careers as royal governor and soldier, he was rated more highly as a practitioner of the political arts than of the martial. In 1770 Virginia governor Norbonne Berkeley, Baron de Botetourt, declared to Wills Hill, Viscount Hillsborough, that Tryon was one of the two "very best Governors upon the Continent" (the other being Guy Carleton, governor of Canada). And although Secretary at War William Wildman Barrington, Viscount Barrington, was no great admirer of Tryon's military abilities, he noted of Tryon a year later, in recommending him to General Thomas Gage, that "he is an excellent man." Even Tryon's worst British critics during the American war admitted that while he was not the best of soldiers, he was still "a gentleman of . . . honor . . . [and] of undaunted courage."[7]

Tryon was also polite and tactful, and he used these attributes to gain the confidence of government officials in both England and America. Many of his successes were due to his tactful handling of persons in power rather than the intrinsic merit of his proposals, and often he defused potentially acrimonious situations with colonials or fellow army officers by means of his ability to conciliate and compromise. He was honest in all his dealings, and no one, except disgruntled rebels during the American rebellion, ever charged otherwise. His regard for the Christian religion was a deep fountainhead of action, containing no trace of bigotry, and although he practiced very little day-to-day personal piety, he was strongly motivated in both public and private life by a love for the Anglican church and a respect for dissenting Christian sects. He put great store in loyalty, a virtue that he always manifested in dealing with friends, family, and monarch. Often Americans excoriated Tryon for his determination to execute royal commands, but in doing so they ignored the fact that his first duty was to his king. Had he acted otherwise he would have been rightly accused not only of violating his sacred oath but also of behaving as a sycophant to colonial opinion.[8]

Tryon was a generous and humane man. In 1774 Ann Hulton, a Loyalist lady, noted a typical example of Tryon's spontaneous generosity. When a poor, persecuted tradesman stood up to a mob of "traitors," Tryon rewarded him with a gift of ten guineas. William Smith, a Loyalist friend of Tryon's, remarked in 1786 that the general's generosity proved he was a man of "vertuous Principles." Tryon expressed his humanity in a number of ways, such as granting a reprieve in 1772 to a counterfeiter who was sentenced to death and recommending a year later that the British ministry not execute a convicted murderer who had extenuating circumstances for his deed. During the bitterly cold winter of 1772–73, he provided free firewood to the poor of New York City.[9]

Not all of Tryon's personal characteristics were positive, however. As both soldier and governor, he impressed many of his contemporaries as being overly zealous in protecting his personal dignity. Allowing for the fact that Tryon had to uphold the majesty of the Crown, he nevertheless appeared too vain for many people's taste. An unfriendly Loyalist in New York once described him to an official in England as "the pink of politeness, and the quintessence of vanity. . . . The man is generous, perfectly good natured, and no doubt brave, but weak and vain to an extreme degree. You should keep such people at home; they are excellent for a Court Parade." General Frederick Haldimand, in his correspondence with his commanding officer, Thomas Gage, also emphasized Tryon's vanity.[10]

Some people went so far as to argue that Tryon had a cruel and vindictive streak, which became especially noticeable after 1776. At that time Tryon emerged as an ardent advocate of predatory war against American rebel leaders, insisting that the rebels would never submit unless they were bludgeoned and torched into acquiescence. Yet Tryon always insisted that the charges, which came from both Englishmen and Americans, were false. In fact, he said, his policy was more lenient and merciful toward the colonists than that of flaccid types who in the name of misplaced decency only dragged out a cruel war to everyone's disadvantage. He did admit to having "a bilious Habit of Body," which caused him to lose his temper often—a fact that William Smith could affirm after observing Tryon at

Council meetings in New York. On more than one occasion the councillor noted in his diary that the governor could barely control his outbursts of temper and petulance.[11] Tryon denied, however, that his short temper ever contributed to any sort of ill-judged behavior, and neither Tryon, his family, nor his many friends ever thought him cruel or vindictive in the least degree.

When the time came for young William Tryon to choose a career, he entered the profession of soldiering. In 1751, at the age of twenty-two, he received a commission as a lieutenant in the First Regiment of Foot Guards. This commission gave Tryon a prestigious position in the British army, a position he could not have secured without the influence of certain well-placed relatives and friends in government. His uncle Sewallis Shirley, a member of Parliament from 1742 to 1761, and comptroller of the household to Queen Charlotte, helped him, as did his friend Thomas Villiers, Baron Hyde, commissioner of the Admiralty from 1748 to 1756 and later postmaster general and chancellor of the duchy of Lancaster. (Tryon was so beholden to Lord Hyde, in fact, that in 1765 he referred to him as his "Sheet Anchor.") Tryon's commission had to be purchased, and the necessary money was supplied by his father, who no doubt considered it money well spent. All his male children had to be provided for, and as William had two older brothers between himself and his family inheritance, Charles Tryon's seeking a position in the military for his younger son was entirely logical and unexceptionable. Young Tryon himself was delighted with his choice of career, and from the start he reveled in the pomp and pageantry of military life. In 1751 he was promoted to a captaincy in the First Foot Guards and seven years later achieved the army rank of lieutenant colonel. During this time he was cementing friendships with many fellow officers, such as Captain Henry Clinton of the Grenadier Guards, under whom he would serve years later during the American war, and Frederick Lord Cavendish, who, among his other accomplishments, served as the duke of Marlborough's aide-de-camp in a British expedition against the French coast during the Seven Years' War.[12]

Captain Tryon must have cut quite a figure as he strolled through London in his splendid Guards uniform, and he caught the eye of at least one female acquaintance, a young woman named Mary Stanton, with whom he had an affair. Their dalliance produced a child, Elizabeth, whom Tryon supported during the remainder of his life and provided for in his will; additionally, he saw to the upkeep of Mary Stanton, although it never occurred to him to marry the woman. In addition he attracted the attention of a much more eligible young lady, an heiress named Margaret Wake, whose family resided on Hanover Street. On December 26, 1757, he and she were wed in St. George's Church, and Tryon instantly acquired her fortune of £30,000 sterling. The new Mrs. Tryon's mother, Elizabeth Elwin Wake, sprang from an old Norfolk family, and her father, William Wake, was a rich merchant with the East India Company in Bombay. Wake's wealth and prominence had recommended him to the authorities, with the result that he secured a position on the Council of Bombay and then from 1742 to 1750 the governorship of that colony. Not only did Margaret Wake Tryon make her husband rich, but she also brought to the marriage an influential family relation, Wills Hill, Viscount Hillsborough, who was president of the Board of Trade and Plantations from 1763 to 1769 and secretary of state for the colonies between 1768 and 1772. It was through Hillsborough's influence that Tryon became lieutenant governor of North Carolina in 1764, governor of the same colony in 1765, and governor of New York in 1771.[13]

Mrs. Tryon was an extraordinary person. She was described as a "finely accomplish'd Lady," with a talent for playing the organ and spinet. One of her acquaintances wrote that she was "a very sensible Woman, & indeed what you call a learned one." But she was also thought to be a little odd. Whenever she could, she ignored women's company, to the mortification of ladies in high society, and involved herself in the conversation of the menfolk. By such practices she created little "incidents" from time to time when she was acting as hostess during her husband's official entertaining. In addition she insisted on being addressed as "Her Excellency" and much preferred to devote her time to reading and writing about military fortifications than to idle social chit-chat. It is no wonder that many people "called her mad," as Janet Livingston Montgomery noted in her memoirs; "she was certainly eccentric." For all her oddities of personality, however, Mrs. Tryon was devoted to her husband and always supported him in his dual careers. To be sure, there were things that Tryon had to overlook in Margaret Wake Tryon, but just as surely there were things that she had to overlook in her husband—not least his support of an illegitimate daughter from a former liaison.[14]

Hardly had the newlyweds settled into their new home on Upper Grosvenor Street in Mayfair, a fashionable section of London, when Tryon was called to active military duty in the Seven Years' War. This conflict, which broke out in 1756 and lasted until 1763, was for England primarily a matter of contesting with France for control of North America. Therefore the British army was engaged in fighting mostly in that part of the world. But when William Pitt became secretary of state in 1757, with full power to prosecute the war, he began to pay more attention to England's assisting Prussia and other Continental countries in counterpoising French land power so that he could concentrate on the conquest of Canada. In addition to granting large sums of money to Frederick II, Pitt ordered the army and navy in 1758 to assist the Prussians militarily by carrying out raids on the French coast, in hopes that Paris would be forced to divert forces to the defense of France's Atlantic and Channel ports. This scheme, which led to amphibious operations against Cherbourg and St. Malo, turned out to be totally unsuccessful and almost cost Tryon his life.[15]

The events leading to Tryon's brush with mortal danger began in the spring of 1758, when the Cherbourg–St. Malo operation was organized under the joint command of seventy-three-year-old Lieutenant General Thomas Bligh and naval captain Richard Howe. Tryon joined the expedition with his regiment, the First Foot Guards, at a camp on the Isle of Wight in May, and he landed at Cherbourg on August 7. After a nine-day British occupation of that port, in which all war-making facilities were destroyed and the neighborhood ravaged, the troops were reembarked for St. Malo. From the first days of September until the eleventh, everything proceeded smoothly in the St. Malo operation. But as the British troops were being withdrawn from the beaches in St. Cas Bay, east of the town, and reembarked in Captain Howe's ships standing by to receive them, things began to go badly. As Tryon described the events of the next few hours in a letter to his friend Captain Clinton, matters became horrific for the British troops, apparently because of tactical blunders on the part of the army's high command, which alerted the French to their withdrawal and caused them to come under intense fire. According to Tryon, the British troops were forced "to the Shore," where their ammunition ran low and the companies became mixed under the volleys of the French soldiers, who fired upon the redcoats from behind a parapet. This musketry was "very severe and the Slaughter great, on Our side," so that finally the troops broke and ran "into the Water to the Boats that were coming up as fast as they could" to rescue the trapped infantrymen. Many soldiers drowned in this melee, but at least "a Prodigious fire from the Ships" forced the Frenchmen to keep their distance behind cover. Finally the boats, under Captain Howe's personal supervision, got close enough inshore to begin loading the desperate soldiers, while all the time the carnage among both infantrymen and sailors continued unabated.

Tryon remained on the beach throughout this intense action, making a dash for the boats only after receiving "a contusion" in his right thigh and finding that "all opposition was of no effect." He waded up to his waist in salt water before coming within reach of a boat and even then could do no more than desperately grab onto "the Ring of the Anchor at the Stern." The boat was fully loaded and "under way." While being dragged through deep water for half a mile, Tryon was struck in the back of the head by a second musket ball, but fortunately it was spent. Rendered "a little Giddy," he was about to lose his grip—and therefore his life—when a soldier in the boat finally noticed his plight and "catch'd hold of [his] hand," pulling him out of the water. Without further misfortune, Tryon and his boatmates reached the safety of a transport ship, the *Richard and Ann*, with the fleet in the bay. The following day, Tryon was delighted to learn that his close friend Lord Cavendish, whom he had feared dead, had instead been taken captive by the French, but he was saddened at the large number of British losses (800 killed, wounded, and captured, he would later learn). He urged Clinton to inform William Cavendish, duke of Devonshire; Sewallis Shirley, his uncle; and one of his brothers (not identified by name) of the "unhappy events of the eleventh."[16]

Five days after the botched British withdrawal from St. Malo, Tryon arrived with the fleet at Plymouth, on England's south coast. From there he wrote an unidentified correspondent to describe his wounds, which, he assured his friend, were superficial. "I am perfectly well," he said, "and the bruise" on his thigh was "already dispers'd by the Sole assistance of some Nerve Ointment." He urged his friend to write Mrs. Tryon, "least the three letters I have wrote to her should be miscarried." In a footnote he added that he had not told his wife about "being Bruis'd," but he neither explained why he had omitted this information from his own letters nor admonished his correspondent to be silent on the matter.[17] In any case, he shortly rejoined his wife in London, where he could give an account of his experiences in person, and he did not take the field again during the remainder of the Seven Years' War. But if he did not campaign in that long conflict as much as some of his brother officers, he nevertheless took pride in the fact that he had performed bravely when called upon to do so on the beaches of France.

With the close of the Seven Years' War in 1763, Lieutenant Colonel Tryon began to give serious thought to his future prospects as a military man. In 1761 his family had increased in size with the birth of a daughter, Margaret, and although his wife's fortune assured him of no worries about maintaining himself and his near relatives in a life of ease and comfort, he still dreaded to think that he might spend the remainder of his days serving in a peacetime army. He was thirty-four years old, vigorous, healthy, and ambitious for his own and his monarch's future prosperity. But given the difficulty of securing promotion without war, his professional life seemed near a dead end. As Tryon noted of this frustrating period in his life, he wished very much "to be placed in a Situation in which I might render my Public Services more beneficial to my Royal Master than my station in the Guards would probably allow Me to do in Time of Peace." Yet he frankly admitted that his other consideration for seeking some new employment "was, that if happily I could, by a diligent discharge of my Office answer the purpose of it, I flattered Myself it would recommend Me to the Kings indulgent Consideration in the Military Line"—in other words, he wished he might be promoted colonel and receive command of a regiment.[18]

It was this frame of mind that led Tryon to offer his "service in America" as a governor of one of His Majesty's colonies. Quite likely he had talked this possibility over with Lord Hillsborough, his wife's relative, who was then president of the Board of Trade, and Hillsborough had suggested the occupation. Certainly, once Tryon had made up his mind to pursue the matter, he received crucial assistance from his powerful patron on the board. When Arthur Dobbs, the seventy-five-year-old governor of North Carolina, petitioned Hillsborough in early 1764 for a leave of absence "to return to England for twelve months, for the recovery of his health, and to settle his private affairs," Hillsborough had the Board of Trade grant Tryon's request and appoint him on April 26 to the office of lieutenant governor to act in Dobbs's place during his leave. Although none of the official documents referring to this arrangement openly stated as much, Hillsborough privately gave Tryon to understand that the old and ailing Dobbs would never return to his post and that Tryon soon would be promoted to the office of governor. Without such assurance Tryon, ambitious and well placed, would not have agreed to accept the relatively inconsequential post of lieutenant governor in one of the Crown's less valuable colonies. Even with Hillsborough's unofficial guarantee, Tryon expressed to Hillsborough; to George Montagu Dunk, earl of Halifax and secretary of state for the Southern Department; and to Edward Sedgwick, Halifax's undersecretary, his earnest apprehensions that Dobbs might change his mind at the last minute and decide to remain in America.[19] Somehow, these men laid to rest his doubts and fears, and thus, conditionally, he accepted his new post.

Soon Tryon and his wife were busy making arrangements for their removal to America. While Mrs. Tryon sorted and packed the household goods—which were numerous and valuable—Tryon transacted two items of business. First, he assisted his mother, his elder brother Charles, and his uncle Sewallis Shirley in arranging for the sale of Norbury Park. The reasons why the Tryon family decided to dispose of the estate are unclear, as are the reasons why Tryon's father was absent from these proceedings, although he was still alive at the time and would be for four years afterward, until November 28, 1768. In light of the fact that Tryon never mentioned his father in his correspondence, it is possible that some sort of estrangement had occurred between the elder Tryon and his family. In any case, William Tryon never alluded to the sale of his beloved Norbury Park except to Shirley, remarking upon "the evident necessity of such a proceeding" and thanking Shirley for his "affectionate and steady conduct in adjusting the intricate state of the affairs of my Mother." Tryon's second item of business was to attend meetings of the Board of Trade in order to be instructed upon his duties as governor of North Carolina, after which he received from John Pownall, the board secretary, a copy of "such observations as had occurred."[20]

Having completed his business in England, Tryon and his family bade farewell to friends and relatives and took themselves—along with John Hawks, an architect, and a servant named George—to Portsmouth. For a time they were entertained there by Admiral Francis Holburne, commander in chief of Portsmouth, and Richard Hughes, a naval officer who later succeeded to a baronetcy and achieved admiral's rank. In July they departed the British Isles in the snow *Friendship*, commanded by Captain John Vernier, bound for the Cape Fear River. Their passage was not uneventful. On August 19, when they were one day's sail from the island of Madeira, where they were to land and replenish their supplies, they fell in with a sinking sloop, the *Tyge*, John Barns master. Although Captain Vernier managed to rescue all fourteen of the passengers and crew before the ship went down, the operation was made perilous by high seas. Tryon, according to a later newspaper account of the rescue, "exerted himself greatly, and was very anxious the whole time" for the safety of the persons on board the *Tyge*. On the following day the *Friendship* reached Madeira, where it remained for a month while Tryon chafed impatiently at the delay.[21]

At last, on October 9, the Tryons reached the mouth of the Cape Fear River. They disembarked the next day at the little town of Brunswick, located fourteen miles upriver. Founded just forty years earlier, Brunswick in 1764 contained only about sixty houses but was the site of Dobbs's official residence, a fifty-five-acre plantation once named Russellborough but now called Castle Dobbs. On October 11 Tryon met Governor Dobbs for an interview and was appalled to learn that his worst fears about the old man staying on were confirmed. As he reported to Halifax, Dobbs told him that he would remain in the governor's chair until the following May, thus leaving Tryon in "an office which is likely to be burdensome to me this Winter, for want of Employ." And Dobbs's decision created other problems as well. For one thing, Tryon had no place to live because, as he reported, the governor "declined letting me his Villa till his departure, tho' the Assembly will detain him at Wilmington till December." Hence, the Tryon family's baggage remained on board the *Friendship* a week after their arrival. For another thing, Tryon found himself without any income from his new position in America. As he told Hillsborough, although he drew interest from his private fortune and received a salary for his service as a lieutenant colonel, "the great Expence of my Equipment and passage to this province" and "the present Establishment of my Family" vastly exceeded what he was taking in. Moreover, he had to maintain his house in London. He had expected to make up for these deficiencies by receiving a salary as governor of £1,000 sterling per annum, in addition to fees for granting licenses and for other governmental transactions.[22]

Tryon was exaggerating his problems considerably, as both he and his mentors in London knew. Given Dobbs's age and infirmities, it would be only a short time before Tryon assumed the governorship in one way or another. If Dobbs went home in the spring, he would never return; if he became infirm or died in North Carolina, Tryon would immediately assume his office. Nor were Tryon's financial problems as great as he pretended. Although it would certainly have been pleasant for him to receive a governor's income, he was more than able to cover his present costs (such as the £25 he paid Captain Vernier for his family's passage to America) from other sources of revenue. Tryon practically admitted that he was overstating his difficulties when he lightheartedly told Hillsborough that he still entertained "flattering Ideas from my Undertaking in this Continent, which are kept alive by the Expectations I entertain of the good offices of my Friends at Home and I do not yet wish to be in Grosvenor Street."[23]

Tryon had arrived in North Carolina only thirteen days before the Council and the Assembly were to convene in Wilmington, fifteen miles up the Cape Fear River from Brunswick. When the time of their meeting arrived, he proceeded to Wilmington to be sworn in as lieutenant governor. Wishing to stage a grand and semimartial arrival for himself at Wilmington, he sent his wife and daughter ahead in the ship *Harriot* on October 18 and one day later came up river himself "in the *Viper* man of war's barge, accompanied by Jacob Lobb, Esq., commander of the *Viper*." According to Wilmington newspaper reports, he was received "with all due respect; a salute of 17 guns being fired from our wharf, which was answered by a discharge of 7 guns from the *Harriot*. . . . The town was illuminated and every suitable Mark of respect shewn on the occasion." On the twenty-seventh Tryon met with the Council, read his commission, and took the official oath of office as lieutenant governor of the province.[24]

For the next few weeks Tryon lapsed into the political and administrative limbo that he had dreaded when he wrote Halifax and Hillsborough in mid-October. As he was not inclined to accept lassitude gladly and had no official duties to keep him busy, he concentrated on other matters for a time, but all with an eye toward readying himself for the role of governor once it came his way. First, he and Mrs. Tryon got to know Wilmington. They leased a house in the town, installed half their furniture (all they had room for) and their newly hired servants, plus George, and proceeded to entertain the local gentry. Tryon did not find Wilmington a very impressive place. It was not much larger than Brunswick, he said, and still retained many traces of frontier rawness. Nevertheless he could discern the beginnings of a town civilization there. A recent visitor had described Wilmington as having regular streets that reminded one of Philadelphia and a number of houses, some made of brick, which were "in General very Good." Second, Tryon studied the province, and from the amount of information he collected and digested, it is safe to say he did his homework well. He learned about the colony's boundaries (many still in dispute) and about its topography, climate, weather, economy, population, demography, extent of settlement, slave system, ratio of whites to blacks, average size of plantation, and exports. Later, when he took up the reins of government, he would find all this information invaluable, and his devotion to such prosaic—not to mention uncompensated—drudgery indicated his commitment to advancing his own and the Crown's interests while he served in America.[25]

By the middle of December, Tryon had learned as much about North Carolina as he could from written records and from informants along the lower Cape Fear River. Both he and Mrs. Tryon grew restless for something to fill their time during the winter. Thus they and Fountain Elwin,

Mrs. Tryon's cousin who had come to North Carolina as Tryon's private secretary, decided to take a long tour of the colony while the heat and fevers of the summer were in abeyance. In fact, as Tryon observed, the cold months were the "only season for travelling in this climate." Still, the roads were dreadful, in many places hardly more than paths, and they wound through swamps, sand dunes, and thick forest. There were numerous rivers to ford or ferry, and public accommodations were often meager or nonexistent. Therefore Tryon and his party often found themselves spending time at private plantations along the way, and much to their surprise, found "more ease and better accommodations" than "could possibly have [been] expected."[26]

Not long before Christmas, Tryon and his retinue departed Wilmington in a "chariot," a closed conveyance similar to a post chaise, designed primarily for a lady's traveling convenience. On the first leg of their journey they wallowed northward 240 miles along what Tryon called "the Sea Board Road," "never being farther from the Sea than Sixty or eighty miles." They reached New Bern on Monday, December 24, and received a splendid welcome from the inhabitants. Their arrival had been anticipated, for they were "met about 8 Miles from Town by a great Number of Gentlemen, who accompanied them to *Newbern*" and conducted them to prepared lodgings. After a nineteen-gun salute, the town was "handsomely illuminated, Bonfires were lighted, and plenty of Liquor given to the Populace." On Wednesday, town officials waited on Tryon with an official welcome, and "in the Evening there was a very elegant *Ball*, in the Great Ball-Room in the Court house, where were present his Honour the Governor, and his Lady, the Mayor, Mr. Recorder and near 100 Gentlemen and Ladies," followed by "a very elegant Collation." After more such proceedings over the next few days (including a lodge meeting of the Masons, which Tryon attended), the travelers departed northward.[27]

Ferrying across the Neuse and Pamlico rivers, the latter two miles wide, Tryon's party reached Bath, which had been settled in 1705 and was the province's oldest town. Two days' travel and a five-mile crossing of Albemarle Sound brought the wayfarers to Edenton, where the Assembly had met from 1720 to 1738. They next proceeded forty miles north to the Virginia dividing line and then westward seventy miles to Halifax. "From thence," said Tryon, he and his companions "took a South and South West Course back to Wilmington where we arrived the Middle of Feby." The entire tour had covered "five Hundred Measured Miles and upwards," through startlingly diverse landscapes: sandy plains covered with pine trees, swamps festooned with "tall Cypress Trees some of six feet in

Diameter, and Seventy feet in height before they shoot a Branch," rich clay lands near Halifax that grew good corn, and wild, hilly forestlands near the falls of the Roanoke River. And even after having seen this much of North Carolina, Tryon realized he had seen only a portion of the province's variegated topography. Farther westward about 300 miles, he was told, lay rolling highlands that merged into the "Blue Mountains." Settlements had already reached to within 100 miles of these mountains and in less than twenty years would lap into the foothills, for the frontiersmen were more industrious than their eastern neighbors and were on the move. All in all, North Carolina's diversity was remarkable and exciting for an Englishman who had hardly known any other than a tamed and gentle landscape benignly verdant under a much milder climate.[28]

With their trip the Tryons had consumed a good part of their slack time before Governor Dobbs's anticipated departure, but the young lieutenant governor and his adventurous wife still needed to find something to keep them occupied for a while. Part of their leisure was taken up with their social life, for they attended dinner parties and dances in both Wilmington and Brunswick. In mid-March they were guests at a party given by Mrs. Justina Dobbs, the governor's eighteen-year-old wife, at Castle Dobbs. Tryon was engaged during the same month in planting and landscaping the grounds of his leased house in Wilmington, even asking the Moravians at Wachovia, in the North Carolina Piedmont, to send him "all kinds of seeds." Tryon was particularly delighted to welcome to North Carolina a visitor, Lord Adam Gordon, colonel of the Sixty-sixth Regiment, then stationed in Jamaica. As he told his uncle Sewallis Shirley, Gordon's visit "gave me no small joy, as he was not only a particular friend, but had the additional merit of being the first person I had seen, even of my personal acquaintance since I left London." As Gordon was on a trip to New York and thus only passing through North Carolina, Tryon immediately set out to accompany the Scotsman from Wilmington to as far as New Bern.[29]

Tryon and Gordon had covered but 74 of the 100 miles' distance to New Bern when they were overtaken by one of Tryon's servants, who bore momentous news. Governor Dobbs, in the midst of "packing up his Books for the passage to England," had died suddenly at Brunswick on March 28. Tryon immediately parted company with his friend and made his way back to Wilmington with all possible haste, only to arrive on the thirtieth, too late for Dobbs's funeral. He was mortified to learn that the governor's last rites had been performed not by an Anglican minister but by "a Majestrate of Peace," there being no clergyman available to read the burial service. This unacceptable situation Tryon vowed to rectify during his tenure as governor, for his deep religious sensibilities, his instinctive feel for what was dignified for a representative of the Crown, and his concern for established order led him to recognize that such lapses were corrosive.[30]

But at the moment more pressing matters prevented him from giving too much thought to this insult to decorum. He proceeded to take into his possession the great seal of the province, the governor's commission under which Dobbs had held office, and as many public papers as he could find at hand from the Board of Trade and the earl of Halifax. On April 1 he informed his superiors in London of Governor Dobbs's death. Two days later he met with the Council at Wilmington, took the oath of office as acting governor, and administered the oath "unto the several Members of the Council." These men, who were recruited from the rich and powerful property owners of the colony, worked harmoniously with Tryon during his entire tenure as governor. Perhaps it was generally true that a governor's appointment of persons to a Council was "a feather wherewith to Tickle the Vanity" of the members and to assure support for British imperial policies; but such was not always the case with Tryon's nominees during the next few years. The Council's first item of business under the new governor was to ratify a proclamation by Tryon, which was published the same day and confirmed the tenure in office of all Dobbs's appointees.[31]

Assuming the position of acting governor, Tryon began his duties with the full understanding that he would soon be promoted to fill the post officially. He was not to be disappointed, for as soon as Hillsborough and Halifax received word of Dobbs's death, they set in motion the appointment of Tryon to the governorship. On July 10, 1765, King George III approved Tryon's promotion to the rank of "Captain General, and Governor in Chief" of North Carolina and that day caused to be sent to him a letter to that effect. Over the next few months Tryon also received a commission as vice admiral of the province and extensive royal instructions, consisting of 119 parts, on how he was to conduct himself in office. Not least important to Tryon, on January 16, 1766, the king finally got around to issuing a warrant to the Treasury to pay the new governor his salary of £1,000 sterling per year in quarterly installments. Tryon, of course, was delighted with all these developments, for they represented the realization of his original designs in assuming American service.[32] His career as a royal governor was now well launched.

CHAPTER TWO

The New Royal Governor

Tryon's initiation into the mysteries of governing a royal colony was immediate and forceful, and for the remainder of his career he never again complained of enforced inactivity. Even before he replaced Dobbs, he had been drawn into a number of political issues in the colony that indicated to him the tenor of his relationship with the Assembly and people of North Carolina, and he had determined in his own mind that once he assumed power he would be an aggressive and reform-minded leader. Although Tryon's tenure in office was marked with considerable harmony between contending institutions and factions, an ongoing, intractable tension nevertheless stood between what Tryon as representative of royal authority wished to accomplish and what the colonials believed to be in their best interests. Also throughout Tryon's administration in North Carolina, sectional tension between east and west simmered and often flared into open conflict. Inevitably, therefore, Tryon's simultaneous attempts to enforce Crown policies and ameliorate frontiersmen's complaints against the easterners who largely controlled the colony's political and economic life brought clashes with those who wished to thwart his schemes. The tension was made worse by the fact that Tryon's governorship commenced just at the moment when Crown and colonial interests began most rapidly to diverge in a way that would lead to constitutional impasse and, finally, civil war within the empire.

Before Tryon departed England in 1764 he had become embroiled in a contest for ascendancy between the governor of North Carolina and the Assembly. The issue involved the relative powers of the governor and the Assembly to appoint a colonial agent to serve the province's interests in London. Tryon's philosophy of appointments, in this case and in all others, was simple: "It is a Maxim with me . . . ," he said, "to look out for

Integrity, Ability and Diligence . . . for I esteem that the Public Offices of a Country lye open to the Virtue of every Member of it. . . . I am of Opinion [that] the less a Man (whose principles are directed to the Public Service) stands connected with private Attachments, and private Interests, the more likely he is to be free from the Biass of self Interested Motives, and more at Liberty to discharge impartially the Duties of his Office."[1] Of course it was one thing for Tryon to articulate high-minded philosophy in the quietude of his gubernatorial study and quite another to stand by it in the give-and-take of North Carolina politics. In 1758 the Assembly had sought to appoint James Abercromby agent, but Governor Dobbs had demurred, wanting instead to keep his own appointee, Samuel Smith, in the office. After a three-year deadlock, the matter was temporarily settled when Dobbs and the Assembly agreed to nominate Cuchet Jouvencal, a clerk in the office of secretary of state for the Southern Department, for a term of two years and to allow some councillors to sit on the Assembly's committee appointed to correspond with the agent. The matter thus came up again just as Tryon was about to leave London for America, and Tryon imprudently boasted to some merchants that he intended to appoint his own agent, William Knox, despite the Assembly's desires. One of these merchants, William Hunter, warned Tryon that Jouvencal was complaining to the Board of Trade about Tryon's "jockeying" and that, regarding the governor's power to appoint an agent, "in a Trice You are as deep in the Mire as ever Old Dobbs Was."[2]

Indeed Tryon was, and he scrambled to send the Board of Trade his own account of these events. It was true, Tryon said, that he intended to nominate someone else to be agent—Knox, although he did not say so— but only because he "found the Province determined to change their Agent, and were in want of a Person to represent them." But if he were to discover upon his arrival in North Carolina that Jouvencal was still acceptable, then, he explained, "I should not have the least Objection." As it happened, the Carolinians did want a new man, so Tryon nominated Knox. But he discovered that the Assembly wanted Thomas Barker, a prominent citizen of the colony then residing in London. Barker was thus chosen by the Assembly but was rejected by the Council, "for reasons best known to those Gentlemen." The Council nominated Edward Bridgen, a prominent London merchant, only to have their choice immediately rejected by the Assembly. Hence, the governor, the Council, and the Assembly each had a preferred candidate, and none could prevail against the others. Moreover, at this point the Assembly reverted to its pre-1761 policy of refusing Council members seats on its committee for corresponding with the agent.[3]

Finally, Tryon felt compelled to submit the entire matter to the Board of Trade for resolution. At the same time, he vigorously protested what he saw as the Assembly's high-handed action in excluding councillors from the committee of correspondence and suggested to the board that it might refuse to do business with the agent if applications came "solely from the Assembly." The Board of Trade analyzed these matters and declined to settle the issue, only threatening to intervene later "if the Assembly should in their next Session not admit a proper Number of the Council to be of the Committee of Correspondence." Meanwhile, the Assembly was complaining to Tryon that the Council (and by implication the governor as well) was thwarting its "right" as "Representatives of the people" to appoint its own agent. Tryon quickly denied such a right existed but immediately added that to "preserve the Tranquility of this province" he would accept any candidate on whom both houses of the legislature could agree. In the meantime, Jouvencal would continue to represent the colony in London.[4]

There the matter rested until 1769, at which time the Assembly approved, but the Council rejected, the appointment of Henry Eustace McCulloh. In exasperation, Tryon fumed to the Board of Trade that it ought to clarify how much power the governor was allowed in the selection process so that he would know how far he could assert his authority. The agent issue, he grumbled, had "caused the principal obstruction during my Administration," and he announced his intention of trying once more to break the Assembly-Council deadlock. Therefore, in October 1769, he urged both legislative houses to act speedily on appointing an agent, and both promised that they would. Amazingly enough, the houses were true to their word, finally resolving their long conflict by accepting McCulloh. They accepted as well Tryon's viewpoint (dictated to him by Hillsborough) that their prerogatives in the process allowed "each [i.e., governor, Council, and Assembly] respectively a negative upon the Bill." To be sure, the governor's powers had proved to be minimal, and Tryon had to concede that in his first political conflict with the legislature he had been totally unable to support the royal prerogative.[5]

When he took over the government from Dobbs in 1765, Tryon assumed responsibility for a number of outstanding administrative problems in the colony, and he undertook to resolve them with vigor and dispatch. One matter that took up an inordinate amount of his time was the Whitehurst-Simpson affair. Thomas Whitehurst, a lieutenant on the ship *Viper*, was challenged by Alexander Simpson, master of the vessel, to a duel as the result of an argument over a woman. In the exchange of fire between the two men, on March 18, 1765, Simpson shattered White-hurst's thigh and pistol-whipped him after he had fallen. Whitehurst died from his wounds and Simpson was arrested for murder. But Simpson escaped from jail, thereby creating problems for Tryon. First, the sheriff of Brunswick County tried without success to board the warship *Diligence*, Constantine John Phipps commanding, and search for the missing Simp-son. Indignantly, Phipps wrote Tryon, warning the governor against al-lowing civilian officers to interfere with ships on the king's service. He then received from Tryon approbation for his refusal to allow the sheriff aboard. Second, Tryon had to write many officers in London to describe the incident to them; he also had to write Francis Fauquier, governor of Virginia, to ask him to watch for Simpson, should he flee to the Old Dominion. The matter was finally resolved when Simpson turned himself in at Wilmington, stood trial, and was acquitted.[6]

Another knotty problem that Tryon inherited was the controversy over land titles created by earlier grants that the Crown had made to individu-als and by the hatred settlers felt toward some persons who controlled these large tracts of land. Probably no other issue in all of North Caro-lina's colonial history was as fertile a breeding ground for problems as were these huge tracts of land, sitting in the midst of the colony almost as semi-independent governments. The Granville District and the Selwyn-McCulloh tracts were the two major ones, and they vexed Tryon, as they had his predecessors, almost to distraction. The Granville District, given by the Crown to John Carteret, Earl Granville, as compensation when he refused in 1729 to sell out his one-eighth share in proprietary Carolina, included a sixty-mile-wide strip of the upper half of North Carolina and two-thirds of the colony's citizens. The Selwyn-McCulloh lands, 1,200,000 acres in all, were located in two separate tracts later encom-passed by Mecklenburg and Duplin counties. The problem for Tryon was that none of these territories rendered his government any revenues in land taxes or land grants because the money went to private owners. Yet, he was expected to assert governmental authority there and to enforce the collection by private agents of the proprietors' and king's revenues. Essen-tially all that Tryon could do about the Granville tract was suggest to the Crown that it be purchased. His advice was not accepted. Consequently, his successor, Governor Josiah Martin, continued to suffer the problem that this huge private domain divided the colony and "fatally embarrassed its policies."[7]

The Selwyn-McCulloh lands were a much greater headache for Tryon. In 1761 Henry Eustace McCulloh, son of the original McCulloh land owner, took up residence in North Carolina with power of attorney from his father to collect delinquent quitrents—small annual fees paid by persons to whom landowners had given holdings, so called because their payment "quit" the grantees of further obligations. Three years later, George Augustus Selwyn gave young McCulloh the same authority within the Selwyn lands. So vigorous was McCulloh in seeking rents from inhabitants of two particular tracts that he was soon hated. In March 1765, when he and a surveying party rode up to Sugar Creek in the Selwyn tract, he was confronted by 140 irate citizens, who destroyed his surveying equipment and chased him away. Two months later another surveying party, this time minus McCulloh, was attacked and pummeled by armed settlers with soot-blackened faces. In April, McCulloh vigorously brought this "War on Sugar Creek," as he was pleased to call it, to Tryon's attention, and the governor forthwith issued a proclamation seeking evidence against those who "Outrageously, and Riotously" assaulted the surveyors. But Tryon's efforts to enforce McCulloh's land policy were lukewarm at best, and nothing ever came of his "search" for the Sugar Creek rioters. McCulloh himself was at last forced by the Crown to forfeit claims to lands that had never been settled, and Tryon, after spending a great deal of time on inquiry and paperwork in the king's interests, in April 1767, effected deeds of surrender for the lands in question.[8]

Early in his administration, attempting to impose his own reformist style on North Carolina's public life, Governor Tryon moved vigorously to have the Assembly enact into law a number of programs that were dear to his heart. In early May 1765 he called the legislature into session at New Bern, the town that, in his opinion, was "at present, the most convenient for holding the general assembly." In his opening address to the Assembly, he proposed a major piece of legislation: the establishment of a postal service. Long before Tryon had come to America, numerous unsuccessful attempts to organize a postal service in North Carolina had been made. In 1764, before Tryon departed England, Hillsborough had instructed him to work on this project, for North Carolina was the "missing link" in a postal route between Charles Town and Suffolk, Virginia. Thus, in late 1764 Tryon proposed a postal system to his patron Postmaster General Lord Hyde and even prevailed upon the Assembly to appropriate £67 proclamation money toward instituting a post road through the province. After becoming governor, he worked even harder on the project, and in two separate legislative sessions in 1765, the Assembly twice appropriated £133 6s. 8d. in order at least to survey a route through the colony. Beyond that the Assembly would not commit itself, so Tryon and a group of private citizens on the lower Cape Fear River agreed among themselves temporarily to support an express service to Charles Town on a fortnightly basis.[9]

Over the next few years Tryon worked energetically to complete his scheme for a postal service. In 1766 he was pleased when the Assembly passed a law compelling ferrymen to keep ordinaries at their ferries, for, as he told William Petty, earl of Shelburne and the new secretary of state for the Southern Department, their presence would benefit the post. He also wrote letter after letter to Benjamin Barons, Peter Timothy, and Peter DeLancey, deputy postmasters general for the southern division in Charles Town, describing his plans and applauding what little progress was being made. By the end of 1769, Tryon could report to London that the postal service had been established through the colony on a semi-monthly basis, and two years later he got the Assembly to enact a law requiring ferrymen to carry post riders free of charge, a measure that improved the service considerably. At last, a postal system was in place in the colony of North Carolina.[10]

Meanwhile, Tryon also worked zealously on matters relating to the Christian religion. The new governor, a warm friend of the Anglican church and the Society for the Propagation of the Gospel in Foreign Parts (SPG), believed that as a matter of both personal faith and state policy, Anglicanism ought to be the established religion in all parts of the British Empire. He discovered, however, that North Carolina had no religious establishment and that, in fact, the Anglican church was languishing. Describing the religious scene in his colony, Tryon informed the SPG that "every Sect of Religion abounds here, except the Roman Catholic." Presbyterians were most numerous, followed by Anglicans. Tryon was convinced that, were there enough exemplary clergy to carry on a good work for the church, "the larger Number of every Sect would come over" to Anglicanism. But as things stood, in the entire province there were only five Anglican clergymen to serve thirty-two parishes, a situation that led to such horrors as Governor Dobbs's burial by a justice of the peace. The colony's only Anglican church in good repair was at New Bern. Those at Bath and Edenton wanted much work, and at Brunswick and Wilmington the buildings were not even completed. The remaining parishes were served by chapels only, with readers officiating in place of regular clergy. Bibles, prayer books, and other religious paraphernalia were virtually nonexistent, and Tryon begged the SPG to send a "Ship Load" of Bibles and other liturgical materials to North Carolina.[11]

Tryon took a personal interest in the completion of St. Philip's, the church at Brunswick. In July 1765, he prevailed upon King George III to provide the church with "Two Flagons, One Chalice, a Patine and a Receiver to take the offering in . . . not Exceeding the Value of Eighty Pounds." He also gave official encouragement to subscription drives and to the sale of pews to local wealthy citizens in order to raise money for the church's construction. Hurrying the work, in 1767 Tryon donated all the sashes, complete with glass, which he had imported from England at a cost of thirty guineas. His gift apparently reawakened community interest in completing the church, for shortly afterward more money was collected for the project. A year later, to Tryon's delight, St. Philip's Church finally was finished and consecrated by its temporary rector, John Barnett, assisted by the Reverend John Wills, rector of St. James's Church at Wilmington.[12]

Tryon also took a personal interest in the quality and lives of Anglican ministers and missionaries sent to North Carolina by the bishop of London and the SPG. He urged the ecclesiastical powers in England not to send "the sweepings of the Universities but some Clergy of Character," and he was generally pleased with the men who came over, for they had "plain Characters" and led "exemplary Lives." The case of one potential clergyman, Edward Jones, in particular engaged Tryon's attention and makes for a poignant story. In hopes of receiving ordination, Jones, a native of Virginia, set off for England with a letter of introduction from Tryon to the bishop of London and another to his sister Ann, in the event that Jones needed assistance. In London, Jones was refused orders by the bishop. In despair he nearly committed suicide, but he was saved by Ann Tryon's spiritual and economic ministrations. Finally the bishop relented so far as to promise Jones "a Place" if Tryon would give the young man a personal recommendation. Tryon's endorsement forthcoming, Jones received the bishop's blessing, returned to North Carolina, and was sent to St. Stephen's Parish in Johnston County.[13]

Tryon's most important work for Anglicanism, and for the religious undergirding of English power in North Carolina, was in getting the Church of England officially established in the province. When he took office he found the Assembly determined to refuse any establishment bill that would allow the governor to appoint clergymen to parishes against the will of local vestries. From 1741 to 1762, four establishment bills had been passed by the legislature only to be disallowed in London because the Assembly, while accepting an Anglican establishment, insisted that patronage to church officials belonged to the vestries. Yet the Crown wanted to control Anglican vestry appointments, and Tryon was instructed to overcome the Assembly's reservations—it was not explained how—against what the house considered to be a too-powerful governor in matters of religion.[14]

In his first address to the legislature on May 3, 1765, Tryon informed the members of his desire for a law "making Provision for an Orthodox Clergy. . . free from the Objections" of earlier enactments. Declaring that he intended no harm to other Christian sects, he nevertheless asserted his political conviction that "for the Happiness of the Country . . . Religion should have but one Head, how many Members so ever there may be, to the Body." Both the Council and the Assembly responded favorably to this speech and in a very short time produced a law which the governor warmly recommended to the Board of Trade in August. The law, entitled the Orthodox Clergy Act, provided salaries and glebes from tax revenues, plus certain payments for conducting marriages and funerals. Complete religious jurisdiction was given to the bishop of London, but the governor was empowered to suspend ministers accused of crimes while they awaited the verdict of an English ecclesiastical court. Most significantly, the law said not a word about who controlled patronage, and so both Crown officials and vestries could interpret the act as a confirmation of their right to nominate ministers. Because of his support for this bill and his acts of charity toward the Anglican church, Tryon, in January 1767, was called by the Reverend Andrew ("Ana") Morton of Northumberland County "the Nursing Father of the church in this province."[15]

In subsequent years Tryon had to deal with a number of consequences resulting from the Orthodox Clergy Act. One was that he had to placate certain authorities in London over deficiencies in the act. Whereas Dr. Daniel Burton, secretary of the SPG, liked the new law, as did the government in London up to a point (the Board of Trade was happy that Tryon had gotten a law passed that covered the "most essential Interests" of both Crown and colony), the king was anxious about the lack of clarification on who exercised the right to appoint clergy. Although the board was willing to let that matter pass, it insisted on one change in the law, namely to allow replacement clergy to receive an incumbent's salary in the event that a minister were suspended. Tryon immediately recommended to the Assembly that it amend the law on that minor point, and on January 10, 1769, he reported to the earl of Hillsborough that the change had been accepted.[16]

The patronage question, however, the most vexing religious issue for Tryon, was not to be resolved during his tenure as governor nor, in fact, by the time of the onset of the Revolution. Tryon very much wanted to establish once and for all the right of the governor, acting for the Crown and the bishop of London, to appoint ministers to parishes as he pleased. He basked in the praise of men like Councillor James Murray, who asserted that Tryon, by getting the Anglican church established, had "done more good for the Province in your first Session than any, nay than all your Predecessors together since the settlement of the Colony." Yet the governor knew how tenuous his authority was to assert a royal prerogative of appointment under the new law. Indeed, he realized that the only reason the clergy bill had gotten through the Assembly was precisely because of its silence on who controlled clergy appointments. Therefore he established a policy, which he explained to Dr. Burton in October 1766, of appointing "ministers as they arrive, into those Counties where the Inhabitants are most willing to receive them." He also sent a copy of this procedure to the Right Reverend Richard Terrick, bishop of London, expressing his hope that the policy meet with his approval.[17]

This system, with the bishop's tacit acceptance, worked fairly well for Tryon, and in the years after passage of the Orthodox Clergy Act, he got fourteen ministers, either British or American and all approved by the bishop of London, inducted into parishes. But some of the ministers he chose were unacceptable to the vestries, and a few vestries stubbornly insisted that they, rather than the governor, must appoint their clergyman. In October 1766 Tryon appointed the Reverend James Cosgreve to Pitt County, only to learn that the inhabitants, as he reported to the bishop of London, were "as jealous of any Restraint put on their Consciences as they have of late shewn on their Property" (a reference to the Stamp Act turmoil that had just ended). Many Pitt County citizens and Carolinians in general insisted, said Tryon, that the clergy act did not give the bishop and the governor the right to the patronage of "Livings," and therefore the Crown could not claim that right. "Some Delicacy therefore," Tryon wrote to the bishop, "your Lordship I hope sees is necessary in the Establishment of the Clergy here." Hence, he appointed the Reverend Mr.

Cosgreve for a trial period of three months, in hopes that the Anglicans of Pitt County would warm up to the man over time.[18]

The vestry of St. Philip's Church in Brunswick also balked at the notion of accepting Tryon's choice of a minister. Although the citizens of Brunswick were grateful to Tryon for his assistance in building their church, they voted in 1769 to refuse a living to the Reverend John Barnett after he had been presented by the governor and even installed. Furiously, Tryon insisted to Barnett that he (Tryon) had a "just right" from the Crown to appoint ministers, and he was ready to force the matter. Some vestries, he fumed to Dr. Burton, "idly imagine the power of presentation is still invested in them; because say they, neither the Crown nor the Governor is in express words declared to have the right of presentation." Tryon was more than willing "to bring this matter . . . to tryal that they may be convinced of the obstenancy and error of such a notion." But Barnett asked to be sent elsewhere, as he was obviously unwelcome at Brunswick, and Tryon (no doubt with some relief) "acquiesced" to the minister's wish to serve in Northampton County. Other parish vestries, such as those of St. Luke's Church in Rowan County and St. James's in Wilmington, rankled Tryon in the manner in which they accepted his nominees. Although they found the governor's choice of ministers satisfactory, they worded their letters of approval in such a way as to let Tryon know that they, and not he, had made the choice of clergymen.[19]

A final problem that Tryon had to contend with under the Orthodox Clergy Act was dissent by non-Anglican religious sects. When Tryon presented his establishment bill to the legislature in 1765, he made clear that he saw no connection between religious intolerance and favoring the Church of England. "I hope no persons of a different persuasion," he said, "will imagine, I am an Enemy to Toleration: I profess myself a warm advocate for it. . . . Yet I must inform Them, I never heard Toleration in any Country, made use of, as an argument to exempt Dissenters from bearing their Share of the Support of Established Religion." If he had not heard it before, he certainly was to hear it now, for there were many religious dissenters in North Carolina who defined tolerance quite differently. It was true that many Presbyterians, Moravians, Baptists, Lutherans, and Quakers quite openly admired Tryon's personal spirit of religious tolerance and knew that he was no narrow sectarian bigot. They were well aware of his many gestures of support for dissenting religions. In 1766 he had the legislature change the marriage law to allow Presbyterian ministers, as the Moravians already could, to perform the ceremony (under license of the governor) rather than leaving marriages of Presbyterians mostly in the hands of Anglican priests. A year later he and his wife visited the Moravian community of Wachovia in the backcountry and dazzled those people with many acts of generosity and expressions of admiration. In 1771 Tryon alone paid another visit to the Moravian community, where he had made many friends during his earlier visit. For Lutherans he showed his sympathy by seconding a petition to the bishop of London from a congregation in Rowan County that it be allowed to have its own minister and schoolteacher, a right specifically guaranteed only to Anglicans under the establishment law.[20]

Despite all Tryon's concessions to the dissenters, however, they refused to grant that he, as a representative of the state, had a right to tax non-Anglicans to pay salaries of Anglican clergymen. Especially in the western counties, where Presbyterians and Baptists predominated, the governor encountered strong resistance to the establishment. Presbyterian ministers in particular ignored marriage laws, even the liberalized law of 1766, and conducted their affairs without asking leave of Tryon or the bishop of London. Tryon complained bitterly about the resistance of these religious groups to his policy, going so far on one occasion as to suggest to the SPG (with uncharacteristic spleen) that the Baptists were "Enemies to Society, & Scandal to common Sense." He also protested to the legislature the Presbyterians' refusal to conform to the marriage law, because, he said, such defiance was not only an open repudiation of Crown authority but also caused him to lose license fees allowed under the marriage act. For his pains, he was forced to watch impotently while the Assembly rejected his requests for redress—ironically enough because he had tried to grant certain immunities to the Presbyterians in order to meet their dissentient objections, and the legislature thought he had compromised too much.[21]

Tryon also was made to understand that the Presbyterian citizens of Mecklenburg County did not want an Anglican minister. Andrew Morton arrived in the colony in 1766 with the intention of preaching in Mecklenburg, but Tryon dissuaded him from going to a place where he would only be humiliated by the Presbyterians. As Morton wrote the SPG, the people in that county "looked upon a law lately enacted in this province for the better establishment of the Church as oppressive as the Stamp Act and were determined to prevent its taking place there." Three years later the Mecklenburg Presbyterians petitioned Tryon to be relieved of having to support an Anglican establishment, wanting instead to use their tax money to pay the salaries of their own ministers—who, they pointed out, were of the same denomination as the established church of Scotland. Many of the Presbyterians had only recently migrated from Virginia and Pennsylvania to escape what they viewed as religious persecution, and they would have nothing to do with an Anglican establishment in North Carolina. Perhaps curiously, however, from 1768 to 1771 many frontier Presbyterians did support Tryon's efforts to uphold royal sovereignty by suppressing the movement known as the "Regulation," which Presbyterian leaders in Orange County called an "Infection."[22]

Tryon also had trouble enforcing the Orthodox Clergy Act among dissenters in Rowan County, a vast western territory stretching indefinitely into the Smoky Mountains and Cherokee country. The problem in this case, interestingly enough, arose when the small number of Anglicans in Rowan County petitioned Tryon to send them a minister and to appoint for them a vestry composed of adherents to the Church of England. They made their request despite the fact that a slate of candidates whom they had put up for a vestry had been defeated in a county election by non-Anglicans who refused to swear an oath "to the national church," as required by law. Although Tryon did not oblige the Rowan Anglicans in their request for an appointed vestry (such a measure was illegal, and obviously unwise), he did allow an Anglican minister, Theodorus Swaine Drage, to enter that hornet's nest of dissension in order to serve the Anglicans there. The results of this appointment were almost predictable. When the poor, gentle Drage went among the dissenting Presbyterians and attempted to enforce the establishment law on marriages and burials, they simply ignored him. Reporting his problem to Tryon, Drage noted that the dissenters in Rowan County saw a connection between the governor's attempts "to intrude on their civil rights" and "any intrusion on their religious rights." This maxim, wrote Drage, "I presume dangerous in itself not with respect to this county and the neighbouring counties, but to the whole Back Frontier of America," because the territory was "principally settled with Sectaries." Although Drage struggled manfully to secure election of an Anglican-controlled vestry, he did not succeed. Disgustedly he told Tryon that the Rowan voters were "rotten nuts," and he pleaded with the governor to intervene on the side of the Anglicans.[23]

Tryon's response to Drage's pleas for aid and comfort were, to say the least, equivocal. Whereas he assured the beleaguered minister that the dissenters' opposition to him was "unjustifiable," and that Drage's upholding the establishment was "laudable and Virtuous," the governor had to be careful about a too-rigid application of the laws. "I confess," Tryon candidly told Drage, "I have a pleasure in acknowledging myself greatly obliged by the Support the Presbyterians have afforded Government in my administration." To be sure, the dissidents in Rowan County were in "manifest Violation of the Rights and Liberties" of the Anglicans, but Tryon believed the best approach to "these Gentlemen" would be to "appeal to [their] reasons and judgment, and not [their] Passions." If argument did not prevail, then Drage could present a "Memorial" to the next legislature to have his salary paid from the colonial treasury rather than by the taxpayers of Rowan County.[24] Had the Reverend Mr. Drage suspected that Tryon was wavering in his devotion to upholding Crown authority, he might have been forgiven; but such doubts would not have been fair. The governor, as Tryon freely admitted, simply had to take into account all aspects of this problem and do the best he could under severe handicaps (not least was his lack of coercive power) to uphold the best interests of North Carolinians, the king, and himself.

In part because he favored Anglicans, but also because he disliked the "Incapacity" under which North Carolinians labored because of their lack of education, Tryon worked toward a better (and Anglican-dominated) educational system in the province. In his royal instructions, he was admonished by the king to "recommend to the Assembly to enter upon proper Methods for the erecting and maintaining of Schools," all of which were to employ only teachers licensed by the bishop of London. Therefore early in his administration he made inquiries of John Ashe, speaker of the Assembly, as to why the Board of Trade had objected to a law of two years previous for establishing public schools. Ashe's reply was that the board had discovered difficulties in the act and had not yet explained them. In any case, in 1766 Tryon proposed to the Assembly and had enacted into law a measure to adopt an academy at New Bern as a province-supported school. This institution, begun in 1764 by Thomas Thomlinson, was highly regarded by the citizens of New Bern and Craven County, so much so that they recommended to the governor in 1765 that he apply to the SPG for money to support it. Tryon gladly complied, soliciting "The Society's Bounty and Encouragement" for Thomlinson's educational efforts, and when no assistance was forthcoming, Tryon proposed in 1766 the law that made New Bern Academy public. The law required the master of the school and its faculty members to belong to the Church of England, in effect requiring dissenters to pay taxes for the upkeep of an Anglican school.[25]

Tryon did not direct all his educational efforts toward benefiting the eastern part of the province and Anglicans. In 1766 he and Mrs. Tryon expressed to a Moravian visitor at Brunswick a warm appreciation for that sect's educational efforts at Wachovia. Four years later the governor manifested an even more direct support for a non-Anglican school, despite his royal instructions, by encouraging the legislature to establish "a public Seminary in some part of the back Country of this Colony, for the Education of [Presbyterian] Youth." This recommendation, first proposed to the governor by the Presbyterians of Mecklenburg County, led to a law, which Tryon approved on January 15, 1771, establishing Queen's College in Mecklenburg County. Although the law stipulated that the president of that college be Anglican, it was assumed that the teachers and trustees would be Presbyterian. Tryon strongly urged that the Board of Trade accept this measure on account of the Presbyterians' support of his efforts against the Regulators, but the board refused on the grounds that Tryon had ignored royal instructions that all school teachers must be licensed by the bishop of London. In addition, the board had a general fear that a flourishing Queen's College would weaken Crown sovereignty even more in a colony that already seemed all too inclined to independent thinking. Tryon, chagrined that London viewed his support of the law as a breach of his unwavering support for the king's interests, nevertheless continued to advocate Queen's College. He went so far in late 1771—once Crown assent had been secured for the college's mere existence—as to propose that it be "erected" into a university.[26]

While Tryon in his first years as governor was devoting much time to public business, he was also attending to the private affairs of himself and his family. On May 19, 1765, Tryon dispatched a letter to General Thomas Gage, commander in chief of the British army in North America, informing Gage that he had married "an Old Tunbridge acquaintance of yours under the Nomination at that time, of Miss Wake," and that she now desired to be remembered to him. Later that summer he and his wife entertained John Bartram, the king's botanist, when Bartram stopped by Brunswick during an extensive collecting tour in England's southern colonies. The matter of housing took up a great deal of Tryon's time. As he told his uncle Sewallis Shirley, because the province had no fixed capital, he must rent four houses in order not to show himself "particularly partial to any particular Spot of the Country or people." Tryon used his house at Wilmington "when I hold the Land Office, which is twice a year"; the one at New Bern during his attendance at "the Genl Assembly and the Courts of Chancery"; and another just outside New Bern "for the purpose of raising a little Stock and Poultry for use of the family." Shortly after the death of Governor Dobbs, Tryon leased the fourth house, Castle Dobbs, or Russellborough, in Brunswick, and moved his family into the place. This estate, which Tryon considered his permanent home and which he purchased two years later from its owner, Edward Brice Dobbs, the former governor's son, he renamed Belle Font. The house, as Tryon described it to Shirley, sat on 55 acres of land; was built of wood; measured 45 by 35 feet; had two stories and a cellar, a parlor, and drawing room each 20 by 15 feet; and was adjacent to Brunswick. A piazza surrounded the house on both stories "with a Balustrade of four feet high, which is a great Security for my little girl." A stable and coach house stood out on the grounds, and although the house lacked a good kitchen, Tryon felt he could have a good one built "for forty Pounds Sterling." The estate provided the Tryons with apples, peaches, nectarines, figs, plums, melons, and fresh vegetables of every sort.[27]

Before the family occupied its new home, Mrs. Tryon, following her penchant for "Neatness," required that the interior be scoured, new whitewash and paint applied, and the outside also painted. Thereupon, Tryon oversaw the "opening and unpacking [of] half the furniture we brought from England," the rest having by then been scattered among his other three houses. All these operations were hindered by "the Sickness and indolence of the Workmen in this Hot Climate," for of all his servants only George and "a little French boy I got here" were well. His French chef, Pierre Le Blanc, "Turner, the farmer," and "the girl we took from my Farm" were all ill from the "fevers" and were taking chinchona bark as a febrifuge. With so many of his servants incapacitated, Tryon felt the need to bolster his domestic help by purchasing a "negro man Tom" from James Murray, a former councillor who had moved to Boston. Fortunately for "Mrs. Tryon and the little girl," they were escaping all the sickness, but "As to Myself I cannot say so much, having been sharply disciplined with a Bilious disorder in my Stomach and Eruptions of the Rash kind, on my Legs." This illness, which dogged Tryon for the next six months, and from which he never completely recovered, sometimes temporarily reduced his ability to work and even forced him to delay sending dispatches to government officials in London. But his administrative abilities were never seriously impaired by the disease. Upon reflection, he accepted these "inconveniences," noting that "every newcomer must experience in this Colony" what the locals called "a seasoning." Nevertheless, he remarked ruefully, "Surely it has a little too much of the Kian Pepper in it."[28]

Financially, Tryon was doing quite well in his position as governor. Besides his annual salary of £1,000 sterling from the king, he also was collecting fees, the long-standing right of royal governors, from the licensing of ordinaries and public houses and for granting marriage licenses, land warrants and patents, ships' registers, and commissions for various public officials. By July 1767 Tryon reported to the earl of Shelburne that he had received £4,390 proclamation money from all these sources, over and above his regular salary. Nevertheless he found these revenues inadequate to his office and duties, and he resented having to collect the proclamation money, hat in hand as it were, "from at least forty or fifty different hands, in which Number there must be some deficiencies." He did not believe that the province was "capable of adding any considerable addition to the fees," for the collectors' "inclination is as slack as their ability is weak for such a step." Only the income he derived from his £30,000 fortune saved him from sinking into "Mean and shabby" poverty. But despite these problems with money, Tryon was pleased that he was finally settled, "at great charges both of Labour and expense," in his new home, and he was optimistic that he could exercise "a large Field for good offices, If the People are reasonable." He looked forward to rendering "His Majesty as much Service in this Colony as in any other more settled."[29]

Certainly His Majesty intended that Tryon earn his pay, for the governor was inundated with work. From the beginning he took great interest in the economic affairs of the colony, spending much time and effort in schemes to increase its value for the good of its citizens, the king, and his own reputation and wallet. Tryon, unlike his predecessor Dobbs, generally believed that the Navigation Acts were favorable to North Carolina's trade, but he thought they needed some minor adjustments. Even as lieutenant governor he had encouraged the royal navy to use North Carolina pine planks in warship construction. He also proposed to the Board of Trade that the government increase its bounty on pine planking in order to increase exports of that product from his province. He also suggested that Carolina cypress trees would make excellent water pipes "to supply all the Conduit Pipes in London." Although nothing came of these efforts, Tryon continued to encourage the exploitation of the province's vast forests, and in 1767 he was delighted to receive from the Royal Society of Arts a model of an improved sawmill that had been designed by James Stansfield in a prize competition.[30]

During his tenure as governor of North Carolina, Tryon observed that the major economic activities of the colony centered around agriculture and the exploitation of pine tree products. In the maritime counties slaves provided most of the labor and often outnumbered whites five to one, but in the backcountry, people were too poor to own slaves, or owned only one to three, and lived a more marginal life. "A Plantation with Seventy Slaves on it," Tryon reported to Shirley, "is estimated a good property." The slaves' "chief employ" was in growing corn on the plantations and in producing barrels, shingles, posts, pails, ships, turpentine, tar, and a "Great Quantity of Lumber," which was exported to the West Indies. About forty sawmills were turning out boards. In addition to wood products, the colony also exported deerskins, pork, beef, beeswax, and tallow; it imported sugar, rum, molasses, slaves, and finished goods from England. Tryon did much to encourage these economic activities, and when necessary—such as during a corn shortage in 1766 and 1767—embargoed the export of a product in order to relieve "the poor and labouring people in General" from distress. He also expended a considerable amount of effort in attempting to divert trade by the Moravians and other backcountry settlers away from Charleston and toward Brunswick. Unfortunately for the economic health of the lower Cape Fear River, his labors met with little success.[31]

One of Tryon's most time-consuming tasks as governor was collecting information for officials in London on various activities in his colony. In August 1766 the Board of Trade ordered him to work up "a particular and exact account of the several Manufactures" in North Carolina. This was not a challenging request because, as Tryon reported in early 1767, there were only a few ship builders, weavers, and tanners at work in the entire province, and most new businesses had to do with the processing of pine trees. Responding to another order from the board in July 1767, Tryon compiled a list of all taxable persons in North Carolina. At the same time he also forwarded to Shelburne a lengthy paper, "A View of the Polity of the Province of North Carolina . . . ," that he had caused to be compiled. Meanwhile, the Treasury requested that he work up an account of all government expenses and revenues, which he did at great effort in time and labor and sent off in a bulky dispatch to the Lords of the Treasury. Then the earl of Shelburne solicited information on fees charged by various officers, on the "Annual charge of Maintaining and Supporting the entire Establishment of His Majesty's Colony of North Carolina," on how lands were granted in the province, and on how far in arrears proprietors were in paying quitrents on lands already granted. With the first parts of Shelburne's order Tryon complied easily, for he worked up a list of fees charged and received from Robert Palmer, surveyor general of the colony, and an explanation of how lands were granted; these he sent in two reports to Shelburne.[32]

Tryon was in for a surprise, however, when he began to look into the matter of quitrent collections. Upon inquiry he discovered that John Rutherfurd, receiver general of quitrents in North Carolina, had no list of those who owed rents and no law to guide him in collections. Rutherfurd's modus operandi was to appoint deputy collectors in all the counties and pay them a 5 percent commission from all collections, but the deputies were greatly hindered by lack of a rent roll. As Tryon reported to Shelburne, with considerable understatement, Rutherfurd's department stood "in need of some further Assistance . . . before the Receipt of Quit Rents can bear any proportion to the great Number of Patents that have been granted." Shortfalls in annual collections were somewhere between £7,000 and £28,000 proclamation money.[33] This discrepancy was the sort of oversight that really angered Tryon, for he had obviously discovered a glaring problem with orderly colonial administration, one that was costing his sovereign a great deal of money.

Hence, he set out, with an enthusiasm that was typical of him, to repair the damage. First he polled all officials in North Carolina who were connected with rent collections on how the king's revenues could be better secured. Then he inquired of Virginia's attorney general, John Randolph, how that colony handled the matter and was told that the enactment of a law providing for a roll and penalties for nonpayment of rents, plus restraints on collectors, was the most effectual way to guarantee that quitrents would be paid, even by sensitive Americans alarmed by any "Law which appears to lay a restraint on Property." Finally, in 1771 Tryon proposed such a law to the Assembly, only to have it fall short of adoption because of technicalities. Even at the end of his tenure as governor of North Carolina, however, Tryon was assuring Hillsborough that the bill, free of objections, "may be carried into execution in a future Session." Despite Tryon's ultimate failure to reform quitrent collections, both the king and Hillsborough were impressed by their subordinate's efforts to promote an increase in revenues for the Crown.[34]

Having been given the customary titles of captain general and vice admiral in the province upon assuming the governorship of North Carolina, Tryon was obliged to handle military and naval matters along with his other duties. By training and inclination, he found these responsibilities familiar and enjoyable. On May 18, 1765, he informed General

Thomas Gage that he was now in charge of the colony's military affairs, and he proceeded to look to his defenses. To his dismay he discovered that his province's only defensive post, Fort Johnston on the Cape Fear River, was in deplorable condition and that its commandant, Captain John Dalrymple, had been compelled by Governor Dobbs, through no fault of Dalrymple's, to flee the province rather than serve time in jail. Two other forts, Granville and Dobbs, had been commissioned but were only half built. Tryon immediately proceeded to appoint a temporary commandant for Fort Johnston, informing Welbore Ellis, secretary at war, that he was placing in that position a North Carolina native, Robert Howe, until the pleasure of his superiors in London could be known. He then made a survey of the fort's artillery and stores, only to have confirmed his worst fears, that the post was deficient to the point of helplessness in personnel, powder, flints, musket balls, cannon shot, and ordnance. Concluding to the marquis of Granby, master general of ordnance, that the fort was "a Disgrace," he nevertheless doubted whether "this Country will . . . at present be at any further Expense in the Rebuilding."[35]

Tryon's gloomy assessment turned out to be not entirely accurate, for over the next three years the military posture of Fort Johnston improved. By order of the Board of Trade, Tryon twice requested of the legislature, and had enacted on the second attempt, a measure to purchase three acres of woodland near Fort Johnston for use by the garrison. He also managed over a period of two years to prod the legislature into increasing the fort's manpower by one-third, from ten to fifteen soldiers. In 1769 Tryon achieved a major goal when he finally pushed through the Council and Assembly a bill "establishing a Militia in this Province." The new militia law provided for pay to both officers and soldiers called out on public service and for better regulations "for the good Order and Discipline of the Men." And finally he managed to secure a permanent commandant for Fort Johnston, first by persuading Captain Dalrymple to return to North Carolina and then, when Dalrymple died in 1766, by appointing Captain John Abraham Collet, a skilled cartographer who later achieved fame as the producer of many maps of various sections of North Carolina.[36]

Despite these improvements in the defensive posture of North Carolina, Tryon remained dissatisfied throughout his gubernatorial tenure with the ability of the colony to defend itself against external attack. He had good reason to be worried, for as he told Hillsborough in 1769, the Assembly, after having provided funds for the bare-bones rearming of

Fort Johnston, and after having made provision for a militia army on an emergency basis, had twice refused any expansion of funds for military improvements. Tryon was convinced the steps so far taken would prove wholly inadequate, "were war to break out." Yet the legislators doubted that war would indeed break out. North Carolina, they said, was "enjoying the blessings of peace" and would be wasting money by going beyond the few things already provided for. Disgustedly Tryon noted to Hillsborough "that the Argument on which they founded their refusal[s] was the Reason why they ought to have granted an aid for that Service." Hillsborough, in the meantime, encouraged Tryon to try again at a later date to get the legislature to spend more on the province's military establishment, especially powder and shot for Fort Johnston, lamenting "the obstinacy of the Assembly, in persisting to refuse to make Provision for the security & Defense of the Colony."[37]

Matters came to a head in late 1770, when Tryon received word from Hillsborough that the Spanish governor of Buenos Aires had sent an expedition against "His Maty's Subjects . . . at Port Egmont in Falkland Islands." War now seemed imminent between Britain and Spain, unless the Spanish Court disavowed this "open Act of Hostility," and Tryon was to look to the defenses of his province, so long neglected by the legislature. With this information to reinforce his requests for more defense money, Tryon went to the Assembly in December and received quick action. Within two weeks funds were appropriated for the purchase of "Six Thousand Weight of Gun Powder [and] Two Thousand Weight of Musket Balls & Shot." Tryon now quickly turned his attention to getting Fort Johnston into a state of defense. He also pledged to General Gage his full cooperation in implementing a new law of Parliament to assist any army recruiting parties that "may come into this Province by your Order." In the end his flurry of military preparations was unnecessary, for as Hillsborough informed him in early 1771, "his Catholic Majesty," the king of Spain, had disavowed the Falklands attack and thus public tranquility would continue.[38]

As vice admiral of North Carolina, Tryon was charged by the king, through "the Ordinances and Statutes of Our High Court of Admiralty of England," to enforce all laws relating to maritime commerce in the colony. Tryon, in a letter to Shelburne in 1767, explained that he met this responsibility by appointing a one-person vice admiralty court in North Carolina, which heard cases growing out of "Seizures made by the Officers of the Customs for breach of the Acts of Trade" and also "Suits brought by Mariners for their Wages." The court seldom met, said Tryon, "as grievances of that Nature dont often occur." A few cases did arise, however, such as those resulting from the condemnations of the ships *Samuel* and *Fox* after they had been seized on suspicion of breaking the Navigation Acts. The *Samuel*'s illegal cargo of molasses was sold, as were both the *Fox* and her cargo of illegal wine, all with Tryon's hearty approbation. But in another case, the seizure of the sloop *Lucy* and her cargo of rum by Captain Jeremiah Morgan, commander of the sloop of war *Hornet*, Tryon decided that a decree by the vice admiralty court requiring payment of duties on the rum might be ex post facto, and he referred the matter to Shelburne for clarification. The case languished before the Board of Trade during the remainder of Tryon's tenure as governor of North Carolina.[39]

While Tryon applauded the vigor of Captain Morgan "in preventing the Commerce of Smuggling," at the same time he found Morgan's boisterous conduct in other respects hardly such as to endear Carolinians to the royal navy. In 1764 Captain Morgan had had a "Scuffle" with Maurice Moore, an assemblyman, after which Morgan challenged Moore to a duel. The assemblyman refused, but Morgan continued to smart from his alleged "loss of honor." Two years later he confronted the entire Assembly as it was "returning from the House" and berated the legislators in a threatening manner, even though they were under immunity while the legislature was sitting. Furious at this breach of decorum, the Assembly ordered Morgan's arrest, whereupon he escaped seizure by returning to his warship, thus passing beyond the authority of the province's civil government. As Tryon noted to Shelburne in describing the confrontation and Morgan's "retreat," "this latter part of his conduct" had freed the governor "of the Dilemma I might have been under had he been taken into Custody." Indeed, which authority, civil or military, would Tryon have been compelled to uphold had he been faced with the arrest and incarceration of a naval officer, even one who reflected "no Honor to His Majesty's Service"? As things now stood, Tryon would uphold Morgan's claim, well founded in precedents such as Captain Phipps's earlier refusal to allow a sheriff aboard his warship, that a British naval officer was supreme upon his own decks. The legislators reluctantly acquiesced to Tryon's interpretation of the law—at least for the moment.[40]

CHAPTER THREE

Stamps and Boundaries

By far the most serious crisis that Governor Tryon had to confront in the first years of his administration was resistance by North Carolinians in 1765 and 1766 to the Stamp Act. This political storm, which had been brewing since the end of the Seven Years' War, resulted when the government of Britain decided to maintain an army of 10,000 men in North America and the West Indies and have Americans pay for its upkeep through taxes laid on by Parliament. The first step in this program, the Sugar Act of 1764, hardly affected North Carolina, but the Stamp Act, which was apparently first proposed by North Carolinian Henry Eustace McCulloh, passed Parliament on March 22, 1765, and was to go into effect on the first day of November, was a different matter altogether. The law required that stamps or stamped paper, costing from half a penny to £10 and collectible only in specie, be affixed to newspapers, legal documents, bills of lading, college diplomas, dice, playing cards, tavern licenses, and many other items. Stamp distributors were to be appointed for each colony, and anyone who broke the law would suffer the penalty of heavy fine and forfeiture, to be divided among the governor, the informant, and the Treasury. Cases arising under the statute were to be tried either in the provincial courts "or in any court of admiralty."[1]

Although Tryon and other British officials, including Prime Minister George Grenville, were aware that Americans adamantly opposed the Stamp Act, they believed that once passed, it would be peacefully promulgated. They were surprised, therefore, when a storm of American protest arose against the law on the grounds that it impinged upon the colonists' English right of no taxation without representation and that it allowed vice admiralty courts, operating without juries, to try freeborn Englishmen accused of violating the law. Tryon, although a supporter of monarchical privilege, was no tyrant, and in his first address to the Assembly upon taking office in 1765, he declared, "I shall ever think it equally my Duty, to preserve the People, in their constitutional Liberty; as to maintain Inviolate, the Just, and necessary Rights of the Crown." But as he witnessed during the summer of 1765 the rising tide of opposition to the Stamp Act in several colonies, he became uncomfortably aware that the time was fast approaching when he must support the one or the other; in the eyes of North Carolinians he could not possibly maintain both. When colonial protest resulted in October in the meeting of the Stamp Act Congress, Tryon heaved a sigh of relief that North Carolina's legislature had not been in session to elect delegates. Therefore the colony, along with Virginia, Georgia, and New Hampshire, was not represented. Nevertheless local resentments against the law were powerful and took early form in a pamphlet by Maurice Moore, assemblyman and judge of Superior Court, entitled *Justice and Policy of Taxing the American Colonies in Great Britain, Considered* (1765). In this tract, Moore asserted that English citizens could be taxed only with their consent and excoriated the notion that colonists were "virtually represented" in Parliament, ideas later bolstered by another Carolinian, James Iredell.[2]

On October 19, as Tryon "lay extremely Ill of the Fevers of this Country," the "General Alarm which was spread against the Stamp Act" in North Carolina finally erupted at Wilmington into the public protest that the governor so long had dreaded. By evening of that day, a Saturday, about 500 people had converged upon the courthouse at Wilmington to demonstrate against the Stamp Act. They began by burning an effigy of the earl of Bute, who they mistakenly believed was responsible for the hated measure, and then proceeded to rout out all the men in the town to observe the fire. They spent the remainder of the evening drinking toasts to "LIBERTY, PROPERTY, and No STAMP-DUTY." Twelve nights later, on Halloween, Tryon was disturbed when another crowd assembled in Wilmington for a second protest. The members of the mob placed an effigy of Liberty in a coffin and with this gruesome symbol of lost freedoms, marched solemnly to the churchyard, while "a Drum in Mourning beat before them, and the town Bell, muffled," tolled "a doleful Knell" in accompaniment. Finding at the last moment that Liberty still had signs of life, the people seated the effigy in a chair next to a bonfire, "and concluded the Evening with great Rejoicings on finding that LIBERTY had still an Existence in the COLONIES."[3]

Tryon knew only too well that he had no coercive power to bring the

North Carolinians into what he considered a due submission to British law. Nor, in fact, did he feel that use of military might was necessary or desirable in his province, particularly if the king's authority could be enforced against "the more formidable Colonies to the Northward," thus bringing a more "ready Acquiescence in the Southern Provinces." Therefore he attempted to secure submission to the Stamp Act in North Carolina with a shrewder strategy than any other royal governor devised. Believing that the Assembly might follow the lead of Virginia and pass resolves against the law, he declared that the legislature remained prorogued. In the meantime the stamp receiver in North Carolina, Dr. William Houston, after being confronted by about 300 fellow citizens, agreed to resign his office. Also, a crowd had compelled Andrew Steuart, printer of *The North-Carolina Gazette*, to agree to publish his newspaper without using stamped paper, "Rather than run the Hazard of Life . . . or have his Printing-office destroy'd." Following these incidents, Tryon invited about fifty of the leading gentlemen of Brunswick, New Hanover, and Bladen counties to meet with him for dinner at his home on November 18, 1765. Plying them with food and drink, Tryon, in his most diplomatic manner, explained to them that he too disapproved of the Stamp Act. He realized that there was not cash enough in North Carolina to pay the tax for one year, and he felt a particular concern for the people of the colony. Yet he hoped no one would oppose the landing of the stamped paper when it arrived or that anyone harbored a desire to destroy "the Dependence on the Mother Country." Although he was applying to London for a "favorable indulgence and exemption" from the duties for North Carolina, he hoped the people would accept the tax and reap the benefits of the trade that other colonies would lose because of their resistance. Meanwhile, Tryon would pay from his own funds stamp duties on all documents from which he would profit as governor, and also for a number of wine licenses for some towns in the colony.[4]

Although Tryon had cleverly presented the leaders of the colony with a tempting smorgasbord of self-serving proposals in hopes that they would break ranks with other Americans and obey the Stamp Act, his plan did not succeed. The next day, the gentlemen firmly refused his offers, even though they expressed great respect for his honor and sincerity in making them. They were convinced that the Stamp Act was, in their words, "destructive to those Liberties which as British Subjects we have a right to enjoy in Common with Great Britain," and although they were loyal and obedient servants of the king, "Submission to any Part of so oppressive &

as we think so Unconstitutional Attempt [at taxation], is a direct Opening & Inlet for Slavery. . . . An Admission of part would put it out of our Power to refuse with any Propriety a Submission to the Rest; and as we can never Consent to be deprived of the invaluable Privilege of a Tryal by Jury which is one part of that Act we think it more consistent as well as securer Conduct to prevent to the Utmost of our Power the Operation of any Part of it." Hence Tryon, to his chagrin, could not get the North Carolinians to abandon what was to them an important principle.[5]

An uneasy calm settled over Tryon's administration after his aborted attempt to persuade North Carolinians voluntarily to accept the law. With the inception of the law on November 1, no stamped paper had yet arrived from England, and ships ceased to clear the ports while courts of law were closed. Twenty-eight days later, the sloop *Diligence*, Captain Phipps commanding, arrived at Brunswick with stamped paper on board, but because Houston had resigned the distributorship, there was no one to receive it. Hence the paper remained on board. Reporting this "Stagnation of Public Business, and Commerce" to London in late December, Tryon declared that unless the stalemate were broken soon, the "Consequences to this Colony" would be "fatal." He noted the dearth of specie in North Carolina and flatly stated that "the Stamp Duty in All its Parts [was] impracticable." These considerations were what had led him, he wrote, "to make my Proposals for the ease and Conveniency of the People, and to endeavour to Reconcile them to this Act of Parliament." Although North Carolinians had rejected his suggestions, they continued to hold him in high regard. When he went up to Wilmington on December 19 officially to proclaim himself governor (his commission had just arrived in the colony), he was received cordially by the gentlemen of the borough as he arrived on the barge of the *Diligence* in company with Captain Phipps. In addition, 2,000 militiamen from the neighborhood discharged seventeen pieces of artillery in his honor.[6]

Shortly after his warm welcome to Wilmington, however, Tryon's ceremonial accession to office was spoiled by an ugly incident. Captain Phipps, it seems, had taken offense because ships anchored in the Cape Fear River off the town had not struck their colors in his honor as he arrived. He ordered his men to seize all the colors, despite the futile arguments of the ships' masters that they had flown their flags and pennants in honor of the governor, there being no king's vessel in sight. Affronted by Phipps's churlish behavior, the townsmen and sailors hurled epithets at him as he strode to his lodgings, hauled his barge up to the courthouse, and would have set it afire had not Frederick Gregg, the mayor of Wilmington, interceded. The populace then dragged the boat underneath Phipps's window and yelled insults at him until Tryon, who was also in the house, harangued the people from a window and caused them to lose temper at him as well. Finally the sullen crowd gathered around an ox and some barrels of punch that Tryon had provided for their refreshment, broke open the barrels so that the punch ran into the street, cut off the ox's head and put it in the pillory, and gave the rest of the carcass to slaves. Tryon, furious at this affront to his dignity, refused to hear apologies from the Corporation of Wilmington, whose members were acutely embarrassed by this whole affair. Henceforth, swore the governor, he would favor the town of New Bern over Wilmington in all his official dealings. Phipps, meantime, threatened to bring up the *Diligence* and cannonade the town, but he was finally dissuaded by shallow water in the river and cooler heads than his.[7]

In early 1766 Tryon realized that the confrontation between himself, representing royal power, and the people, united in opposition to the Stamp Act, was reaching a climax. The law, he reported to the Board of Trade, had "been as generally rejected in this Province as in any Colony on the Continent," and he was only too happy to cooperate with Captain Lobb, commander of the sloop *Viper*, and Captain Phipps, commander of the sloop *Diligence*, in forbidding any ships entering or clearing the Cape Fear River until they could prove that they had affixed the required stamps on their papers. Before long the blockade bore fruit. On January 14, 1766, Captain Lobb seized the incoming merchant ships *Dobbs* and *Patience* that had sailed from American ports without the necessary stamped paper, and shortly thereafter Lobb detained the sloop *Ruby* for the same reason. Lobb sent all these ships' papers to William Dry, collector of customs at Brunswick, who thereupon asked Robert Jones, the attorney general, for a ruling on the legality of proceeding against the vessels. Jones's decision, which he handed down on February 15, was that the seizures were legal and that Dry should prosecute the cases in the vice admiralty court in Halifax, Nova Scotia.[8]

Following hard on the attorney general's ruling, Tryon was faced with a firestorm of opposition from the citizens of the lower Cape Fear. On the evening of February 16, he was visited by Dry, who informed Tryon that he had been warned by many prominent men in a letter of the fifteenth that "the People of the Country [would] come down in a Body" should he suffer any of the seized vessels "or the Papers belonging to them to be carried out of the River." Because Dry had promised to meet these citizens and discuss the matter, Tryon strongly urged him first to put all the ships' papers on board the *Viper* for safekeeping, as Tryon "apprehended . . . those very Subscribers would compel him to give them up." Dry's answer was that "they might take them from him, but he would never give them up without Capt. Lobb's order." On February 18 "the Principal gentlemen, Freeholders and Inhabitants" of the lower Cape Fear elected leaders and signed an "Association" against the Stamp Act, vowing "at the Expence of our Lives and Fortunes" to fight against "the Oppressive and Arbitrary Tendency" of the law.[9]

The following afternoon, several hundred of the Associators armed themselves and proceeded to Brunswick to make their grievances known to Governor Tryon. Between the hours of six and seven o'clock they collected near his home, then sent George Moore and Cornelius Harnett to call upon him with a letter signed by John Ashe, Thomas Lloyd, and Alexander Lillington, informing him that the people intended to secure "redress of their grievances, from the Commanding Officer of His Majesty's Ships." In the meantime, to protect Tryon's person, property, and family from "Insult," and if "agreeable to Your Excellency," the letter said, "a Guard of Gentlemen shall be immediately detached for that purpose." The governor, knowing that the guard was designed not to defend him but to keep him at home while the crowd did its will, vigorously protested that the protection "was not Necessary, or Required." Nevertheless, after Moore and Harnett withdrew, Tryon found his house "surrounded with Arm'd Men, to the Number I estimate, of One Hundred and fifty." He now learned from "some of the Gentlemen" that their real intention was to find Captain Lobb, who they had been told was in Tryon's house. After refusing to swear that Lobb was not under his protection, Tryon melodramatically declared to the North Carolinians that "as they had force in their Hands . . . they might break open my Locks & force my Doors." Demurring from this course of action, they soon learned that Lobb was on board the *Viper* and departed to search for the captain, leaving a guard to watch Tryon's house.[10]

That evening at eleven o'clock, Tryon slipped a message by one of his servants to Captain Phipps on board the *Diligence*, anchored nearby in the Cape Fear River. In his note he urged Phipps and Lobb to assist Captain John Dalrymple, commandant of Fort Johnston, "should any Insult be offered of His Majesty's Fort or Stores." Poor Dalrymple had only five men in his garrison at the time and stood "in Need of all the Assistance the *Viper & Diligence* Sloops can give." If necessary, Tryon asserted pugnaciously, the naval officers and Dalrymple were "to Repel force with force," or remove to their ships whatever stores of ordnance and ammunition they thought necessary for the good of the service. Phipps replied with expressions of regret for any "uneasiness" that this "Accident" had given Tryon but assured the governor that a five-man naval party was already on the way down to Fort Johnston with spikes for Dalrymple's guns if he needed them. Then Phipps worked out a system of light signals that Tryon was to show from his windows to let Phipps know that his message had arrived safely.[11]

Soon after Tryon had "put up the Lights required," Phipps himself arrived, "the Guards having quitted the Posts they had taken round the House." Spouting fire and brimstone, Phipps offered Tryon the use of his ships' cannon if he wished to obliterate the town of Brunswick and its "mob," but Tryon assured him that his only duty was to protect Fort Johnston. To that end Tryon wrote a note to Dalrymple, which he put in Phipps's hands, ordering the commandant to obey the commands of either Phipps or Lobb; in the early morning hours of February 20, Phipps delivered this message safely. Shortly thereafter Lobb, fearing that the constantly growing crowd of disgruntled citizens in Brunswick intended to seize the fort and turn its guns on His Majesty's ships in the river, ordered Dalrymple to spike the guns as a precaution. The order was duly executed.[12]

After a night of little rest, Tryon received a note from Captain Lobb at noon on February 20 requesting the governor's presence on board the *Diligence* for a conference. When Tryon arrived for the meeting, he found Lobb, Phipps, Dry, and Thomas McGuire, judge of the local vice admiralty court, awaiting him. He now learned from Dry that the night before armed citizens had broken into Dry's desk and forcibly taken the unstamped papers of the *Dobbs*, *Ruby*, and *Patience*. Additionally, Lobb told him, a committee of citizens had visited Lobb on board his ship and demanded that he turn over to them "Possession of the Sloops he had Seized." The committee had given him until that afternoon to decide whether he would comply. As he told Tryon, he was willing to part with the *Dobbs* and *Ruby*, but he had no intention of letting go of the *Patience* and, in fact, was demanding that the purloined papers of the *Patience* be returned to him. Not even the fact that the citizens of Wilmington had cut off all supplies to the *Viper* and *Diligence* was enough to shake the captain's resolve. Tryon heartily approved of Lobb's stance and urged him not to consider in any way the governor's pride, family, or property in his execution of his duty; for Tryon "was greatly sollicitous for the Honor of

Government, and His Majesty's Interest in the present exigency." After
returning home, however, Tryon received word that Lobb, contrary to his
protestations of only a few hours before, had in fact released all three
vessels. Disgusted, Tryon wrote Secretary of State Henry Seymour Conway in London. "I could not help owning [that] I thought the detaining
the *Patience* became a Point that concerned the Honor of Government,"
he said, especially because the opponents of the law seemed to be carrying
every point, and his ability to enforce the Stamp Act was becoming
weaker. In fact, Tryon soon learned that the Associators were exacting
promises from officials that they would make no more attempts to enforce the Stamp Act. In this measure, as in all others, the Associators were
successful, except that William Pennington, comptroller of the port of
Brunswick, refused to accede to their demands and sought refuge in
Tryon's home on the evening of the twentieth.[13]

The following morning, Tryon was mortified to discover upon glancing
out a window that Pennington was leaving his home with James Moore.
Calling these two men back, Tryon demanded to know what was going
on and was informed by Moore that the armed citizens, still embodied
nearby, wished to speak with the comptroller. Tryon frostily told Moore
that he, Tryon, "had Occasion to employ" Pennington on dispatches
relating to "His Majesty's Service" and could not let him go. Moore
thereupon departed, and Tryon, accompanied by Pennington, went back
inside his house. About five minutes later Moore returned with about 500
men, surrounded Tryon's home, and dispatched Cornelius Harnett, a
leader of the crowd, to knock on the governor's door and ask for a short
conference with Pennington. When Harnett was admitted, he informed
the comptroller that the people insisted that he take the oath not to
enforce the Stamp Act. At that point Tryon interrupted to reiterate to
Pennington that he was under the governor's protection and that he need
not swear any oath of which he did not approve. Thereupon Harnett
bluntly informed Pennington that if the governor did not let him go, the
citizenry "were determined to take him out of the House" by force, and
this was an insult they did not wish to offer Tryon if they could possibly
avoid it. Angrily, Tryon replied that one more of their insults "would not
tend to any great Consequence, after they had already offered every Insult
they could Offer." Pennington, however, had grown more and more uneasy during this conversation and finally blurted out that he chose to go
with Harnett. Reminded by Tryon that his offer of protection stood,
Pennington wretchedly declared to his host that if an oath were exacted it

would be gained only by compulsion and that he would rather resign his office than do anything contrary to his duty. Tryon quickly seized upon this point and told Pennington that he had better resign, whereupon paper was brought and his resignation secured. At that point Tryon said, "Mr. Pennington, now Sir, you may go." Hence, Pennington and the entire band of Associators retired from the governor's house and shortly thereafter dispersed to their homes. Almost immediately, Captains Lobb and Phipps began receiving provisions for their ships, and tensions eased in the lower Cape Fear region.[14]

Despite his impotence in the affairs of the past few days—or perhaps because of his impotence—Tryon in late February and early March 1766 was in no mood merely to forgive and forget the "insults" that he and his family had suffered both personally and as representatives of royal authority. On February 21, after the Associators had departed Brunswick for their homes, Tryon went on board the *Viper* and vented his spleen against Captain Lobb for having given up the sloop *Patience* after he had vowed to the governor that he would not. Lobb insisted that he had acted honorably, although the governor remained skeptical. Then Tryon suggested to Lobb that the latter had been too hasty in spiking the guns of Fort Johnston, and again Lobb defended his actions as being necessary and within the letter and spirit of the governor's orders. Tryon then left Lobb's ship and proceeded to Fort Johnston, where he ordered the spikes drilled out of the cannon, an operation, he noted with relief, that was executed "without Prejudice to the Pieces." Although Tryon still believed that Captain Lobb had not comported himself well in the recent crisis, and although he had that officer write out his justifications for his actions in case of proceedings against him in the future, Tryon took no further action in the case.[15]

Tryon then proceeded to act against other persons who he believed had acted irresponsibly in the past few days. Smarting because Maurice Moore, a prominent judge, had taken such a visible role in opposing the Stamp Act, Tryon removed him from office and commissioned Edmund Fanning to take his place. Then he lashed out during a Council meeting on February 26 against Andrew Steuart, editor of the *North-Carolina Gazette* and public printer for the province, for having published during the recent unpleasantness what Tryon called an "inflammatory" letter. Thereupon the governor declared Steuart's commission as public printer suspended. In the same meeting Tryon announced that the legislature would remain prorogued until the fall of 1766, and he issued a proclamation "strictly charging and commanding all officers both civil and Military to exert their Authority in suppressing all such illegal proceedings" as had just taken place. Rather enigmatically, he ended his proclamation by declaring that any officials refusing to do their duty "shall answer the Contrary at their peril."[16]

Given Tryon's recent inability to control events, his threatening proclamation might have been dismissed by the citizens of North Carolina as idle bombast. If so, they underestimated their governor, for in March and April he wrote both Secretary of State Conway and the Board of Trade seriously suggesting that the government send "Military force into this Colony" to quell defiance against the Stamp Act. If such action were taken, as Tryon seemed to hope would be the case, then the troops ought to arrive in the fall, after the weather had cooled. Two regiments of regulars, supported by two sloops of war, Tryon suggested, would be an adequate force "to give Law to the commercial Interest of this Government" and "to secure His Majesty's Stores and Artillery at Fort Johnston." Although he hoped that "the Inhabitants [would not] be so Weak, in the Vain Imagination of their Strength" as to make their situation any more desperate than it already was, he was fully prepared to support the king and ministry should they decide that the North Carolinians already deserved military chastisement for their unlawful and haughty defiance of Britain's will.[17]

Governor Tryon now had to deal with but one last unpleasantness—Wilmington's cutting off of supplies to Lobb's and Phipps's warships during the recent confrontation. Writing a cold note to Moses John DeRosset, mayor of Wilmington, Tryon demanded to know why a contractor's boat loaded with provisions for the *Viper* was detained at Wilmington during the crisis. DeRosset replied that the supplies had been held up as part of the Associators' agreement to compel release of the seized merchant ships, but "Since the Accommodation of Matters with the commanding Officers of the King's Ships," a supply of provisions had been sent the warships, "and Your Excellency may be Assured of the best Endeavours of this Corporation to forward His Majesty's Service." In closing, however, DeRosset whined that the citizens of Wilmington could not help but notice "that Your Excellency... on every Occasion, [laid] the whole Blame for every Transaction relative to the Opposition made to the Stamp-Act on this Borough when it is so well known the whole Country has been equally concerned in it." This gratuitous comment Tryon allowed to pass in contemptuous silence, but he tucked it into his memory as one more mark against a town for which he had already developed a considerable aversion.[18]

Even while Tryon was dealing with the crisis of colonial opposition to the Stamp Act, the measure was in the process of being repealed by Parliament. On March 1 Conway informed Tryon that a repeal measure had been introduced in the House of Commons. Thirty days later he officially announced the demise of the Stamp Act and the passage of the Declaratory Act, asserting parliamentary supremacy within the empire "in all matters whatsoever." At the same time, Charles Stewart, duke of Richmond, secretary of state for the Southern Department, notified Tryon that Parliament was indemnifying all persons who had incurred financial losses because of attempts to enforce the stamp law, and the Board of Treasury wrote to request the return of all the stamped paper in Tryon's possession. Tryon was delighted with this news, for he had believed from the first that the Stamp Act was a mistake. Moreover, as he informed a number of persons, he had continued to meet with total resistance to the law in North Carolina. He was particularly pleased that Parliament was providing indemnities for citizens who had suffered economically in enforcing the law because William Houston, the North Carolina stamp commissioner, was still being boycotted and ill treated by his neighbors. Tryon knew, of course, that money could not restore the standing of a person like Houston in the community, but at least it could indicate to him and to his fellow citizens that the king, Parliament, and Tryon himself recognized his honor and worth.[19]

On June 25, 1766, Tryon officially proclaimed in North Carolina that the Stamp Act was repealed, and congratulations were exchanged all around. If citizens were uncomfortable with the Declaratory Act, they muffled their criticisms amidst the general euphoria over having successfully resisted what they perceived to be an unconstitutional exaction of taxes without their consent. If Tryon was unhappy with the feeling that Crown authority and parliamentary supremacy had suffered grievous blows at the hands of American protesters during the past year or so, he kept his disquiet to himself. He could not help being a little ruffled, however, when the citizens of Wilmington, in their address of congratulations on repeal of the Stamp Act, suggested once more that Tryon had picked them out for special censure. In his reply, therefore, he frostily denied doing any such thing, thus bringing from the Corporation of Wilmington a hasty assertion that they had meant no disrespect to the governor in their previous remarks. Only then did Tryon express his willingness "to forget"—but pointedly not to forgive—"every Impropriety of Conduct . . . the Town of Wilmington have shown . . . toward me in the late Commotions."[20]

As the Stamp Act crisis came to its inglorious and somewhat ambiguous end, Tryon turned his attention to many other matters engaging him as governor of North Carolina. A continuing problem that he had been attempting to resolve was the settling of a boundary line between North Carolina and South Carolina. When he assumed office, a temporary boundary line, which had been run in three parts in the years 1735, 1737, and 1764, separated the colonies as far westward as the lands "claimed by the Catawba Indians," on the Salisbury-Charlotte road. But authorities in England were aware of a pressing need to extend the line, for land disputes were rife along the uncertain border. Even before Tryon left England in 1764, he had been instructed by the Board of Trade to cooperate as governor of North Carolina with William Bull, lieutenant governor of South Carolina, in determining what would constitute a "proper final Boundary." In the meantime he and Bull were to abide by the dividing line already run.[21]

Tryon pitched into this assignment with his usual verve and enthusiasm, writing Bull in February 1765 about his instructions and spending his spare moments over the next hectic months analyzing the problem. On January 27, 1766, during a lull in the Stamp Act troubles, Tryon wrote up a report of his findings for the Board of Trade, which included a number of remarkable recommendations. His first proposal, that the line of 1764 be extended westward by 106 miles to the Saluda River, was not unexpected. But his second one was, for he rejected claims by North Carolinians to lands north of Winyah Bay and the Pee Dee River, declaring that to incorporate those lands into North Carolina "would too much Contract the Sea Board of the South Government" and be detrimental to South Carolina's development. This was a statesmanlike act, and in April 1767 Tryon encouraged the new governor of South Carolina, Lord Charles Greville Montagu, to support his proposals before the Board of Trade. When Montagu visited Tryon a year later, he told the North Carolina governor that the plan was acceptable and probably would be approved by "the South Govt.," whereupon Tryon vigorously renewed his recommendations to London.[22]

Then in December 1768 Tryon received from Montagu an entirely new proposal, one that was totally unacceptable to North Carolina and therefore brought all progress on resolving the boundary dispute to a halt. In his new plan Montagu suggested that the boundary line be extended westward to the Catawba lands, around those lands to the Catawba River, along the Catawba to its southern branch, and finally along that branch to its source in the "Cherokee Mountains." Tryon vehemently protested to Montagu and Hillsborough that this plan, if adopted, would cut off North Carolina's access to the west and reduce the colony's size by one million acres. The North Carolina Council and Assembly also dissented strongly against Montagu's proposals. In response, the South Carolina Council asserted that Tryon's arguments against the new plan were untenable, then proceeded to reject his proposals of 1766 and to urge the government in England to accept Montagu's suggestions. While this haggling was going on, the Board of Trade took action on the border dispute, and in April 1771 it recommended to the Privy Council a compromise line, which was accepted. Thereupon the governors of both Carolinas were ordered to appoint commissioners to survey the proposed new line. By that time, Tryon had left North Carolina for his new position as governor of New York, but the issue continued to vex his successor, Josiah Martin, even until the outbreak of the American Revolution.[23]

Another matter that occupied Tryon at great length was Indian affairs, both in his own colony and in North America at large. In May 1765 he informed General Gage that he was just beginning his education on Indian matters, but within the year he was deeply immersed in that multifaceted business. In late 1765 the Board of Trade ordered Tryon to have the North Carolina legislature defray part of the expenses that a surveyor, Samuel Wyley, had incurred during his survey of the Catawba lands in 1764. After accomplishing that task, Tryon turned to a request by chiefs of the Tuscarora tribe; they wanted to sell part of their lands in North Carolina and join the Six Nations near Lake Oneida in New York. With the approbation of John Stuart and Sir William Johnson, respectively superintendents of Indian affairs in the Southern and Northern departments, as well as that of the North Carolina legislature, Tryon permitted the Tuscaroras to execute their removal from the colony. In return for Tryon's assistance in these matters, Diagawejee, the Tuscarora sachem, honored Tryon by conferring upon the governor his own name.[24]

Tryon also became involved in questions regarding the Indian trade within his colony, for in 1764 the Board of Trade had proclaimed that this business was to be regulated by the Indian superintendents and that all the colonies' laws dealing with Indian affairs were to be stricken from the books. When Stuart notified the southern governors of this plan, they all acceded to it rather readily, except for Tryon, who informed the Indian superintendent in February 1767 that he could not go along with the plan unless the North Carolina Assembly gave approval. Despite this caveat, Tryon did issue a proclamation from the king in July, ordering all Indian traders in North Carolina to conform to the new regulations. He hastened at the same time to issue another proclamation, at the behest of Shelburne, ordering all North Carolinians west of the Proclamation Line of 1763 to remove themselves eastward forthwith and to cease molesting the Cherokees. In 1768, when the Board of Trade reversed itself and returned the business to the governors, Tryon resumed regulation of the Indian trade in his colony.[25]

The constant encroachments of North Carolinians upon the Cherokee's hunting grounds led Tryon to support Stuart's idea of a boundary line to separate the two races. By 1766 Stuart had managed to get the South Carolinians to survey such a line for that colony to a northern terminus on the Reedy River, and the Cherokee had requested that the boundary be extended through North Carolina and into Virginia as far as Chiswell's Lead Mine. Stuart first proposed the idea to Tryon in February 1766, but the governor responded equivocally, declaring that he had neither instructions nor funds for running such a line. Moreover, illness had kept him from studying the problems confronting North Carolina's western settlements. Nevertheless, when he had received "such particular Informations" as he had "sent for from the Back Counties," he would address Stuart's proposal more fully. Stuart responded by sending Tryon an overwhelming amount of material to show that North Carolinians were abusing the Cherokee in violation of the Proclamation Line of 1763 and that the Cherokee were becoming extremely restive under these infringements. Thereupon Tryon was converted to support a boundary line to delineate the lands of the Cherokee and whites, insisting only that it leave on the eastern side parts of Rowan and Mecklenburg counties that had already been settled by North Carolinians. His Council also accepted the proposal, and Tryon, Stuart, and the Cherokee agreed to meet in September 1766 to arrange details.[26]

For a variety of reasons, Tryon and the other principals were not able to keep the September appointment, but plans for running the boundary line did not abate. In November the North Carolina Assembly granted Tryon £100 proclamation money to defray the expenses of boundary commissioners, and during the spring of 1767, Tryon himself decided to accompany the commissioners, John Rutherfurd, Robert Palmer, and John Frohock, when they proceeded westward to their task. At last Tryon and

Stuart made final plans to meet on June 1 for a conference with the Cherokee on the Tyger River in northern South Carolina. Although Stuart, to Tryon's disgust, was forced in mid-May to cancel his own attendance because of other business, the governor and his party set out for the North Carolina backcountry during the latter part of the month, accompanied by two regiments of Rowan and Mecklenburg county militia. Without undue incident Tryon's party reached the Tyger River in late May, and on June 1 Tryon commenced talks with a Cherokee chief named Ustenaka, or Jud's Friend, about a boundary.[27]

During the conference Tryon assured the Cherokee that the proposed boundary line would help him keep white men off the Indians' land, as he had been ordered to do by "His most gracious Majesty King George." The Indians agreed through their spokesman, Ustenaka, that a boundary was needed in order to control the "Rogues among your People and among my people." After bestowing upon Tryon the name of Ohaiah Equah, or Great Wolf, the Cherokee readily agreed to commence surveying the line. Quickly Tryon made arrangements for the Cherokee to go to Salisbury and receive presents at government expense from John Mitchell, a merchant, and on June 4, 1767, the work began. For two days Tryon accompanied the boundary commissioners in their tasks, then departed for Brunswick with part of the militia in escort. After suffering no worse mishap than having one of his horses stolen, and after visiting the Catawba Indians at their camp on Fishing Creek, Tryon reached home in June. He had traveled a total of 843 miles.[28]

In early July Tryon reported to Shelburne that the commissioners had completed their work on the boundary line. Proudly he boasted that his labors had produced results answering all His Majesty's intentions of "maintaining Peace and Harmony" between white North Carolinians "and the bordering Indians under His Protection." Although Tryon had spent the large sum of £1,490 proclamation money upon this venture, he thought the result was worth the expenses, not least because it had helped him regain the prestige he had lost during the Stamp Act crisis. The boundary commissioners, in fact, had named a mountain peak near the boundary in his honor. The only irksome thing in the entire project, he told Shelburne, was that Stuart, after "fair Promises . . . of meeting me on this very important Duty . . . should omit joining this Service." Tryon was aware, of course, that Stuart had begged off because of genuinely pressing business, but apparently the governor's vanity was wounded because Stuart had not dropped everything to meet him for an interview.[29]

CHAPTER FOUR

Tryon Palace and Reform Measures

E arly in his tenure as governor of North Carolina, Tryon began to emphasize as part of his reform measures the importance of establishing a permanent capital for North Carolina and of constructing a home for the royal governor at provincial expense. He was aware that these issues had been addressed by a number of his predecessors, but with no success. Edenton had once been designated the capital, as had New Bern. Tower Hill, a site about thirty miles west of New Bern had once been considered as a possible permanent location for the seat of government but had not been developed. By the time Tryon came on the scene, the Assembly was as likely to meet at one place as another, depending upon the whim of the governor, and the colony's records had to be carted from place to place. Tryon, although he resided most of the time at Brunswick, had to move about to other places in order to do the colony's business. Obviously the system was in need of an overhaul. Additionally, north-south sectional tensions in North Carolina, which Tryon discovered upon his arrival had created a rupture in the colony, were being magnified by arguments among citizens about whether a "northern" town like Edenton or a "southern" one like Wilmington would make a better capital. Hence, Tryon thought it imperative that settlement of a capital site, and the erection of "a convenient building" to house the governor, be made a major part of his administrative agenda.[1]

It was obvious to Tryon that a centrally located, hence convenient and sectionally "neutral," town site must be chosen. Thus he wrote the Board of Trade on April 1, 1765, only four days after Dobbs's death, "I . . . am determined in my Opinion that the public Business . . . can be carried on no where with such Conveniency and Advantage to far the greatest part of the Inhabitants, as at Newberne." His choice of New Bern over another contender, Wilmington, was reinforced during the Stamp Act controversy when he concluded that he had been unjustly accused by Wilmington's mayor, Moses John DeRosset, of punishing that town for sins committed by the entire province. Although Tryon's plans for settling the capital issue were delayed by the necessity of proroguing the Assembly for almost a year during the Stamp Act crisis, he finally managed to call the legislature into session in November 1766. At that time Edmund Fanning, an Assembly member from Orange County, introduced a bill "for erecting a Convenient building within the Town of Newbern, for the residence of the Governor." On December 7, with remarkable ease considering the long and vexatious history of the colony's wrangles over where to locate the capital, the bill passed, along with a measure appropriating £5,000 proclamation money to begin construction of the governor's new home. Also remarkable was that Tryon was entrusted by the legislature with the building project, the sole instance in the years after 1740 that such a major public work in North Carolina was not given to commissioners appointed by legislators jealous of their powers and suspicious of royal officials. Obviously Tryon's reputation for honesty and fair dealing with the people, which he had quickly established in his early months as governor, had not been eroded by the Stamp Act controversies.[2]

In early January 1767 Tryon appointed John Hawks, the architect who had come over with him on the *Friendship* in 1764, to design and oversee the construction of "a Convenient Dwelling House" for North Carolina's governors. Immediately Hawks set out for Philadelphia on a shopping trip for supplies, while Tryon awaited approval of the project in London. That endorsement forthcoming from Shelburne in August 1767, Tryon had Hawks proceed with construction. By December Tryon was compelled to inform the Assembly that the original appropriation was exhausted and that £10,000 more would be needed to complete the house and its outbuildings. Without opposition, the legislature passed the appropriation in early 1768, and Tryon boasted to Shelburne in March that visitors from other colonies were already calling the house, even in its uncompleted state, "the Capital Building on the continent of North America." Nine months later Tryon told Hillsborough that the edifice was covered and roofed, that plumbers were busy, and that joiners were at work inside the house. In early summer 1770 the governor and his family moved into the still-unfinished mansion, after unsuccessfully petitioning the king to provide him with new furniture, as Tryon's was "so absurd, that it would disgrace even the upper story of the Edifice."[3]

In December 1770 Tryon gratefully thanked the Assembly and people

Tryon Palace at New Bern, in an early-nineteenth-century representation. This building, constructed under Tryon's guidance during his tenure as governor of North Carolina, was one of his great accomplishments in office. (Courtesy of the North Carolina Collection, Wilson Library, University of North Carolina at Chapel Hill)

"for their Gift of this very Elegant and Noble Structure . . . , a Palace that is a public Ornament and Credit to the Colony, as well as an Honour to British America." But even while the governor was expressing gratitude for gifts already received, he was in the process of accumulating yet more house-related expenses. Already he had saddled the colony with a loan from Samuel Cornell, a merchant, for construction costs when tax collections did not keep up with the carpenters. Now he billed the Assembly for £134 to defray moving expenses for himself and the public records, and he also requested that the legislators purchase from William Dry "a few hundred acres of land conveniently situated to the palace" for the sum of £1000. Whereas the Assembly accepted his moving bills, it refused to spend money for the land because "the present exhausted state of the public funds renders the Country incapable of making such a purchase." Indeed the legislature did not exaggerate, for Tryon's final accounts for the Palace—as he now called the new governor's mansion—showed that it had cost only £140 14s. 3d. less than the total appropriation of £15,000.[4]

Because Tryon had expended huge sums of money in building his Palace, he was accused unfairly by detractors, especially in western North Carolina, of gratifying his vanity at the expense of both North Carolina taxpayers and his own honor. He had constructed a mansion, said one critic, "worthy the Residence of a Prince of the Blood," an "elegant

Monument" with no purpose but to give the ministry in London an example of his "great Influence and Address" with the citizens of North Carolina—and this "In a Colony without Money, and among a People almost desperate with Distress." Unfortunately for the people under his dominion, he had been "bred a Soldier" and had "a natural, as well as acquired Fondness for military Parade." Although these statements contain elements of truth about Tryon's character and motivation, they convey the erroneous impression that North Carolinians were somehow duped by this smooth-talking courtier into a building program that was too extravagant for their means. In fact they went along with the plan from start to finish without demur or complaint that they were not getting their money's worth. The Assembly spoke for many citizens when it told Tryon that the Palace was "truly elegant and noble" and that to Tryon's "unwearied attention and influence and the Abilities and diligence of the Architect, the Inhabitants of this Country owe that Honour and Credit, It may reflect upon them." Despite the controversy over the costs of the project, Tryon and his family delighted in the opulence of their new home, and the governor congratulated himself on a task well done.[5]

The discontents that Tryon faced over the financing of the governor's Palace were a small part of larger fiscal issues that plagued his administration from beginning to end. In 1765 he had inherited from Dobbs a squabble between the Council and Assembly over the power to appoint public treasurers for the colony. Already Dobbs had conceded that the governor did not exercise that authority—a situation that Tryon did not like at all—and so when the Assembly and Council deadlocked on an appointment in 1765, Tryon appointed speaker Samuel Swann, a popular choice with the lower house, to serve until the legislature agreed upon a candidate. Because of the Stamp Act troubles, Tryon delayed calling the Assembly into session, but when it met in November 1766, it complained about the Council's subverting its right to name treasurers. Finally the Council accepted the Assembly's choice of John Ashe, but only for a two-year period, at the end of which time the problem would arise once more. Tryon attempted to resolve the deadlock once again by appealing to Shelburne on three separate occasions during 1767 for a ruling on the matter, but he received no instructions. So when the legislature met in the fall, the issue remained unresolved. However, the Council finally accepted the Assembly's nominees, John Ashe and Joseph Montfort, at least for the following five years, and Tryon did not have to deal with the matter anymore.[6]

Tryon also tried to reform the process whereby taxes were collected and accounted for. As the poll tax was the basic source of tax revenue in North Carolina, and almost exclusively the way in which persons on the local level were assessed, there was considerable anger among Carolinians, particularly frontier Carolinians, about supposed inequities of the system. Even worse for the fiscal health of the province, however, the system of tax collection and accounting was both inefficient and corrupt, especially because Tryon had no control over accounting procedures or appointments of tax officials, and because these officials were paid by fees and commissions that were not set by the governor. Another problem was that the entire system was controlled by a small number of ruling families in the eastern part of the colony and was used as a means of dominating the political and social life of North Carolina. Tryon, then, was faced with a paradoxical situation in his attempts to systematize the collection of taxes, for any change he proposed might weaken the very power structure that gave most support to his own efforts to strengthen the king's authority in the colony. He never fully resolved this dilemma, and therefore his fiscal reform efforts never came to fruition. His failure contributed to the Regulator discontents that broke out so forcefully in 1768.

Yet Tryon tried to effect changes, for by the time he took office as governor, sheriffs who collected the taxes were in mass default to the government. As for the treasurers' financial statements, they were a complete muddle. Tryon told Shelburne in July 1767, "The Treasurers have hitherto shewn so much ill judged Lenity towards the Sheriffs that . . . [they] have embezzled more than one half of the Publick Money ordered to be raised and collected by them. It is estimated that the Sherriffs Arrears to the Publick amount to Forty thousand Pounds Proclamation Money." Clearly reforms were needed, and already Tryon had taken some steps to correct abuses. In 1765 he issued a proclamation ordering officials to cease extorting citizens through "Exorbitant Fees," and for two years running, 1766 and 1767, he encouraged the legislature to reform the system by raising sheriffs' salaries, thus removing any cause for their having to steal from the public, and by forcing treasurers to submit their books each year to an audit by the governor and the Assembly. The legislature finally complied with Tryon's requests in 1768, and in the case of the sheriff's law actually enacted a requirement that Tryon had not called for, that sheriffs annually account to treasurers for collections.[7]

Even as these laws were being enacted, however, Tryon practically admitted to the Assembly that he believed the legislation inadequate and doomed to failure. "I humbly submit it as my Opinion," he told the legislators, "that no Provision will be found effectual against these Abuses, as long as a Jealousy subsists of the Chief Magistrate's being particularly informed of the Receipts and Disbursements of the Public Money; and until his Freedom of Inspection and Examination into the state of the Funds ... is admitted, and acknowledged as necessary." Nonetheless he declared his unwillingness to pick a quarrel with the Assembly "on a Subject of this delicate Nature" and thus left the matter entirely to that body's "Wisdom and Discretion." Tryon's unwonted tentativeness in handling the issue of access to the accounts, even though he recognized it as crucial to the success of his reform efforts, was due in part to his desire to maintain his support among the ruling citizens of the colony, especially because rising discontents among the Regulators required him to look for allies. But Tryon's hesitancy was also due to his knowledge that his predecessor, Dobbs, had fought a losing battle with the Assembly over the legislators' taking the accounts out of his hands. Tryon did later present the Assembly with a plan for regularizing accounts, which he had put together after long study of the Virginia system, but he was careful to leave the accounts under control of a committee of the lower house. Even this measure was rejected. Finally the Assembly itself commissioned a study of accounts, and upon learning that large sums indeed had gone missing, passed a law requiring treasurers to keep better records. Tryon, however, never gained any control over accounting procedures; hence his efforts at fiscal reform were largely unsuccessful.[8]

A financial conundrum that dogged Tryon's administration from 1766 until its end was the colony's paper money woes. The governor was forever being petitioned by the legislature to be allowed to utter new emissions, because older emissions were constantly eroding in value due to counterfeiting and thus needed to be replaced. Tryon always had to refuse the legislators' requests for the same reason that he constantly had to fend off their pleas to be allowed an expansion of the colony's paper money supply: Parliament's Currency Act of 1764. This law, which extended to all colonies a measure passed in 1751 to prohibit legal paper tender in New England, flatly denied the Carolinians and their governor any leeway in emitting new paper money, even to the point of threatening Tryon with the loss of his position, exclusion from future employment by the Crown, and a fine of £1,000 sterling if he violated the law. Although Tryon was completely sympathetic with the Council and Assembly members when they pleaded with him for new paper money, he dared not violate a prohibition so specific and so immune to "interpretation."[9]

During the first years of Tryon's administration, the quantity of paper money in North Carolina was adequate; emissions made during the Seven Years' War continued to fulfill the province's needs. Therefore neither Tryon nor the legislature had to bother with confronting the prohibitions of the Currency Act. But in late 1766 inhabitants of Pasquotank County petitioned the governor to allow more paper money into circulation. Tryon promised to take up the matter up with Shelburne, and early in 1767 he informed Shelburne that whereas North Carolina needed for its thriving commercial activities a circulating medium of at least £200,000 proclamation money, at present only £70,000 was in use. Although Tryon had received clear instructions from the Crown upon taking office that he was not to allow any further paper money emissions, he decided in early 1768 to go along with the legislature when it petitioned the Crown for authority to emit new paper money for purely domestic commercial transactions, while guaranteeing that all bills due "the Crown, or to Merchants or others residing in Great Britain . . . Shall be made Payable at the full Sterling Value." Sending along this petition to the Board of Trade with a long cover letter favoring emission of more paper money, Tryon assured officials in London that the proposal could have nothing but salutary effects.[10]

By assenting to this measure, Tryon revealed himself as being not only a supporter of paper money but also a shrewd politician, for at no risk to himself he had sided strongly with North Carolinians in a matter dear to their hearts (and purses). But he did not deceive himself into believing that the petition would be favorably received in London, even though he wrote his London financial agent, Drummond and Company, to order paper and copperplates for printing the currency, should the request be granted. He was correct in his assessment, for Hillsborough, who had just assumed the newly created office of secretary of state for the colonies, forcefully reminded Tryon in a letter of April 16, 1768, that Parliament had settled that matter once and for all—and rightly so as far as he was concerned, for "Paper Currency with a legal Tender is big with Frauds, and full of Mischief to the Colonies." Undaunted by this rebuff, Tryon in June asked Hillsborough to reconsider the matter in light of the Regulator disturbances going on in North Carolina at that time and suggested that new emissions of paper money might dampen the protestors' complaints. Hillsborough remained unmoved, only responding that "I have already

. . . been so full and explicit upon the Application made by the Council &
Assembly of North Carolina for a Paper Currency, that I have nothing to
add upon that Subject."[11]

When the Assembly met again, in late 1768, Tryon passed on this
information to the legislators, but they were so desirous of relieving the
money shortage that they wanted to pursue the matter further. Hence
they enacted two currency laws, one calling for a new emission of
£20,000 in "debenture notes" to pay troops used in suppressing Regulators the summer before, the other continuing in circulation legal tender
currency that remained from earlier emissions. When they asked for
Tryon's ongoing assistance in getting London officials to grant their requests for more paper money, the governor reluctantly complied with the
debenture notes bill because it could perhaps be interpreted as not falling
under the prohibitions of the Currency Act. (Officials in London later
accepted his interpretation and approved the "special" money.) Tryon
vetoed the other law, however, because it clearly violated the act. Meanwhile, he wrote Hillsborough twice in early 1769, renewing North Carolina's petition for new paper money emissions, only to be told bluntly,
"No Petition that prays for Paper Currency as a Legal Tender can meet the
success you wish."[12]

Although Hillsborough relented a bit in a letter to Tryon of June 7 by
suggesting that officials in London would not automatically "preclude
the fullest consideration" of any Assembly proposal, Tryon gloomily
reported to the legislature in October that the outcome looked grim. He
was correct. When Tryon wrote Hillsborough in January and July 1770 to
suggest reconsideration of North Carolina's financial position, Hillsborough refused, noting that the colony's money supply was "fully sufficient
to answer the purpose of circulation." Tryon and the legislature heartily
disagreed with this assessment, as they had for three years past. Hence the
Assembly attempted once more early that year to renew the struggle by
asking Tryon to support parliamentary repeal of the Currency Act. Also,
the legislators petitioned Parliament in early 1771 to exempt North Carolina from the provisions of the act. But these efforts came to naught, and
there the matter rested when Tryon's administration came to an end.[13]

While Tryon dealt with fiscal issues, he also ran into difficulties with
North Carolina's judicial system. His instructions from the Crown were
to fix courts in the colony by executive ordinance, and he was in fact
enjoined from following his predecessor Dobbs's practice of allowing
courts to be established by the Assembly. Yet in reality both he and the

Crown had to ignore this part of the royal prerogative and make the best of it when the Assembly established by law courts that were acceptable to officials in London. These officials, and Tryon as well, were afraid that if they did not go along with the Assembly, they would have another constitutional fight on their hands, and such a clash they did not want or need for various reasons. Of greater importance to Tryon was the desire to gain control of county clerk appointments, for as he told Shelburne in 1767, clerks were "very remiss and neglectful" in providing the governor with "any Informations necessary to be required and obtained." Shelburne's only response to Tryon's complaints was a suggestion that the law regarding clerks' appointments be changed by the Assembly. But as Tryon believed such a proposal would only create a new quarrel with the legislature over Crown authority, he let the matter drop.[14]

Tryon also became involved in a wrangle with the Assembly over North Carolina's foreign attachment law, but in a curious and peripheral way. Foreign attachment, a procedure whereby a creditor could place the property of a defaulted debtor in the hands of a third person until the debtor appeared in court to settle claims, was used in England in the eighteenth century and had been adopted in North Carolina in 1746. Because attachment was practically the only remedy a creditor had against a defaulted foreign debtor, the citizens of the province believed that the exercise of that right was vital. Hence they were terribly concerned when in 1770 the Board of Trade questioned the law's legality and urged Tryon to have the Assembly amend it drastically or even eliminate it when it expired in 1773. By that time, of course, Tryon had become governor of New York; when Josiah Martin, the new governor of North Carolina, tried to effect the necessary changes, the Assembly wrote Tryon urging his intervention against Martin as the legislators renewed the old law pretty much as it had been before. Tryon wisely refrained from being dragged into this imbroglio, and Martin, angered by the Assembly's petitioning Tryon and bound by royal instructions, rejected the measure entirely.[15]

Although a great part of Tryon's time as governor was taken up with controversial and divisive matters that brought him into conflict with both the Assembly and officials in London, some of his business involved less significant—but to him no less personally important—matters. Beginning in 1766 and continuing throughout his tenure as governor, he devoted much effort to encouraging the labors of North Carolina mapmakers, especially William Churton, Claude Joseph Sauthier, and John Abraham Collet. In 1767 he followed a well-established custom of many

American colonial governors by sending the king an exotic native animal, in this case a panther, which, upon its arrival in England, was lodged in a royal menagerie in the Tower of London. Between 1768 and 1770 he approved the Assembly's creation of five new counties, Guilford, Wake, Surry, Chatham, and Tryon, the second of which was named in honor of his wife and the last in honor of himself. The formation of these new counties, all in the western part of the colony, was for Tryon of much more than mere symbolic importance. He hoped that by bringing self-government closer to western settlers he might alleviate some of their discontents toward the eastern part of the province. Finally, he reported to Hillsborough in 1769 on a hurricane that struck the Carolina coast in September, causing extensive damage to New Bern. He speculated that the storm may have been caused by a "blazing Planet or star" (a comet), which was visible in the evening sky just previous to the time of the storm.[16]

While he dealt with what seemed an endless multiplicity of public business both significant and minor, Tryon generally attempted to keep his private life separate from his official role. Sometimes, as during the Stamp Act troubles when crowds gathered about Belle Font and appeared to endanger the governor's wife and daughter, his family life inevitably merged with his public affairs. Tryon's family was on public display during official celebrations, during travel, or when official entertainments were held at the governor's residence. But mostly the Tryons' family life proceeded along in considerable privacy as its members shared both pleasures and sorrows. In early 1769 Tryon learned that his father, Charles Tryon, had died on November 28 of the year before, but this news seems to have affected him only little. However, the death of his infant son, who died just weeks after his birth in late 1768, touched both Tryon and his wife profoundly (they never had any more children). Still, they carried on their lives by continuing to entertain and correspond with a wide network of friends and acquaintances. In April 1769 they welcomed Waightstill Avery, an attorney from Salisbury, into their home to dine, and during the same month Tryon wrote Major Horatio Gates, bantering with him about army life. Major Gates, a British army officer, had seen service in America and now lived in Bristol. A few months later, Tryon wrote his old friend Henry Clinton, congratulating him on his recent marriage and reflecting on the vicissitudes of being a royal governor in America.[17]

From time to time Tryon and his family got away from the rush and bother of official business by taking trips of varying lengths. As has already been noted, they visited the Moravians at Wachovia on two separate occasions, and in July 1769 they traveled to Williamsburg to visit the governor of Virginia, Lord Botetourt, for a month. Anne Blair, the daughter of John Blair of Williamsburg, left a delightful account of the Tryons' taking tea at her home while enjoying this extended vacation. During this visit Miss Blair at first was rather reserved with Mrs. Tryon, for she had heard rumors that the governor's wife "took no notice of the Ladies." However, as the visit wore on, Mrs. Tryon melted Miss Blair's reserve with her charm, and soon the young hostess was cooing about what a "fine accomplish'd Lady" Mrs. Tryon was. Yet Miss Blair could not refrain from remarking, rather cattily, "They say she rules the Roost, it is a pity, I like her Husband vastly." She also pitied the Tryons' little eight-year-old daughter, Margaret, who was "stuck up in a Chair all day long with a Coller on," apparently so cowed by the ominous Mrs. Tryon that she dared not "even . . . taste Tea, fruit Cake, or any little Triffle offer'd her by ye Company." Another excursion of the Tryons' was a sailing trip in September and October 1770 "between Beaufort and Portsmouth" in order that Tryon might recover his health and "view the Sea Coast." The governor was badly in need of restoration by that time, for another bout of fever had debilitated him terribly, nearly to the point of death.[18]

While Tryon was vacationing in Virginia during the summer of 1769, he none too subtly began to prod Hillsborough for advancement in military rank. He reminded the secretary of state of his motives in coming to America on the king's service, recalling that his first ambition had been to render public service to his "Royal Master." He believed he had been successful in that duty, for both Shelburne and Hillsborough had approved his spirited and reform-minded public conduct. His second ambition, to be promoted to colonel in the British army, had not yet been achieved, and he was desirous of receiving either "a Regiment" or an appointment as one of the king's "Aid De Camps." When Hillsborough received Tryon's letter, he hastened to lay it before King George III, along with his own glowing recommendation of Tryon's "Merit and Services as governor of North Carolina." But, as Hillsborough told his protégé, "Further, I durst not presume to venture" because Tryon's request related to "a Service which entirely belongs to other Departments of Government." There the matter rested, unfortunately for Tryon, because the king did not choose at that time to favor Tryon's petition for promotion. Yet Tryon was not totally disappointed, for as he told Hillsborough, he had "lodged in [his] Royal Master's breast" the notion that a deserving servant wanted and merited an advance in rank. Now he must wait patiently for the seed that he had planted to grow and bear fruit, as he believed it assuredly would do in due course.[19]

Even before he commenced maneuvering for military promotion, Tryon faced his most serious conflict with the North Carolina legislature since the Stamp Act crisis, this time triggered by the Townshend Acts. These problems, which in American history came to be known as the Townshend crisis, were important in bringing on the Revolution, but they were also of great significance to Tryon personally, for they led ultimately to great changes in the course of his career. The crisis arose when Charles Townshend, chancellor of the Exchequer, pushed through Parliament in 1767 three laws designed to tighten England's imperial hold upon America. The first was to raise £40,000 sterling in annual revenues from the colonies by placing new customs duties on wine, lead, glass, painters' colors, and tea. The second stipulated that the duties so collected would be used to pay salaries of imperial officials who heretofore had depended upon colonial assemblies for their pay, thus making them less a burden on the king's exchequer and at the same time more independent of colonial assemblies. The third created a Board of Customs Commissioners to bypass colonial juries and to ensure that both the new duties and those already in force were paid.[20]

Throughout most of 1768, Tryon had no trouble with North Carolinians over the Townshend Acts, not because the citizenry accepted them but because the Assembly was not in session to act upon them. In the summer of 1768, Tryon received from Hillsborough a copy of the Massachusetts circular letter, written by Samuel Adams as an invitation to all the colonial assemblies to unite in resistance to the new laws. Tryon also received Hillsborough's admonition to exert his "utmost Influence, to defeat this flagitious Attempt to disturb the Public Peace, by prevailing upon the Assembly of your Province to take no Notice of it," or simply put, to prorogue the Assembly if it began to get out of hand. In May and July, Hillsborough sent Tryon further orders to assist customs collectors, who were meeting "great Obstructions . . . in the Execution of their Duty." Then in November, Hillsborough sent Tryon a copy of King George III's opening speech to Parliament in which His Majesty, to Hillsborough's delight, had sworn "to preserve entire and inviolate the supreme Authority of the Legislature of Great Britain over every part of the British Empire." Tryon was to adhere in his conduct to the very same principles.[21]

Tryon needed no encouragement from London to bolster his devotion
to the Crown's dignity and prerogatives, and he had every intention of
seeing that the Townshend Acts were enforced. But at the same time he
could not devote his full attention to this important objective, for he was
distracted by a lingering fever and by a number of other problems such as
boundaries, Indian affairs, and quarrels with Regulators. In fact, Tryon
rather urgently needed the Assembly to act on some of these matters,
especially to pay troops and to attend to Regulator grievances. When he
took a chance in early November and called the Assembly together to deal
with a prearranged agenda, he quickly discovered that the legislators also
intended to address themselves to the Townshend laws, and in a way
inimical to the views of king and Parliament. Nevertheless he did not
prorogue the Assembly, for he felt he simply must have action on the rest
of his program. The result was that the Assembly, after acting on the
matter of paying troops, took up discussion of the Massachusetts Circular Letter, which had been sent to Speaker John Harvey. By December 2
the house agreed to send "an humble, dutiful and loyal address" to the
king, protesting against the Townshend duties on the ground that they
were unconstitutional and asserting that Americans had a basic right to
trial by a jury of their peers. Thereupon Tryon prorogued the Assembly.
But the damage had been done, for North Carolinians had flatly denied
Parliament's right to levy import duties for the purpose of collecting
revenue and to have Americans tried by Crown agents rather than their
own courts. On December 15 Tryon rather lamely and inconsistently
explained to Hillsborough that he had felt it necessary not to dissolve the
Assembly "before the Business of the Session was ended," because its
response to the Massachusetts circular letter had been so "moderate."
Yet, in fact, Tryon's "Business" had not been fully taken care of before he
was compelled in any case to bring the Assembly to an end, for Regulator
grievances had not been addressed. Moreover, it was obvious that the
Assembly had not acted with much "moderation." Be that as it may,
Tryon now assured Hillsborough—if rather belatedly—that he would in
the future exert himself to "the fullest . . . of [his] Abilities in the support
of . . . the Acts of Trade."[22]

During the summer of 1769, Tryon had no further problems from
North Carolinians over the Townshend Acts, except for some resolutions
passed by a few "sons of liberty" in the Cape Fear region, because the
legislature was not in session during that time. The governor even began
to hope that the controversy would not be renewed if he called the

Assembly together in October, for he had received word from Hillsborough that Parliament was rescinding all the new taxes except the one on tea and that neither the king nor Parliament had any further plans to tax the colonies for revenue. Tryon gladly accepted Hillsborough's admonition to explain these points to North Carolinians and "remove the prejudices which have been excited by the misrepresentation of those who are Enemies to the peace and prosperity of Great Britain and her Colonies," for as Tryon told his friend Henry Clinton, should the controversy over taxes continue, his administration would be endangered in both its "Success, and Duration." In fact, he said, he was angry at the ministry in England for not repealing the Townshend duties "last Session." If the taxes were indeed "Contrary to the true Spirit of Commerce," as Hillsborough now declared, then they certainly should not have remained on the law books as an irritant to the colonists and a vexation to royal officials who were expected, beyond all reason, to enforce them.[23]

When the Assembly met in late 1769, Tryon's hopes for a peaceful session were quickly dashed. On October 23, while he was in the grip of another of his seemingly endless bouts of ague, Tryon sent to the legislators a lengthy list of items needing their attention, such as Regulator grievances, colonial defense, the systematizing of public accounts, and the sinking of old paper money emissions. He also informed them of Hillsborough's assurances that the Townshend duties would be repealed and that no new taxes for revenue would be laid upon Americans, news which both the Council and Assembly found pleasing. Therefore Tryon found no reason to worry about the legislators' doing anything regarding the Townshend laws that would be offensive either to him or to London, and for a time the Assembly went quietly about doing the governor's business. Great was Tryon's surprise, however, when on November 2, Speaker Harvey laid before the Assembly a copy of resolutions recently passed by the Virginia legislators (who met as a "convention" because they had been prorogued by Lord Botetourt), organizing a nonimportation association and urging other colonies to do the same. Without a dissenting vote the North Carolina Assembly adopted the Virginia resolutions almost verbatim. Then it proceeded to draft another protest to the king regarding Parliament's taxing Americans for revenue and its violations of colonial Englishmen's right to trial by jury.[24]

When news of the Assembly's latest actions reached the fever-ridden but nonetheless alert Tryon, he was furious. Fuming later to Hillsborough that the entire witches' brew of half-truths and misrepresentations contained in their odious message to the king had been concocted by an unholy alliance of "People who never were in Trade" and "a few Merchants" who shielded their baser motives behind "Sham Patriotism," he called the Assembly to the Council chamber on November 4. There, in a tense confrontation, he accused the legislators of a personal attack against himself, for they had ratified their mean resolutions in spite of his assurances to them in his opening speech that the Townshend duties, as well as any new taxes upon colonists for revenue, would soon be made dead letters. Thus, Tryon fumed, the assemblymen had "sapped the foundations of confidence and gratitude." They had "torn up by the roots every sanguine hope" he had entertained "to render this province further service." They were to consider their so-called "legislation" vetoed, themselves dissolved, and their unpleasant presence in the governor's proximity no longer required.[25]

If Tryon expected his troubles with assemblymen to end at this point, he was in for yet another surprise. Instead of dispersing to their homes, sixty-four of the seventy-seven legislators met extralegally as private citizens in the New Bern Courthouse, elected John Harvey "Moderator," and proceeded to readopt the nonimportation resolutions that Tryon had spurned. When Tryon informed Hillsborough of these proceedings, he swore that he would schedule no new Assembly elections until he was so instructed by "His Majesty's Commands" and until he had received news that Parliament had repealed "those Acts . . . laying Duties on Paper, Glass and Colours in America." Some time in mid-1770, Tryon did learn that the Townshend taxes on all goods except tea had been repealed. Not long afterward he noted to Hillsborough that the North Carolina Association was moribund and that life had returned to normal, except that the citizenry were boycotting tea upon which duties had been paid and were drinking instead tea that had been smuggled into the province.[26]

In the meantime, the assemblymen had attempted to mollify Tryon by begging him not to impute their "Resolves . . . to a loss of Confidence in Your Excellency or for want of a very Grateful Remembrance of those Signal Services You have rendered this Province." The legislators were only too happy, they wrote to Tryon, to "take this Public Opportunity of declaring to the World, the Benefits this Province had Received from Your Excellency's Administration" and the warm "Sensations of Gratitude" they felt toward a man whose excellent "Administration . . . must Deservedly obtain You the Blessings of Posterity." Although Tryon was too gracious not to thank the assemblymen for their "honorable opinion" of him, their sweet words did not restore to him the pleasure he had formerly experienced in serving as governor of North Carolina. Thus, on the very day that the Assembly, as Tryon believed, violated its trust in his word, he commenced to lay plans for departing the colony, either by taking extended (and likely permanent) leave in Britain, or by assuming the governorship of New York in the place of Sir Henry Moore, who had died in 1769 and whose place Hillsborough had hinted might be his for the asking. "I wish I could say," Tryon wrote Hillsborough on January 8, 1770, "that my Prospect Brightens." But he could not, for the "Proceedings of the last Assembly" had wounded his "sensibility." "Confidence, my Lord, that delicate polish in Publick Transactions, has received an ugly scratch, and I fear we have no Artist Here who can restore it to its original perfection." Therefore he requested that Hillsborough lay before the king his request either to be allowed "the Government of New York" or permission to return home on leave.[27]

In early summer, Tryon's future prospects seemed determined when John Murray, earl of Dunmore, received the post in New York and Tryon was told by Hillsborough that the king had graciously consented to allow Tryon "to return into this Our Kingdom of Great Britain for the Space of Twelve Months." Bitterly disappointed at losing the New York governorship, Tryon lamented to Hillsborough in July 1770 that "The Repeated Assurances Your Lordship has given Me of the favorable Sentiments You entertained of my Conduct in my Public Station, and the honourable manner in which You have expressed those Sentiments to our Royal Master . . . but naturally led me to Hope I should have gathered some Fruit from such promising Blossoms." At the same time he also shrewdly understood that he had "lodged in [his] Royal Master's breast" another request like the one for a colonelcy in the British army that might in future lead to success. So he politely thanked Hillsborough for the king's indulgence in allowing him leave and suppressed his ambitions until he should find a more propitious time for expressing them.[28]

CHAPTER FIVE

The War of the Regulation

During the remainder of his tenure as governor of North Carolina, Tryon was hardly an idle spectator marking time until he should depart the colony. In fact, he was having to deal with the so-called Regulator problem, which had vexed his administration from the beginning and built to crisis proportions in 1768 and again in 1770–71. Western North Carolinians had numerous grievances against their eastern neighbors, many of which Tryon had attempted to ameliorate, usually with little effect. The eastern oligarchy, having control of the legislature and giving Tryon much of his support for governance, collected revenue from the citizenry largely by imposing poll taxes and quitrents, which fell heaviest on poor farmers. The eastern rulers also charged heavy fees for certain government services and were so unregulated in their collection procedures that frontiersmen considered them practically extortioners. All these monies were expected to be paid in legal currency that was in extremely short supply. Because taxes and fees were collected by inefficient and corrupt sheriffs and treasurers, often outsiders, unchecked by gubernatorial or legislative audit, the monies received were embezzled. In addition, the westerners were galled by the method of tax collection, for a sheriff could descend upon a person's home without warning and demand payment, and if he did not receive it, he could distrain the citizen's property and auction it to satisfy the tax bill. Finally, many frontiersmen profoundly resented having to pay extra taxes for the construction of the new governor's mansion at New Bern and for the upkeep of the Anglican establishment.[1]

Since his arrival in North Carolina, Tryon had been confronted with outbreaks of violence from westerners protesting these abuses, outbreaks that were only portents of worse things to follow. In 1765 he had been compelled to deal with unauthorized settlers driving McCulloh's surveyors from lands intended to be demarcated for purposes of imposing quitrents. Two years later a group of Orange County citizens attempted to organize formal machinery for dealing with protests from the people, but their efforts were blocked by uncooperative government officials. Meanwhile, Tryon, who felt considerable sympathy for frontiersmen's complaints, labored mightily to reform abuses in tax and fee collections by sheriffs and treasurers. He had done all within his limited powers to have provisions of the Currency Act of 1764 rescinded for his colony in order to increase the money supply. In all these efforts he had been at best only marginally successful and at worst had sometimes only increased resentments. In 1768 he approved a bill enacted by the legislature that, while reforming some of the worst abuses of the sheriffs, stipulated that these officials might collect taxes in only five places per county and levy an extra fee of 2s. 8d. against anyone not paying at the designated places. At about the same time, he accepted legislation calling for an extra 2s. 6d. poll tax to finance construction of the governor's mansion.[2]

Angry that Tryon and the Assembly once again appeared to be callously disregarding their complaints, westerners reacted in April 1768 by organizing the Regulator Association with the intention of "regulating" their own affairs. The movement, first established in Orange County, spread rapidly, with its adherents demanding that sheriffs give account of collected taxes and fees and asserting that without such accountability they would withhold their levies. On April 8 an Orange County Regulator refused to pay his taxes, whereupon the sheriff seized his horse, bridle, and saddle and prepared to sell them in order to collect the tax. Outraged, a group of about 100 Regulators rode into Hillsborough, the county seat of Orange County, tied up the sheriff, rescued the horse, and fired two or three shots into the house of Edmund Fanning, register of deeds and a prominent judge in the town. In response, Fanning ordered the arrest of three conspicuous Regulators and called out seven companies of Orange County militia to restore law and order. But when only 120 militiamen answered the summons, Captains Francis Nash and Thomas Hart of the Orange County militia recommended to Fanning that he call upon Governor Tryon for outside assistance. Fanning did so on April 23.[3]

When Tryon received Fanning's letter, indicating that "an absolute Insurrection of a dangerous tendency" had broken out in Orange County, he quickly took an extremely hard line against that form of protest, despite his earlier concerns for westerners' grievances. Immediately he had his Council issue a proclamation admonishing the participants "in

Edmund Fanning, a close friend of Tryon's who served under him in both North Carolina and New York. Fanning was particularly disliked by the Regulators. (Courtesy of the North Carolina Collection, Wilson Library, University of North Carolina at Chapel Hill)

such Insurrections to disperse." Also, he ordered the militia commanders of eight western counties to call out their troops against the "insurrectionists," and he named all members of his Council and many other high government officials justices of the peace to execute the law and confine anyone who had "Committed any Treasons, Felonies, . . . Trespasses and Extortions" against the people of North Carolina. As for taxes, Tryon made no suggestion that he would attempt to lower them, for he was convinced, with considerable evidence to support him, that the poll tax in North Carolina was not all that onerous. The "Indispensable Lot of Mankind who lives in Society," said Tryon, is "to give a part of their Property to that Government, which affords them a secure and quiet

Employment of the Remainder." Anyone refusing to pay a just part forfeited the right to government's protection, left "his Family and Property" prey to "Lawless Associates; and himself at the Mercy, of the Laws of His Country." On April 27 Tryon wrote Fanning declaring his readiness at any time "to come up, & join you against all your Opposers. . . . Therefore, do not hesitate to Inlist me in the defence of the Laws of the Country." In the meantime he received word from Samuel Spencer, assemblyman from Anson County, that Regulators were becoming more and more unruly there. Hence, he issued a proclamation against the Anson dissidents.[4]

In early May Tryon received another letter from Fanning, informing him that the Regulators had calmed down and that only the Orange Militia would be needed to quell the unrest in that county. Conditions in Hillsborough, however, belied Fanning's optimistic assessment, for the Regulators there had just spurned his offer to intercede before the Assembly on their behalf. Moreover, they had forced Fanning to free on bond Herman Husband, the chief penman for the Regulators, and William Butler, ostensibly the leader of the Hillsborough crowd earlier in the year, after Fanning had arrested them with the intention of sending them to New Bern to stand trial. Later in the month, Tryon received from the Orange County Regulators a petition protesting government officials' overcharging for fees, as well as a narrative of the events since 1766 that had led the westerners into rebellion against constituted authority. The governor was profoundly disturbed by the Regulators' claims that officials were gouging them, and he immediately ordered the attorney general to begin proceedings against extortionists. But he also forcefully warned the Regulators to obey the law, and when in June he received word that they still were defying the government, he wrote Hillsborough that he intended to "go up into the back Country among them . . . for the hot Months."[5]

As good as his word, Tryon marched into Hillsborough on July 6 at the head of militia regiments from Rowan, Mecklenburg, and Granville counties. After waiting ineffectually for almost a month to hear that "the clamour of Faction" had been hushed, he issued a proclamation on August 1 ordering government officials to post lists of legal fees and Regulators to pay their taxes. His appeal to the citizens had no effect, for the Regulators near Hillsborough continued to band together illegally and even threatened to "kill any Person that should distrain [property] for their levies." Then on August 10, Tryon received word that about 500 irate citizens were assembled at the home of Jesse Pugh, some forty miles from Hillsborough, with the intention of marching on that town and burning it if the governor refused their demands. Immediately Tryon ordered out patrols "to watch the Motions of these Insurgents," and he was informed on the eleventh that they "had Advanced upwards of twenty miles nearer the Town." He now sent expresses thundering into the countryside to rally as many militiamen as could reach Hillsborough the following day and by evening of August 12, he had gathered about 250 troops. After a parley with dissident leaders, Tryon had the satisfaction of seeing them disperse, if but reluctantly, to their homes.[6]

Neither Tryon nor the Regulator leadership had backed down permanently, and the governor's latest problem was that the insurgents were threatening to disrupt the Superior Court, which was to meet at Hillsborough in September to hear the cases of Husband and Butler. On August 16 Tryon warned the dissidents not to disturb the courts and asked them to meet him at Salisbury, where he would visit for the next few days to post bonds against any such intentions. When the Regulators rejected his proposals, Tryon set out for Salisbury, now planning to mobilize the Rowan and Mecklenburg militia to forestall any threat to the court. He arrived in Salisbury on the nineteenth and was welcomed by "a great many gentlemen . . . with Expressions of great satisfaction." After entertaining the Rowan Regiment with "Provisions and Drink," he rode on to Mecklenburg County. There he reviewed a regiment of 900 men and then proceeded back to Salisbury, where on August 26 he was met by eleven companies of the Rowan Regiment. At a review of these troops, Tryon asked them to volunteer for service under the "King's Colours" in defense of the Superior Court. Only one company refused his appeal. Moved by this support, Tryon assured the militiamen that "their conduct had made a deep Impression on his mind." The governor was also pleased to receive a letter from four prominent backcountry Presbyterians, promising "to prevent the Infection" of insurgency "spreading among the People of our Charge."[7]

During early September, Tryon lingered in and about Salisbury, gathering more militia strength for defense of the Superior Court at Hillsborough. On the fifth, he received a letter from Judge Richard Henderson of Granville County, promising that the militia of that county would support the government. Then on September 12 he rode toward Hillsborough at the head of the Rowan and Mecklenburg militia forces, arriving there on the nineteenth despite having been "taken ill" on the march. Two days later, his army was augmented by the arrival of the Orange and Granville militia, swelling his forces to 1,461 men. The next day, Tryon learned that 800 "Insurgents" were only a mile from Hillsborough, apparently ready to disrupt the Superior Court, which commenced its proceedings on that day. But in the face of Tryon's army, the Regulators did nothing more than send the governor a letter, asking for terms of pardon. Thereupon Tryon called a council of war, at which he and his militia commanders agreed that all insurgents except seven leaders would be pardoned, if the Regulators would deliver up the seven for trial, lay down their arms, and swear to pay their taxes. Faced with these terms on the evening of September 23, all the backcountrymen, except thirty who accepted the governor's offer, simply dispersed to their homes without any response, even though their numbers by that time had swelled to twice those of Tryon's militia army in Hillsborough.[8]

Meanwhile, to Tryon's satisfaction, the Superior Court proceeded with its trial of Husband and Butler, as well as two other Regulators who had been arrested. The court decided that Husband was to be released, but Butler and the others were convicted. At the same session, and in fulfillment of Tryon's promise that the attorney general would proceed against government officials who were extorting money, Edmund Fanning and the county clerk were "found guilty of Taking too high fees." Both were given modest fines and required to pay court costs, and Fanning was forced to resign as register. Although many Regulators thought Fanning, the focus of their discontents, had escaped too lightly, subsequent analysis of evidence indicated that he was guilty only of a misconstruction of the law.[9]

The Regulator troubles subsided after the events of September 23 and 24, but Tryon remained in Hillsborough until the middle of the following month. Part of his reason for lingering was his illness, which had increased in virulence by September 24 to the point that he had to give command of the militia to Lieutenant General John Rutherfurd. In fact, the lingering sickness would plague him on into November. But his primary reason for remaining in the backcountry was to make sure that the insurgency was not about to flare up again any time soon. He believed, as he told Hillsborough in December, that the Regulators' primary objective had been not merely relief from unfair levies and fees but the entire "Abolition of [all] Taxes and Debts"; therefore he must make absolutely sure that "the Mischief" intended by the insurgents against the town of Hillsborough, the Superior Court, and the civil government had been irreversibly thwarted. Being in this frame of mind, he welcomed a sermon preached by the Reverend George Micklejohn of St. Matthew's Parish, Orange County, to the troops on September 25, wherein the reverend exhorted the Regulators, on pains of "the DAMNATION OF HELL," to follow Paul's admonition to "be subject unto the higher powers." Recognizing, however, the limits of coercion in effecting his aims, Tryon shortly thereafter released Butler and the other two Regulators from jail and issued a proclamation of pardon for all but the most prominent of the rioters. He also dismissed the militia and sent them home. "This lenity," he told Hillsborough, "had a good Tendency, for the insurgents, finding their Ardour opposed and checked and that they were not the Masters of Government, began to reflect that they were misled and in error, and as a proof of their change of Disposition they have since permitted the Sheriff to perform the Duties of His Office."[10]

Tryon arrived back at his home at Brunswick on October 17, "in so weak and reduced a State of Health" that even eight days later he could hardly scratch out a few lines to Hillsborough about his adventures in western North Carolina. As he gradually recovered his strength, he began to lay plans for addressing Regulator grievances and for securing finances at an upcoming session of the legislature to pay for his recent military expedition. On November 7, when the Assembly convened, he encouraged the legislators to inquire into the validity of frontiersmen's protests and make remedy in law as need be. He also reported to the Assembly that his calling out of the militia had cost the colony £4,844 proclamation money, a huge sum which somehow must be funded. To his satisfaction, the Assembly proceeded to discuss bills introduced by Fanning as representative of Orange County for debtor relief and for creating new counties in the west in order to bring county governments closer to the people. He was disappointed, however, when the session produced very little remedial legislation, for he knew that westerners' grievances remained strong toward both the provincial and county governments. Regarding payment of the militia, the Assembly finally passed a law emitting new nondebenture paper currency to effect that aim; as has already been noted, Tryon accepted this legislation with considerable unease because he thought he owed the troops their pay as "a principle of Justice," and he barely managed to squeak this measure by officials in London. Once these pieces of legislation were passed, Tryon hastened to prorogue the Assembly on account of its support for colonial protests against the Townshend Acts.[11]

Because the Assembly of 1768 had not dealt adequately with Regulators' grievances, Tryon continued to be vexed with backcountry discontents. In December 1768 he suggested to Hillsborough that a general pardon, covering all the insurgents save Husband, be issued, and when he received from that official approval not only for the pardon but also for his conduct in "the suppression of the Insurgents," he proceeded to declare all Regulators forgiven. In the meantime, however, Tryon began to accumulate evidence showing the frontiersmen in no mood to accept the governor's leniency quietly. As an example, Tryon received in October 1769 á petition from 260 citizens of Anson County reiterating all the old Regulator grievances and declaring that they had "too long yielded [themselves] slaves to remorseless oppression." At about the same time, petitioners from Orange and Rowan counties protested to Tryon that they had "long . . . labored under many and heavy exactions, Oppressions and Enormity, committed on us by Court Officers of every Station," and they wanted the governor to support changes in the laws granting court clerks "perquisites" instead of "yearly stated salaries."[12]

When the legislature met on October 23, 1769, Tryon did not urge as he had the year before much remedial action to address the Regulators' complaints. He did propose that the Assembly establish procedures to systematize and regulate public accounts so that "the Community will then chearfully pay the public Levies, satisfied that they are fairly adjusted and applied to the Services intended." But he asked for no further legislative attention to western discontents, and the Assembly, which now contained numerous Regulator sympathizers—not least Herman Husband—did not enact either Tryon's proposed reforms or any other law to redress western dissatisfaction. In fact, the Assembly acted exactly the opposite, by passing a resolution calling for severe treatment for "all Persons who shall oppose Sheriffs in the Execution of their Office." This neglect of reform on the part of Tryon and the legislative majority was due in part to their need in late 1769 to deal with choosing a colonial agent and emitting paper money. A more important reason was that Tryon and the Assembly got into another confrontation over the Townshend Acts and the governor once more had to prorogue the legislature. But the most important reason of all was that both Tryon and the larger part of the Council and Assembly were in no mood further to conciliate the backwoodsmen. To the governor and the legislators, the Regulators were, as Speaker John Harvey put it, "a set of men . . . forgetful of their duty they owed their Sovereign, insensible of the Happiness" that Tryon's administration had brought to North Carolina, "and in Defiance of the Laws under which they Lived." In this matter, then, if not in many others, Tryon the royal governor and the colonial Whig aristocracy of eastern North Carolina were on the same side of the political, social, and cultural fence.[13]

Soon Tryon and the eastern Carolina gentry felt the effects of their having neglected to address western discontents. In March 1770 Tryon learned from Maurice Moore that Regulators in several western counties again were hampering the sheriffs in their attempts to collect taxes. The governor quickly issued a proclamation "strictly requiring" that the sheriffs do their duty and that any who were "Obstructed in the Execution of their Office" attend the next meeting of the legislature to report personally upon such obstructions. In April Tryon reported to Hillsborough that the Regulators continued "in a state of Disobedience to the Laws of their Country," but that he expected the Assembly at its next session "to bring these people within the discipline of Government" by passing legislation to curb them. In late September Tryon received ominous news from various sources in Orange County that the Regulators in the backcountry had once more erupted into open defiance of government. On the twenty-fourth, insurgents had gathered in force at Hillsborough Court House under the leadership of Husband and three other men and had packed the Superior Court room where Judge Richard Henderson was presiding. In only a short time, Henderson later informed Tryon, the crowd became a mob, took charge of the session, and began beating a lawyer, John Williams, "with Clubs and sticks." After Williams finally escaped, the rioters grabbed William Hooper, assistant attorney general, and dragged him through the streets, treating him with "contempt and insult." Then they turned their fury on Fanning, seizing him "with a degree of Violence not to be described, from off the bench where he had retired for protection and Assistance." They dragged him out the courthouse door "by the Heels," while others beat him with such severity that Henderson feared for his life. Finally, Fanning broke free and ran into a nearby building, thus saving himself "from immediate Dissolution." But his "Mansion House" in the town was not so fortunate, for the mob gutted its interior furnishings and then demolished it with axes. Over the next two days, the crowd's fury raged unabated. Judge Henderson and many other inhabitants of Hillsborough barely managed to preserve their lives by fleeing from the town.[14]

When news of the Hillsborough riots reached the capital, Governor Tryon was away from New Bern on the previously mentioned coastal trip for his health. But upon his return on October 7, he instantly called a

Council meeting to ponder what would be a reasonable response to the Regulators' behavior. At the same time, he asked the attorney general, Thomas McGuire, to render a legal opinion on the seriousness of their activities. In his response McGuire adjudged that some of their actions amounted "only to a Riot," others to high misdemeanors, but that nothing they had said or done was "Sufficient to Convict a Man of High Treason." Therefore McGuire proposed to Tryon only that he convene the legislature to enact laws appropriate to the occasion, and that he muster the militias of affected counties to serve as a police force until statutory correctives could be secured. Upon advice of the Council, Tryon carried out these recommendations while additionally ordering by proclamation that justices of the peace collect depositions from eyewitnesses to the late riot in Hillsborough for use by the Assembly when it met.[15]

While waiting for the Assembly to convene, Tryon had more troubles with the Regulators. On November 12 the backwoodsmen burnt Judge Henderson's barns and stables in Granville County, destroying a number of horses and a large quantity of corn. Two days later they put the judge's house to the torch. Tryon responded by issuing a second proclamation, promising a reward of £100 proclamation money to anyone apprehending the perpetrators of these lawless acts. Then, on the twentieth, Tryon heard rumors that the Regulators intended to march on New Bern to disrupt the upcoming Assembly session, and he ordered militia colonels John Simpson, Richard Caswell, and John Hinton to be prepared for such a contingency. Finally, Tryon received a petition from John Butler, sheriff of Orange County, asking that he be relieved of tax-collecting duties until the Regulators ceased threatening his life. The governor's response to Butler's appeal is not recorded, but it is unlikely that Tryon reacted favorably to what he very likely would have seen as a dereliction of duty on Butler's part.[16]

Tryon opened the Assembly session on December 5 by requesting that the legislators address themselves to the Regulator troubles. To ameliorate the sufferings of the backwoodsmen in the matter of "Abuses in the conduct of the Public Funds [and] the General Complaints against Offices and Officers," he proposed reforms in the accounting system. To stem the erosion in the value of circulating currency because of counterfeiting, he advocated measures for "tracing . . . up, the Authors of this Iniquity." But he also called for authority to raise "a sufficient Body of Men, under the Rules and Discipline of War, to march into the settlements of these Insurgents, in Order to Aid and protect the Magistrates and Civil Officers" and restore "Public Tranquility." Both the Council and the Assembly welcomed his recommendations and proceeded to enact a large number of new laws. That the assemblymen were terrified of the Regulators by late 1770 was indicated by the fact that they first proceeded against Husband, one of their own but a man closely associated in their minds with the western mob, by accusing him of sedition and libel for supposedly having written a threatening letter to Maurice Moore. Although Husband denied authorship of the message and declared that if he were imprisoned, his friends from the west would come down and free him, he was expelled from the Assembly and thrown into the New Bern jail. Then the Assembly enacted into law a measure known as the "Johnston Act," introduced by Samuel Johnston, allowing the attorney general for one year's time to prosecute rioters in any Superior Court in the colony simply by a change of venue. The measure also declared anyone who did not answer a summons of the court within sixty days to be an outlaw and liable to be killed on sight. In addition, the Assembly empowered Tryon to call militiamen to arms to enforce the laws.[17]

To Tryon's relief, the Assembly did not rest on its laurels after passing coercive measures against the Regulators. It also proceeded to enact a number of laws designed to redress grievances of backwoodsmen that were seen obviously to be genuine. It outlined in greater specificity provisions for the appointment of sheriffs and what their duties would entail, regulated the fees of officers, set attorneys' fees on a definite and published scale, made provision for speedier collection of small debts, put the chief justice of the Superior Court on a salary and took away his power to draw income from fees, and created a number of new western counties. Tryon was delighted with the tenor and substance of these many reforms—even though they were not as extensive as he wished—and he wrote Hillsborough on January 31, 1771, "They will tend much to quiet the General Discontents of the Inhabitants and probably make it less difficult for Administration to suppress the Insurgents in the back Frontiers."[18] So, Tryon dared believe that he might escape these troubles without again having to resort to armed force, a measure both terribly expensive and in some degree an admission that other policies had failed.

Meanwhile, Tryon made provision for the possibility that the Regulators might attempt to rescue Husband from the New Bern jail. As he told Hillsborough, he had alerted "the Commanding Officers of the several Regiments of Militia" around the town to be prepared to take arms at short notice, should the insurgents be reported on the march eastward.

He also issued a proclamation banning the sale of shot and lead in the colony "'til further notice." In fact, the Regulators were gathering in large numbers at Hillsborough and were publicly announcing that February 11 was the day they would commence their march toward New Bern. On February 8 Tryon's problem of keeping Husband incarcerated was solved when a special court of oyer and terminer, Chief Justice Martin Howard presiding, released Husband from custody. The governor was disgusted with this outcome, for, as he told Hillsborough, the court was stampeded into action by fear that the Hillsborough mob was going to lay the town of New Bern in ashes. Tryon himself was criticized by some citizens for having refused Husband bail in the first place and of bringing on the crisis, but Tryon's decisions throughout this affair were supported by the counsel of the chief justice and deputy attorney general, both of whom believed that it was both legal and necessary for public tranquility that Husband be held for trial.[19]

Dissatisfied "with the Temper and disposition" of the court that had discharged Husband, Tryon dissolved it on February 28 and called another to meet on March 11 to hear charges against sixty-two men accused of rioting the previous September at Hillsborough. He directed sheriffs to choose jurymen only from "Gentlemen of the first Rank, Property and Probity," and he sent a personal representative up to Hillsborough to assure witnesses of governmental protection from the Regulators. Because of his careful attention to the selection of the jury, upon embodiment it proceeded to do as he had wished and find true bills against sixty-one of the defendants, whereupon under the Johnston Act they were given sixty days to surrender for trial or be declared outlaws. When at the end of this waiting period they had ignored the indictments—in fact were actively recruiting westerners into a Regulator army—Tryon realized that his government's dignity, and perhaps its very existence, depended upon his bringing armed might against the insurgents. Therefore, according to his account, he promised the jurors, much to their delight, "to compel the Insurgents," by force if necessary, "to Obedience to the Laws."[20]

On March 16 Tryon began issuing orders to militia commanders of various North Carolina counties to embody volunteers for service against the backcountry insurgents. At the same time, he decided that it would be a mistake to petition General Thomas Gage, commander in chief of British regulars in North America, with headquarters in New York, for assistance in the form of regular army troops. Shortly thereafter he received word from John Frohock, Alexander Martin, and Griffith Rutherford of Rowan County that they had agreed with a group of Regulators encamped near Salisbury to arbitrate differences over fees already collected by the officials. Immediately Tryon repudiated their arrangement as being "unconstitutional, Dishonourable to Government and . . . dangerous to the peace and Happiness of Society," and he suggested almost sarcastically to them that if they were guilty of gouging the citizenry, as they seemed to be tacitly admitting, then it was their personal responsibility "to give Satisfaction and make restitution to the injured." As for himself, he told them, he entertained "a Just Abhorrence of the conduct of that Man who is guilty of Extortion in the execution of His Public Character."[21]

During the next six weeks Tryon immersed himself in military matters as he organized his militia army. To keep the Assembly abreast of his preparations, he wrote Speaker John Harvey on occasion, while at the same time keeping careful records of military disbursements from the treasury. To be his second in command he appointed Hugh Waddell, a veteran of frontier warfare, and he chose Thomas Hart and Richard Blackledge as his commissaries. For his artillery officers he selected Colonels James Moore and Robert Schaw. On March 19 he wrote General Gage, informing him of his preparations and asking for four British flags, two light cannon, and six drums. These materials, which Gage dispatched on April 14, arrived in New Bern twelve days later. While General Waddell proceeded into the backcountry to organize militia forces there, Tryon arranged volunteer companies arriving from nine counties into a presentable army at New Bern. Finally, on April 27 Tryon was prepared to march westward, and after bidding his wife and daughter good-bye, he swung into the saddle and rode to meet the Regulators.[22]

Over the next three weeks Tryon marched at a leisurely pace toward the main Regulator camp on Alamance Creek, west of Hillsborough, all the time augmenting his army with militia volunteers who joined him in his adventure. On May 3, at Union Camp on the Neuse River, he reviewed the seventeen companies that comprised his army, then proceeded over the next two days to march farther inland. He was joined on the sixth by the Wake Regiment, and although sixty of those troops agreed to volunteer, the other forty refused and were "dismissed, much ashamed both of their Disgrace, & their own Conduct which occasioned it." That day, Tryon requested from his officers returns on the number of troops under his command and learned that he now had 970 men. By September 12 he had marched through Hillsborough and forded the Haw River, much to his relief, as he had "expected the Regulators would have opposed the passages of the Royalists over this River." He now learned that on the ninth General Waddell's troops had been forced by superior numbers of Regulators to retreat, shortly after having crossed the Yadkin River in their march toward a rendezvous with Tryon's army. Moreover, Waddell had had two powder wagons blown up by insurgents in Mecklenburg, was short on powder, and for the foreseeable future was simply eliminated from the campaign.[23]

Undeterred by Waddell's misfortunes, Tryon called a council of war on the evening of May 12, at which time it was decided that the governor's force would march rapidly forward and join General Waddell if possible. Without undue incident, by the afternoon of the fifteenth Tryon had rapidly closed with the Regulators' encampment on Alamance Creek, but the hoped-for rendezvous with Waddell had not taken place. Nevertheless Tryon drew up his men in lines, swore the newly joined Orange County militia to an oath of fidelity, and ordered his troops to remain under arms during the night, for he had "determined that the Army should march against the Rebels early the next Morning." That evening he attempted to send the Regulators "a Letter offering them Terms," but his messengers met "with Insults" from their outposts and "returned back to Camp with the said Letter." Thus, a battle between Tryon's forces, now numbering about 1,300 men, and the Regulator army, about 2,500 men, had become almost inevitable.[24]

At seven o'clock on the morning of May 16, Tryon marched his troops out of their camp toward the Regulators and within two miles of the rebels formed his army into two lines of battle. By ten o'clock he had advanced to within half a mile of the Regulators, whereupon he halted while he sent emissaries to the backwoodsmen with a letter requiring them to lay down their arms and "Surrender up their outlawed Ringleaders." The insurgents countered with demands that Tryon punish provincial officials they believed guilty of cheating them, terms which Tryon considered "wholly inadmissible." By this time, the two armies had drifted to within 300 yards of each other, and according to anti-Regulator accounts, the insurgents were behaving "in a most daring and desperate manner," even "daring [their enemies] to come on." In the midst of this growing tension, Tryon attempted to effect a prisoner exchange, but after he had waited half an hour for the Regulators ostensibly to fetch prisoners from "a Distance in the Rear," he became "suspicious that they were only protracting the Time that they might out wing his Flankers." Hence, he

Governor Tryon confronting the Regulators, by Felix O. C. Darley. Created by
the artist about 1876, this is a fanciful view of Tryon at a climactic moment in
his career as governor of North Carolina. (Courtesy of the North Carolina Collection, Wilson Library, University of North Carolina at Chapel Hill)

sent a courier to them with a warning "to take care of themselves as he
should immediately, at the Return of the Messenger, give the Signal for
action."[25]

Tryon accordingly ordered this prearranged signal, "a Discharge of the
Artillery," and the battle of the Alamance commenced. The cannon were
"instantly seconded by a Discharge from the whole of the [militia] first
Line," and there "ensued a very heavy and dreadful Firing on both Sides."
The action, said Tryon, "was hot" for about two hours, although "the
Rebels soon took to the Trees." The Regulators were "sorely galled by the
artillery, which played incessantly on them with grape shot," and soon
"their Fire slackened considerably." At that point, Tryon directed his
cannon to cease firing and his troops, "in the best Order the Circumstances would admit of," to advance. Soon the insurgents were driven
from their cover, "and the whole Rebel Army Fled in great Confusion,
leaving behind them near twenty Prisoners taken in the Field, Fifty
Horses, with Saddles, provisions, and a small quantity of Ammunition."
After pursuing their fleeing foes for about a mile, Tryon's militiamen
collected on the battlefield at half past two o'clock in the afternoon and

returned to their previous night's campsite. That evening, Tryon assessed his own and his enemies' losses, discovering that 10 of his men had been killed and about 60 wounded while 9 Regulators had been killed, "a very great number wounded," and "about 20 or 30 made prisoners."[26]

In the days immediately following the battle of the Alamance, Tryon slowly came to the conclusion, as he told Hillsborough on May 18, "that the Advantages now gained over a set of desperate and cruel Enemy, may . . . finally terminate in giving a Stability to this Constitution which it has hitherto been a stranger to." Yet Tryon was so unsure about the will of the insurgents being broken completely that on the evening of the seventeenth he decided to strike even more terror into their hearts by summarily executing James Few, "an Out Law . . . taken in the Battle." This poor, luckless man, to the "great Satisfaction" of Tryon's troops, was "hanged at the Head of the Army" under the legal cloak of summary justice allowed by the Johnston Act. Tryon's tactic was unnecessary, for the Regulator movement had been crushed on the sixteenth; but as he noted later, he carried out the execution in part to appease his troops who were clamoring for the immediate application of public judgment against "the Outlaws that were taken in the Action." In addition, his troops were threatening mutiny against him and mayhem against any insurgents they might meet in future, should they not receive instant satisfaction of their demand for vengeance.[27]

Tryon now proceeded to restore the western counties of North Carolina to a semblance of the king's peace. On the day after the battle he issued a proclamation of pardon to all insurgents, except those already outlawed, who would surrender, swear an oath of allegiance, and promise to obey the laws. Responding to these proclamations, which Tryon renewed four times through mid-June, the Regulators began to submit in large numbers. By May 27 about 1,400 of them had surrendered, and by June 7 some 2,000 had taken the required oaths. The Regulator movement was clearly at an end, and Tryon, perhaps more than anyone else in the colony, was delighted at the result. In the meantime, however, he continued to march through the backcountry with his forces. On May 21 he took possession of Herman Husband's plantation and seized what he called "A large parcel of Treasonable papers found in his Home." He was joined by General Waddell's army on June 1, and three days later he reached Bethlehem. After resting there until the ninth, and after detaching Waddell and 600 men to march westward into Rowan and Tryon counties, Tryon directed his army toward Hillsborough, which he entered on June 13.[28]

By that time Tryon's service in western North Carolina was nearing an end. He now issued a proclamation offering a reward of £100 proclamation money and 1,000 acres of land to any person "who will take Dead or alive and bring into Mine or General Waddell's Camp" one or more of the insurgent leaders Husband, James Hunter, Rednap Howell, or William Butler. He also was pleased to see the results of a trial by a special court of oyer and terminer of twelve Regulators, who were convicted of treason; six were hanged and the others, at Tryon's request, reprieved. That duty done, he dubiously asserted to Hillsborough that the inhabitants were "Cheerfully" paying their taxes and that "they are much happier by loosing the Victory, than they would have been had they Defeated His Majesty's forces." On June 20, 1771, Tryon handed over command of his army to Colonel John Ashe, and after expressing to his officers "the warm Sense of his Gratitude" for their service "and receiving in Return from those Gentlemen the most Affectionate Expressions of Respect & esteem," he rode for New Bern. Four days later, he reached home and was welcomed by not only his wife and daughter but also the citizens of New Bern and Craven County, who saw him as their deliverer from potential anarchy and chaos. Although it was "late in the evening before he arrived, yet as soon as it was known, the whole town was instantly illuminated, and a bonfire kindled. Many Gentlemen met, and spent the remainder of the evening in festive joy, for the safe return and happy deliverance of his Excellency's person from the imminent perils to which it had been exposed in the late battle with the Regulators." Two days later, the entire town collected "in a Body and waited on his Excellency at the Palace with a congratulatory Address, to which he returned a very polite Answer." Clearly Governor Tryon was a hero to eastern North Carolinians for having suppressed "a most wicked and dangerous insurrection and rebellion."[29]

But not all Americans agreed with these people's assessment. Given the fact that Tryon, an ardent advocate of royal authority in the colonies, had cowed colonials by armed might—even colonials that were in rebellion against other colonials—it was not surprising that he got into trouble with some Americans in the politically feverish 1770s. As General Gage noted, in writing to Sir Jeffery Amherst in August 1771, "There is a licentious spirit too prevalent" in most of Britain's North American colonies. On June 27, 1771, a writer named "Leonidas" in the *Massachusetts Spy* blasted Tryon as "a Traitor and a Villain," accusing him of impoverishing his province to build himself a palace, of being in cahoots with a

"Banditti of Robbers, . . . Judges, Sheriffs, and Pettifoggers" to impoverish the people, and of discharging artillery at the Alamance "while under the sacred Bond of a Treaty." A month later, the *Boston Gazette* sarcastically reported that in the "Spirit of naming Children &c. after great Folks, . . . a Gentleman the other Day, named a favorite Spaniel Puppey of his, TRYON." Another diatribe was directed against Tryon in the November 7 issue of the *Virginia Gazette* when "Atticus," generally thought to be Judge Maurice Moore, lambasted the governor for many crimes against "the people" of North Carolina. Richard Henry Lee of Virginia declared that "in the mildest view of it," Tryon's suppression of the Regulators was "dirty work," and Thomas Jones, a contemporary historian of New York, grumbled that "republicans" in that colony "taxed his excellency [Tryon] with being a murderer, and called him . . . 'Billy the Butcher.'"[30]

Notwithstanding these Whiggish criticisms, Tryon was adjudged by the vast majority of Americans at the time, and by later historians as well, to be a man who had acted with maturity and judgment during his tenure as governor of North Carolina, including his dealings with the Regulators, despite his relative youth and lack of administrative experience before he took office. Without any doubt he was the most successful and finest of the five royal governors who had served in the province from its inception as a Crown province in 1729 to the outbreak of rebellion in 1775. Colonial citizens in the 1760s, and historians since, understood much too well the harsh realities of North Carolina politics from 1765 to 1771, including the Regulator problems and Tryon's reluctant part in thwarting them, to accept his critics' statements as the final word. To be sure, when events at Boston in 1773 would force their hand, many of the leaders who now openly defended Tryon would side with the revolutionaries against Great Britain. But in 1771 they remained the governor's friends. In August, for example, a writer calling himself "Phocion" carefully and systematically refuted in the *Massachusetts Spy* many of the criticisms that had been raised against Tryon by "Leonidas."[31] His sentiments received widespread acceptance.

Officials in London were also delighted with Tryon's crushing of the Regulator movement, and they hastened to see that the governor received special preferment from the Crown for his services. On August 2 the earl of Rochford, writing for Hillsborough (who was visiting Ireland at the time), informed Tryon that his action against "a body of lawless Insurgents stiling themselves Regulators" had received "the King's entire Approbation." The battle of May 16 had "fully answered the just expectations which were entertained from the wisdom & Spirit of the measures pursued by you for crushing in their Infancy, the Dangerous & desperate Designs of those lawless disturbers of the public Peace." But Tryon received more than mere kind words from his sovereign for his martial activities in North Carolina. In the following year, with the assistance of General Thomas Gage and Secretary at War Barrington, he received promotion to a colonelcy (without command of a regiment) in the British army. Tryon was extremely pleased with these marks of the king's favor but was somewhat disappointed that His Majesty had not seen fit to grant him pecuniary recompense as well. Therefore in April 1773 he wrote Postmaster General Lord Hyde requesting "some solid reward" for his services, but his appeal fell on deaf ears.[32]

Tryon's suppression of the Regulators was his last public service as governor of North Carolina, for he was leaving that province to assume the governorship in New York. Tryon had known since early in 1771 that he was the recipient of this new post, for late the previous year his good friend Lord Botetourt, governor of Virginia, had died, and Tryon's patrons in London had maneuvered to have Lord Dunmore transferred to Botetourt's old position. Tryon was then appointed in Dunmore's place with his salary unchanged, and Josiah Martin was chosen (with Tryon's assistance) to assume the governorship of North Carolina. Both Tryon and Martin were delighted with this arrangement (although Tryon at one point would have been satisfied to be given the government of Virginia). Dunmore, however, was not, and he attempted to persuade Hillsborough to have Tryon sent to Virginia instead of New York. On June 4, 1771, Dunmore wrote the secretary of state that as Tryon was "perfectly a Stranger to both Countries, he cannot have a reason for choosing other than that, which is esteemed to be most advantageous as to Emolument." Dunmore concluded his letter by saying that he would remain in New York until he heard from Hillsborough, even if "Mr. Tryon should repair to this place, in consequence of his appointment." Dunmore knew, of course, that Tryon's departure from North Carolina had been retarded by his having to conduct a campaign against the Regulators.[33]

Because of this delay, New Yorkers and others were allowed ample time before Tryon's arrival at his new post to speculate about the man and form conclusions about his abilities. General Gage wrote Tryon in April to welcome him and Mrs. Tryon to their new post, but, he added, "Lord Dunmore likes it so well, that he declines Changing this Government for that of Virginia. I don't know . . . how it is likely to terminate." Tryon replied that he was sorry his "Worthy Friend" Dunmore was disappointed with London's new arrangements, but he made absolutely clear to Gage that he intended to take the new position. In the meantime, James Rivington, later a famous publisher of the *New-York Gazetteer*, was writing Sir William Johnson, superintendent of Indian affairs at Albany: "Lord Dunmore must soon give way to Mr. Tryon, an amiable Gentleman, finely accomplished for Government." Goldsbrow Banyar, secretary of the province of New York, was noting his pleasure at Tryon's appointment, for "He is sensible, affable and of a most engaging Address." And the Rhode Island Friends were passing at their yearly meeting a resolution thanking Tryon for the "justice and equity" of his actions as governor of North Carolina and welcoming him to New York.[34] Tryon seemed to have every reason to hope that his new post would bring him success and laurels. Only the future could tell him whether his expectations were warranted.

CHAPTER SIX

Governor of New York

On June 30 Governor Tryon and his family, accompanied by his newly appointed secretary, Edmund Fanning, and the cartographer Claude Joseph Sauthier, embarked at New Bern in the sloop *Sukey* and sailed northward toward New York, in high anticipation of what life would hold for them in their new home. After an uneventful voyage, they arrived seven days later in lower New York harbor at about three o'clock in the morning. Tryon's appearance was something of a surprise (it being unknown to New Yorkers when his exact arrival would take place); thus officials who normally would have welcomed him personally were unprepared. According to Councillor William Smith, "Dunmore was absent in Jersey," looking over some land with William Alexander, Lord Stirling, and when notified that Tryon had appeared, took a rowboat to Paulus Hook, engaged an oyster piragua, and went out to the *Sukey* to fetch Tryon and his family up to the city. About noon, they all arrived at lower Manhattan and landed, but "No Gentlemen" were there to greet them. About half a dozen persons raised a ragged cheer while "a salute was fired at the Battery"—but that was the full extent of Tryon's welcome. Thereupon Dunmore conducted Tryon's party to the Governor's Mansion in Fort George.[1]

It soon was apparent to Tryon that Dunmore was not reconciled to leaving New York and that getting along with him was going to be difficult until he accepted the inevitable and departed for Virginia. Even while Tryon was at sea, Dunmore had renewed his petition to Hillsborough to remain at this present post and stated his intention of trying to persuade Tryon, whom he obviously considered an interloper, to go to Virginia in his place. Therefore Dunmore was hardly even polite to his successor on the first day that Tryon was in New York. John Smith, brother of Councillor William Smith, paid a visit to Tryon at the Governor's Mansion shortly after Tryon's arrival and found a remarkable scene.

"Ld Dunmore," wrote William Smith later, was "walking the Room & reading a Newspaper & Tryon another," while poor Mrs. Tryon sat "neglected in a Couch or Sopha." As soon as Dunmore got a chance, as Tryon later told Hillsborough, he "warmly Solicited" Tryon "to make the Exchange of Governments with him," but Tryon refused on the ground that he could not, "with any possible Colour of Decency, retreat from a Province, to which [he] was appointed to Preside over." Moreover, his health precluded his further service in the South, "without first going over to England" for an extended leave, and in any case, "Mrs. Tryon at that time [was] in so weak a State of health that she could scarce bare the Voyage from North Carolina, & has continued very ill ever since her arrival here." Therefore although Tryon "entertained the most favourable Opinion of the Government of Virginia," and in fact had been willing in late 1770 to settle for it, now it was too late, for he had "cast [his] Lot" in New York. Given these conditions, the hot-blooded Dunmore could only prepare to depart for the South, though he did so with considerable ill grace.[2]

Tryon, meantime, quickly got down to the business of settling his family into its new home in Fort George and of leasing Abraham Mortier's estate, Richmond Hill, on the western side of Manhattan, for a summer house. As soon as Mrs. Tryon's health had recovered sufficiently, Tryon had her oversee the unpacking of the family's copious personal belongings, while he vigorously turned to executing public business, just as he had done in North Carolina. On the day after his arrival, he called the Council together, along with Dunmore, took the oath of office, and swore in the Council members. Then he and the councillors proceeded to the Town Hall, where his commission was publicly read to a crowd that, according to Smith, was neither great nor joyful, and that evening, "tho' the Mayor ordered it, yet the Town was very partially illuminated." Tryon, however, was pleased at his reception by the "Multitude of His Majesty's cheerful and Loyal Subjects" and expressed to Hillsborough his "warmest Gratitude" to the king for his "Distinguished Mark of . . . favor to me." The festivities ended on a rather sour note, for at a party given in honor of Tryon's arrival, Lord Dunmore got drunk, struck Edmund Fanning and Charles Ward Apthorpe, "called Tryon a Coward who had never seen Flanders, & ran about in the Night assaulting one & another." Completing his performance, Dunmore yelled for all to hear, "Damn Virginia— Did I ever seek it? Why is it forced upon me? I ask'd for New York—New York I took, & they have robbed me of it without my Consent."[3]

Tryon also fell into consultation with Josiah Martin, who happened to

A view of Fort George with the city of New York, about 1731–36, possibly by
William Burgis, engraved by John Carwitham. Tryon would have known New
York as it is illustrated here during his residency in the colony. (Courtesy of the
I. N. Phelps Stokes Collection, Miriam & Ira D. Wallach Division of Art,
Prints and Photographs, New York Public Library, Astor, Lenox and
Tilden Foundations)

be in New York recovering from a lingering illness, about affairs in North
Carolina. On July 9 the two governors had long and informative discus-
sions about the state of the colony, especially about the Regulator movement, and although their conversations were limited due to Tryon's involvement with other business and because of the ceremonies attendant
on his arrival in his new government, Martin found Tryon's information
and advice invaluable, acknowledging to Hillsborough his "great obligations to him, for his free, & open communication of which, I should have
more availed myself, if he had not been occupied." In general, Tryon
assured Martin that North Carolina had been left in a "peaceful state"
and that Martin need not rush away immediately. Therefore he postponed
his embarkation "a few days," in order to learn even more from Tryon,
and did not depart until July 23.[4]

In the meantime Tryon was being inundated with welcoming memorials
and speeches from the people of New York. On July 12 the Anglican
congregation of Trinity Church and the Anglicans in New Jersey congratulated Tryon and his family upon their safe arrival and praised the

governor's "extensive Abilities, Experience in public Affairs, and strict Regard to the wholesome Laws of our Country." The city of Albany added its voice to the rising chorus in early August, as did Governor Thomas Hutchinson of Massachusetts. The students of King's College were so carried away with Tryon's arrival that a number of them wrote poems in his honor, and Alexander Colden told Benjamin Franklin that Tryon's "Amiable Disposition leaves no room to doubt we will be happy in having so worthy a Gentleman for our Governor." It seems evident that New Yorkers generally were pleased to have Tryon as their chief executive, even if he had made some enemies by warring against the Regulators and even if he was replacing a man, Dunmore, who was himself popular—and possessor of a title.[5]

Tryon, ever the ingratiating representative of the king whenever political circumstances allowed, reciprocated the affection of New Yorkers by joining wholeheartedly in projects of civic uplift. In late 1771, when the New York Society Library was chartered, Tryon offered the new institution financial and moral support and was made an honorary member. He paid even more attention to King's College, for ever since he had entered public life as governor of North Carolina he had shown an inordinate interest in educational institutions. In 1774 he gave the college 10,000 acres of his own personal land in Vermont for the endowing of "Tryonian Professorships," that "the Principles of Virtue, Literature and Loyalty" might be promoted in the province of New York. The trustees of King's College reciprocated this munificence by awarding Tryon an honorary doctorate in civil law. A year later Tryon submitted to the government in London a request that King's College be chartered by the Crown, especially since the school was affiliated with the Church of England and would help counter the growth of dissenting religious sects and republican principles in New York. The matter was laid before the king in April 1775, but because of more pressing colonial problems brought on by the American Revolution, it was never acted upon.[6]

As a member of the Church of England, Tryon was touched by the memorials he had received from Anglican congregations in both his own province and New Jersey. He considered it fortunate that the Anglican church had been established in New York's four lower counties by the Assembly's passage of the Ministry Act in 1693. Therefore he did not need to go through political and bureaucratic travail, as in North Carolina, to make the Anglican church official in the province. However, he did discover that New York dissenters were every bit as distraught as those in North Carolina over having to pay taxes for supporting an official church. He also discovered that Councillor Smith, with whom he would later become close friends, was a Presbyterian dissenter and a leader of the opposition to church taxes. In fact, at their first meeting Tryon showed Smith a letter he had received from New York's Baptists expressing concern about their new governor's lack of toleration. Smith took the liberty to tell Tryon "that they were full of Fears on Account of a Letter written by him from Carolina to the Society for propagating the Gospel . . . in which he had intimated, that none but Presbyterians & Quakers deserved Toleration, the peculiarities of the sects being in his Opinion, repugnant to Common sense." Tryon explained to Smith that he had written that letter in March 1769 "in a Hurry sharpened agt. the Baptists, as they were the People who opposed Govt. in Carolina." He asked Smith to draft a letter for him to the Baptists, asking forgiveness for his too-hasty act and asserting his wholehearted support for England's Toleration Act. Smith did, Tryon published it, the Baptists subsided, and the governor was helped "over a stumbling Block thrown in his Way" early in the administration.[7]

Tryon's acceptance of toleration for New York dissenters did not in any way weaken his support for Anglicanism as the basis of his personal creed and as part of the foundation upon which royal government was maintained in America. In 1773 he presented Trinity Church with "a complete Set of rich and elegant Hangings of crimson Damask for the Pulpit, Reading Desk, and Communion Table—a Folio Bible, and several Folio Prayer Books, with a full Service of Plate." Tryon's gift, noted the *New York Gazette*, "must endear his Excellency to every Friend of Religion and Virtue." Eighteen months later, Tryon appealed to William Legge, earl of Dartmouth, who replaced Hillsborough as secretary of state in 1772, for Crown funds to establish Anglican chaplains for each of the royal governors in America. The benefits of chaplaincies, he said, would be twofold. First, they would give "an augmentation of strength and influence" to the colonial governments, and as "every Appendix of Dignity to His Majesty's Commission to His Governors in America . . . promotes the public interest," this would be money well spent. Second, such royal generosity "would be a peculiar mark of distinction to the members of the Church of England, who stand in need of every possible aid and protection from Government." His plan was not adopted.[8]

One great service that Tryon rendered to the Church of England in New

William Smith of New York, Tryon's intimate friend and confidant during his governorship of New York and generalship in the British army during the American war. (James Grant Wilson and John Fiske, eds., *Appleton's Cyclopedia of American Biography* [New York, 1888], 5:591)

York was his ruling, as presiding judge of the Chancery Court in 1774, in favor of the Ministry Act of 1693, thus warding off an assault by dissenters upon the Anglican establishment. The case involved a suit between Joshua Bloomer, an Anglican clergyman, and two churchwardens, Robert Hinckman and Philip Edsall, of the predominantly Presbyterian Jamaica Parish. In 1768 the Reverend Mr. Bloomer had been inducted as minister in the parish by Governor Sir Henry Moore, over the opposition of the churchwardens, who did not want an Episcopalian to serve them. When the churchwardens refused to pay Bloomer his salary, he retained James Duane, John Tabor Kempe, and John Jay as attorneys and sued Edsall and Hinckman. The churchwardens thereupon secured the legal counsel of John Morin Scott and William Smith, and the two sides wrangled over the case for the next three years. Finally, in the spring of 1774, Tryon issued a decree in favor of Bloomer, declaring upon the basis of Duane's arguments in court that the Church of England indeed was established in New York. He ordered the churchwardens to pay Bloomer his salary from the year 1768 but divided the costs of chancery between the parties. He warned the churchwardens not to delay the matter any further, or they would be saddled with all the costs. The defendants appealed the case to the Council, but it was never settled because of the interruption of the American Revolution. By that time, Tryon's attention was riveted on matters far more important than preserving and defending the Anglican establishment in New York.[9]

Looking to private financial matters early in his administration, Tryon, who always paid careful attention to his personal fortune, began seeking ways to live within his means as royal governor of New York. His salary from the Crown, as it had been in North Carolina, was £1,000 sterling per year, augmented by various fees from land sales and other governmental transactions. Even though the New York Assembly supplemented this income annually with an appropriation of £400 New York currency for him to purchase candles and firewood to use in his mansion in Fort George, Tryon found the total amount inadequate and in May 1772 complained to Hillsborough that he needed more money. Despite his financial problems, however, he refused an offer from the New York Assembly of a salary supplement of £2,000 New York currency. His instructions from the king forbade such a bequest on the grounds that colonial additions to royal governors' salaries would reduce their independence as representatives of imperial interests.[10] On the other hand, Tryon was not averse to attempting to gain a share of revenues from ships' seizures in New York waters under the Navigation Acts. Already he received one-third of all seizures made on land, but in late 1771 he appealed to Hillsborough to allow him as well a share equal to flag officers of seizures made on water. Hillsborough found Tryon's claims not unreasonable and referred them to the Treasury for a ruling, but at that point the matter became lost in the maze of Treasury bureaucracy and was never acted upon.[11]

Tryon was a loyal supporter of his friends and looked to the interests of his secretary, Edmund Fanning. Early in his administration he appointed Fanning surrogate and register of the Prerogative Court in New York, despite the claim of Goldsbrow Banyar that he, Banyar, had the disposition of that appointment and that the position therefore would go to George Clark. When Banyar appealed the matter to the Privy Council, Tryon wrote two letters, justifying his taking precedence in this appointment because he held the "King's Commission as Commander in chief In & over the province" while Banyar held only "the patent of Secretary of the Province." Clearly for Tryon the issue had become one of precedence and royal authority and not merely a question of giving his friend Fanning a reward for his services against the North Carolina Regulators. Nevertheless, when the Privy Council referred the case to the Board of Trade in 1774, the board ruled in favor of Banyar and Clark, and Fanning found himself without a public salary.[12]

Although Tryon informed Hillsborough in August 1771 that he had not as of yet transacted any public "business of moment," that situation was shortly to change. A month later he was deeply involved in matters of diplomacy with Joseph Solano, Spanish governor of Santo Domingo, demanding that Madrid redress Daniel Frisby, master of the sloop *Hawke* and a New Yorker, for seizure of his boat by an armed Spanish sloop on June 27 while Frisby was in passage from Curaçao to New York with a valuable cargo aboard. He also wrote Hillsborough, notifying the secretary of his actions and requesting that the Spanish ambassador in London be apprised of these untoward circumstances. He received from Hillsborough word that the matter was being pursued through diplomatic channels and from Governor Solano the blunt assertion that Frisby was lying. The last that is heard of the matter is a cryptic note in the Treasury records in London that a copy of Tryon's letter to Hillsborough had been received and calendared.[13]

Tryon was also paying attention to a number of issues relating to provincial defense of the province and to military rank. In November 1771 he received a letter from General Thomas Gage requesting quarters and carriages in Albany for regiments that were to be moved within the province. Tryon laid the letter before his Council, and at the suggestion of William Smith it was decided to require that the mayor and justices of Albany fulfill Gage's requests. "None seemed apprized of the Delicacy of the business," Smith mused, "for this is executing the Obnoxious Act of 5 Geo: III amending the Mutiny Act of which there have been such loud

Complts." Smith's purpose in casting the burden upon the magistrates in
Albany was to prod them into objecting "to the Services & keep[ing] up
as far as we durst the Appearance of Non compliance with the Act."
Tryon obviously did not discern Smith's motive, else he would not have
tolerated such a blatant attempt to defy English law.[14]

During his first New York Assembly session in late 1771 and early
1772, Tryon managed enactment of a number of laws relating to military
matters. He was so successful, in fact, that General Gage practically
purred with delight when he reported to Secretary at War Barrington
Tryon's handling of the legislators. First, Tryon asked the Assembly to
provide £2,000 for "Quarters and Carriages" under the provisions of the
Quartering Act to pay Albany officials for moving Gage's troops. Although there was considerable foot-dragging among the legislators because of controversies over quartering troops in New York, the Assembly
passed the legislation. Moreover, the Assembly in the following year,
upon Tryon's request, renewed its military appropriation for upkeep of
British regulars in the colony, and Gage continued on occasion to require
that Tryon provide his regiments with quarters and transports.[15] Second,
Tryon requested that the Assembly pass a bill for establishing a militia in
New York, and on March 18, 1772, such a law was forthcoming. He
quickly organized militia units "in most of the Counties of the Province,"
and within a year he could report to London that New York possessed a
total of thirty-six regiments. His masters in the ministry were delighted,
especially because Tryon was using the law to reinforce social stratification by giving all officers' commissions to "Gentlemen of the first families
and distinctions" and also by organizing "several Independant Companies" in New York City at the expense of the municipality's richest citizens, with no costs accruing to the government. Thereafter, from time to
time Tryon held splendid reviews for the province's militia companies,
usually in celebration of a holiday such as the king's birthday or some
other momentous occasion. Third, Tryon informed the Assembly that he
needed legislation authorizing him to lay taxes for the purchase of gun-
powder for Fort George's cannon and to rebuild New York City's dilapi-
dated fortifications. Within two months the Assembly provided him with
the necessary laws, and by the spring of 1773, Tryon was reporting to
London that Fort George, the Governor's Mansion, and the battery were
all in excellent repair, the work having been overseen by Captain Thomas
Sowers, His Majesty's chief engineer in America.[16]

While Tryon's military legislation was sailing smoothly through the

Assembly, the governor was embroiled with General Gage in a controversy over the chain of command. It was Tryon's conviction, which he asserted in early 1772, that the governor of New York, acting as the king's ultimate representative on the scene, ought to have control of all British armed forces in the province during peacetime. This viewpoint toward the military on Tryon's part was in fact one element in his larger, and growing, belief (which would not be articulated until a few years later) that royal governors in America ought to exercise the powers and prerogatives of a viceroy. His immediate concerns, however, were that he might need control of regular troops to support his authority in frontier land controversies, such as the one that even then was going on in Vermont. In addition, he perceived that he could curry favor with New Yorkers by asserting "civilian" control over the military in a time when tensions between Americans and Britons over constitutional issues were high.

Tryon opened his campaign against Gage's power as commander in chief by informing Gage that he intended to ask Hillsborough for command of British regulars in New York. This was no new problem for Gage, for he had been compelled in 1768 to fight off similar claims by Governor Sir Henry Moore, one of Tryon's predecessors. At that time Hillsborough had attempted to defuse the issue by ordering Moore and Gage to settle the problem between themselves, insisting all along that "nothing can be more foreign to his Majesty's intention that introducing a military government into his provinces in America." When such appeals failed to resolve the controversy, Lord Barrington in 1770 obtained from the attorney and solicitor general a ruling favoring Gage's authority, and the problem seemed settled. Tryon's reopening the entire issue irked Gage, who believed that Lieutenant Governor Cadwallader Colden, then eighty-five years old but no stranger to controversy, had "set him upon it." But Gage need not have worried, for on October 14, 1773, Tryon was ordered by the Crown to desist in his claims. For the moment the governor reluctantly complied with his royal master's wishes, but two years later he appealed to Dartmouth for a ruling in favor of gubernatorial precedence over the American commander in chief. Dartmouth's only response to this appeal was a terse letter to all royal governors in America, declaring "that it is His Majesty's pleasure that the orders of the Commander in Chief of his majesty's forces in North America, and under him of the Major Generals and Brigadier Generals shall be supreme in all cases relative to the operations of the same troops." Tryon was disgusted with this ruling, for he had engaged "a Man of Law" to draw up his last petition to

Dartmouth and had "conversed with many General Officers of the Army who were of opinion that the Govrs. had Preheminence."[17]

As Tryon set about seizing the reins of power in New York and putting his personal stamp upon his new government, Councillor William Smith was taking Tryon's measure, assessing his strengths and weaknesses, and attempting to determine the best way to deal with him on the Council. Because of sickness, Smith did not meet Tryon until July 29, 1771, and at that time the governor gave him a strange request: "He told me," said Smith, "that he was preparing Notes of his Mother's Rank, & asked me to put them into Form for publication; for he had just then the News of her Death." Smith complied and sent the obituary notices to the local papers. But regarding Tryon's seemingly odd reaction to his mother's demise, he said, "Here I saw his Vanity, for he was anxious to have it known that she was the daughter of Earl Ferrers." Smith was correct in sensing Tryon's vanity, but in this particular case the governor was also acting from policy, for having just undergone a rather unenthusiastic welcome by the citizenry of New York, he was attempting to assuage the people's disappointment in losing an earl as governor by pointing out in this rather unsophisticated way his own connections with nobility.[18]

Tryon needed all the prestige he could muster, for he found himself mired in petty party spirit from the moment he took the helm in his new government. The politics of New York at that time were dominated by two factions, generally coalescing around the Livingston and DeLancey families, with everyone seemingly taking one or the other side. Everything Tryon did as governor became a political matter, for the two factions jealously watched him in the Council and elsewhere and attempted to draw him into one or the other family's orbit. Tryon found this constant bickering to be both infuriating and personally painful. After listening to it for eight months in Council, he exploded with fury on March 8, 1772. In a vehement speech delivered "with great Earnestness" in a trembling voice, he told the Council that his first loyalty was to the empire and that he intended to preserve his autonomy. "I will be your *independent* Govr.," he roared; "I must look up to the Crown—I mean to consult the Interest of the Province, but being the Kings Servant I must have an Eye to his Commands." Later, Tryon explained to Smith, an ardent Livingstonian, why he had waited for six months to lash out against the political bickerers on the Council who were making his life miserable. Quite simply, he had been forced to wait until he could be sure Lord Dunmore would not unseat him from office by appeals to powerful connections in London. Had Tryon made enemies too soon, these persons could have contributed to his overthrow. But now, Tryon was convinced that his position "at Home" was secure and that he could express his personal inclination not to "steer by the Popular voice nor be a Dupe to the Assembly or Council." By remaining free of partisan entanglements, he would uphold both "his Honor & Safety."[19]

Tryon's spirited defense of his personal autonomy as a royal governor may have been the only honorable way that he could serve Crown interests in the province, but his public posture of distancing himself from the Livingston-DeLancey political battles carried a price. By the end of 1772, Tryon was so dejected by the impossibility of pleasing all the rich and powerful leaders in the province that his secretary, Fanning, reported "that he was inclined to give up his government." The "Spirit of Party" was depriving him "of considerable & agreeable Friendships, as the Jealousy he was obliged to oppose to the Jealousy of Parties for the Dignity of Govermt., obliged him to be shy." Being forced "to act as it were alone, . . . he could get no Credit with any Body," and yet he continued to be bombarded with "insolent Requests from both Parties." He was worn out by the "painful Vigilance" that he must maintain; he was overworked by the "various and immense" business that he must conduct; and "his temper would not permit him to neglect any Thing." Only his "Fear of Expence in England" prevented his return home.[20]

Although local party conflicts sometimes made Tryon's life complicated, he vastly overstated his problems near the end of 1772. Some of his vexations, in fact, were self-inflicted, especially in the area of land grants in the upper reaches of New York province. Tryon was so anxious to pocket fees from issuance of such grants, as well as to gain personal possession of vast tracts of unimproved frontier lands, that he sometimes was overzealous in pushing those grants. His biggest headaches were caused by land disputes in the "Hampshire Grants," territory west of the Connecticut River in what later became the state of Vermont, claimed at one time by both New York and New Hampshire. Long before Tryon came on the scene, governors of both provinces had granted overlapping patents in the region, pocketed the fees, and awaited Crown adjudication of resulting boundary disputes. In 1764 the king awarded New York jurisdiction over all lands west of the Connecticut River and north of Massachusetts, but three years later the Privy Council prohibited New York's governors from granting any more lands in territories already granted by New Hampshire's governors until the Crown could sort out rival land claims in the disputed territories.[21]

When Tryon became governor, he was instructed by the Crown to maintain the standing rules on granting lands in Vermont under the government of New York. But he was also faced with armed, organized resistance from farmers in the claims region, notably the settlers around Bennington, led by Ethan Allen and others, who were being told by New York authorities that the New Hampshire patents under which they had occupied their lands were valueless. Many of them were quite willing to settle the whole matter by having the governor of New York confirm their present grants upon payment of half fees, and they had so petitioned Governor Dunmore on December 3, 1770. Seeing this as a sensible solution, Dunmore had interpreted his Crown instructions as allowing him to confirm land patents in Vermont on such a basis. Thus, fifteen were confirmed and twenty-one others were under consideration by the New York Council when Tryon assumed office.[22]

Off and on for about six months, Tryon and the Council debated the question of how Crown instructions on the Hampshire Grants should be interpreted. Tryon even took the liberty of showing the Council a private letter from Hillsborough, dated June 5, 1771, explaining that the Privy Council was working on the matter and would soon make a report. Basing their decision upon that letter, Councillors Smith and Roger Morris insisted that Tryon not follow Dunmore's lead but instead wait for clarification of the matter from London. On the other hand, Oliver DeLancey and his supporters, a majority of the Council, were advising the opposite. Smith was convinced that the DeLanceys were laying a trap for Tryon by encouraging him into at least a technical violation of his instructions; thus the councillor was dismayed when Tryon decided on January 22, 1772, to continue the policy of confirming Vermont patents upon payment of half fees. After that particular Council meeting, Tryon detained Smith, whom he had come to respect and rely upon, to assure Smith that he was not becoming a tool of the DeLanceys. He related an anecdote from Lord Ligonier to the effect that one should obey orders except when the enemy brings the orders, "and then largely Intimated the Propriety of breaking the Instructions." Smith was unimpressed, warning Tryon to be on his guard against further DeLancey advice "to break other Instructions" and to be sure that he, Tryon, was the first person to inform the secretary of state in London about his actions. With good humor, Tryon accepted both of Smith's hints and showed no signs of anger because of Smith's opposition to his decision.[23]

Tryon profited from land grants in Vermont not only by receiving his share of the half fees paid to confirm existing New Hampshire patents but also by securing a large tract of land for himself. On April 14, 1772, he granted a patent for more than 30,000 acres to thirty-two persons, including Fanning, James Elliot, James Deane, and others. Two days later these men signed over their shares in the "Norbury Tract," as Tryon called these lands in honor of his family's estate in England, to the governor for a small sum of money. Tryon had taken this roundabout way to secure Vermont land because he did not want to be too brazen in openly flouting London's strict admonition that American royal governors limit the amount of land granted to 1,000 acres per individual.[24]

Following Smith's earlier advice, Tryon fired off to Hillsborough on February 2 a letter explaining his reasons for confirming New Hampshire patents in Vermont. Admitting that he had acted "in opposition to the letter" of his instructions, he nevertheless insisted that he had "kept strictly upon the spirit" of them, as his only aim was to promote the best interests of both New Hampshire settlers and the Crown. He concluded, "If I, my lord, who am upon the spot, may be allowed to consider and determine what is necessary to restore the Tranquillity of the eastern frontier of this government, I should advise that the whole of the New Hampshire grants should be confirmed under this government," upon the basis of allowing the settlers to pay half fees for certification of their titles. Even before he received this letter, Hillsborough, who was not aware of all Tryon's proceedings regarding Vermont lands, had learned enough by December 1771 to reprimand the governor for some of his actions. He ordered Tryon to send him a full description "of the method of proceeding upon application for grants of land, in order that his Majesty may be informed whether such Method does or does not correspond with the letter and spirit of the Royal Instructions given for that purpose." Hillsborough was particularly perturbed that grants were being made to persons who immediately ceded their claims to another person, in order to give "to any one person more than he is allowed by the King's Instructions." He also expressed his disapprobation of Tryon's having shown one of his private letters to the Council without the king's specific allowance that it was to be so used.[25]

Responding to Hillsborough's chastisements with two letters of his own, Tryon attempted to justify his behavior. He had shown Hillsborough's letter to the Council, he said, because that body was the only source of information that he could draw upon for conducting the business referred to therein. Hence, its members must be kept abreast of the latest Privy Council activities regarding Vermont lands. He had been totally unaware that he was under any admonition to keep the secretary of state's letters secret, and had acted with complete candor; but he certainly would not repeat his mistake in the future. On the more important question of how the Crown could limit land grants to a thousand acres, Tryon did not see any way to keep a person from alienating his claim after he had received it. Land prices were cheap and there were potential purchasers "who had the command of money." Nor did he, as a matter of policy and principle, wish to hinder rich men from acquiring "an unlimited landed property." Large tracts of land ought to be lodged "in the hands of Gentlemen of weight and consideration," who would "naturally farm out their lands to Tenants; a method which will ever create subordination and counterpoise, in some measure, the general levelling spirit, that so much prevails in some of His Majesty's Governments."[26] For Tryon, then, land policy was a tool for the encouragement of social stratification and a concomitant strengthening of royal control of the colony.

While corresponding with Hillsborough about Vermont land problems, Tryon was also in touch with Governor John Wentworth of New Hampshire. On October 2, 1771, he complained to Wentworth about a survey conducted by the New Hampshire government the previous winter on the east branch of the Connecticut River, which seemed to indicate that that colony was going to reopen in London the already-settled question of which province had title to the Hampshire Grants. In addition, Tryon was angry about "the refractory and disorderly behaviour of the grantees under New Hampshire," who "in open defiance of the laws . . . lately by force dispossessed several persons settled under titles derived from this province." Although Wentworth disclaimed any intention of reopening the controversy over which colony had possession of the Hampshire Grants, and although he expressed the hope that the perpetrators of the "outrages" would be punished, he refused to issue any proclamation against the lawbreakers and in fact was proceeding rapidly toward an attempt to have New Hampshire reannex Vermont. In May 1772 the New Hampshire Council approved a memorial to the Crown, asking that the Hampshire Grants be taken from New York and given to New Hampshire.[27]

By spring of 1772, Tryon realized that his attempts to resolve the Hampshire Grants controversy were only getting him into more and more trouble. Not only was open rioting going on there against New York's authority, but also Governor Tryon seemed to be in danger of losing support and confidence in London. In 1771 he had granted a friend,

Colonel Thomas Howard, 10,000 acres of supposedly unimproved land on the Connecticut River, only to learn that the land had been settled years before by New Hampshiremen who refused to relinquish their property. Tryon tried to explain the case to Hillsborough on February 1, 1772, but he fully expected that this grant would be repudiated later in the year by the Board of Trade (which it was). Even worse, Tryon received from Hillsborough in May a sharply worded letter, written the previous month, ordering him to pay "strict obedience to the Instructions that have been already given to you" regarding Hampshire land grants, "and that you do not consider yourself as at liberty from any circumstances whatever to deviate from the letter of those Instructions." Tryon immediately complied with the order by terminating all land grants in Vermont, whether new ones or confirmations of previous New Hampshire cessions, but in September he pointedly informed Hillsborough that unless he were left some latitude to use his own judgment upon the scene, "I am apprehensive, the wisest and most equitable decisions of the Crown, may not extend to all the intricacies of these disputes."[28]

Finding that his hands were tied by Hillsborough but believing that if he did nothing the disorders in Vermont would only get worse, Tryon decided in May 1772 to attempt a conciliation of the New Hampshire settlers. On May 9 he wrote to the Reverend Jedediah Dewey and the inhabitants of Bennington, warning them that their continued violation of the law "must soon draw forth . . . the exertion of the Powers of Government." But as he wished "to avoid compulsive measures" if at all possible, he requested that the citizens of Bennington justify their conduct. For his part, he would give safe conduct to anyone except Robert Cochran, Ethan Allen, Remember Baker, and Seth Warner, all of whom Tryon had earlier proclaimed outside the law, to come forward and explain themselves. He promised that he and the New York Council would "examine into the grounds of your behaviour and discontent with deliberation and Candour, and as far as in us lies to give such relief as the nature of your situation and circumstances will justify."[29]

Tryon was pleased when the Vermont settlers dispatched Captain Stephen Fay and his son to a parley, but he was not so happy when they delivered to him a disquisition, composed by Ethan Allen, upon their "undoubted rights and privileges [as Englishmen]." Swallowing his anger, Tryon agreed in July 1772 to suspend all actions concerning the disputed land grants until the king acted, while also pardoning all proscribed Green Mountain leaders. The Benningtonians, elated at this truce, had only a short time to celebrate before it collapsed, for even while negotiations were going on in New York a body of Vermonters dispossessed several New York settlers at Otter Creek and brought Tryon's wrath down upon their heads. Accusing the citizens of Bennington of being "disingenuous and dishonourable," he declared in August that their actions were "daring insults to government" and "a violation of public faith." He demanded that they immediately restore the settlers' land at Otter Creek. The people of Bennington responded by defending their conduct, and compromise became impossible. Tryon informed Hillsborough of these proceedings and pleaded once more for discretion to offer the New Hampshire settlers confirmation of their titles in New York upon payment of half fees. Were he not allowed this flexibility, he declared, "I am under the firmest persuasion, no effectual measures at present, less than Military Force, can prevent the Eastern Colonies pouring in their Inhabitants between the River and the Lake." He repeated these same sentiments to Dartmouth in late October, when Dartmouth replaced Hillsborough as secretary of state for the colonies.[30]

For the next few months, Tryon waited impatiently for Dartmouth and the Board of Trade to resolve the Hampshire Grants issue. In December he told Dartmouth that speedy action on the matter was essential, not only for public peace and ease of government administration, but also for his own private happiness. Over the next five months, he complained about being so constrained by his instructions that he could not "long keep his ground, or preserve his government in peace." "His Majesty's instructions and His Majesty's interests," he grumbled, "are not all times one and the same thing, and he who in America follows implicitly the letter of the instructions will not best serve the King, and although I am not ignorant that by an implied disobedience to them, I stake the forfeiture of my Government, yet I would rather make that sacrifice than forego any proper opportunity to promote the public concerns of my Royal Master." His temper was not soothed when a short time later he received a circular letter from the Privy Council ordering him entirely to cease granting land in all of New York, not just Vermont, while the Board of Trade reviewed procedures for land grants in the royal colonies. Dartmouth, meanwhile, assured Tryon that the Board of Trade would soon be forthcoming with a ruling on the Hampshire Grants, and in effect he told Tryon to keep quiet until this decision was made, for these lands were the king's to dispose, Dartmouth had made his decision, and that was an end to the matter. Nevertheless Dartmouth assured Tryon that London was "confident of [his] integrity and impressed" by his intentions. All in London were convinced that the royal governor of New York, pigheaded though he may be, had the best interests of the king at heart.[31]

At last, in the spring of 1773, Tryon received the Board of Trade's rulings on the disputed Vermont lands. Although he was pleased with the fact that New Hampshire's claim to the territory was once more denied, he was appalled by the ruling that the only claims to lands in the Hampshire Grants that should be confirmed were those upon which actual settlement and improvement had taken place. Under this ruling, as Tryon told Dartmouth in July, "many hundred thousand acres" of unimproved land would have to be forfeited by New Yorkers, a large number of whom had purchased from the original recipients of grants. Because this "solution" required a favorable vote from the New York Assembly, Tryon assured Dartmouth that the Board's ruling would never be put into effect. The only possible solution he could suggest was that all New Hampshire patents in Vermont be nullified while allowing "all occupants under New Hampshire Grants not covered by New York Patents" to "have confirmations of their Possessions" and "all occupants under New Hampshire Titles, within New York Patent, have such liberal equivalents out of their waste lands . . . as his Majesty shall think equitable." In early 1774 he received additional royal instructions from Dartmouth on how to grant lands in his province, but none of them incorporated his latest suggestions.[32]

Tryon's hopes that the king and his advisers would solve the Vermont land crisis were now blasted, and he concluded in September 1773, because of continuing tumults by Ethan Allen's "Green Mountain Boys," that he must call upon regular British soldiers in New York to restore order. Hence he asked Major General Frederick Haldimand, acting commander in chief of British forces while Gage was taking an extended leave, for military assistance. At the same time he informed Dartmouth of his actions. But Haldimand was reluctant "to employ Regular troops, where . . . the Civil Magistrate can at any time call upon its trained Inhabitants to aid and assist them." Moreover, Tryon was admitting that he could not deal with "a few lawless Vagabonds" without the aid of regulars, a concession that would most certainly weaken the government's authority in the eyes of the citizenry. However, if Tryon insisted upon using regulars, Haldimand needed to know how many soldiers would be required.[33] On September 9 Tryon, with the full support of his Council, notified Haldimand that no matter what the risks, the New York authorities still believed the regulars were needed. Therefore the British commander in chief should concentrate his forces at Forts Crown Point and Ticonderoga in preparation for incursions into Vermont. In the end, Haldimand did not commit the army, for he reluctantly dragged his feet over the next month, killing time until winter was too near to attempt any military operations in the Hampshire Grants. Tryon was forced to "postpone" his request, and shortly thereafter, he received word from Dartmouth that the king was averse to having army regulars support "the Civil power in the Colonies, unless in cases of absolute and unavoidable necessity." Thus the scheme was completely dead.[34]

It seems odd that Tryon, an army officer who had not hesitated to use militia forces against the Regulators in North Carolina, did not do the same against the Vermonters. The probable reason for his hesitancy to call upon the militia of New York was that it was composed mostly of working-class men who had no interest in risking their lives to protect wealthy New Yorkers' land grants and thus might refuse to serve.[35] Another reason was that by this time he had been given leave by Dartmouth to go home because of his health, and he was afraid to run the risks of leading a militia army under such hazardous circumstances, perhaps even into defeat, when soon he would be able to confront the king and royal officials in London and hopefully settle the matter there. Yet, needing to do something to deal with the roisterous Vermonters, Tryon, with the support of the New York Assembly and Council, on March 9, 1774, issued a proclamation against "the Bennington Mob" for its "many atrocious Acts of Cruelty and oppressions." He offered a reward of £100 New York currency for the arrest of Ethan Allen and Remember Baker and £50 for six lesser offenders. That same day, he signed a new law, just enacted by the Assembly, calling for the death penalty for anyone who destroyed property or assumed judicial power without authority in the Hampshire Grants. Neither of these gestures proved successful, for the Vermonters defied them with impunity, so for Tryon the Hampshire Grants crisis remained unsolved.[36] Tryon continued to learn painful lessons about the limitations of his power as a royal governor, limitations imposed by both uncooperative Americans and the king's reluctance to free him from administrative shackles.

CHAPTER SEVEN

Land, Politics, and Tea

G overnor Tryon did not allow his frustrations with the Hampshire Grants to throw a pall over the rest of his administration, for he continued to remain active in a number of ways. In fact, he did not by any means confine his interest in frontier land grants to Vermont alone. He was just as interested in the lands of the Hudson and Mohawk valleys. For old friends such as Henry Clinton, who wrote him in early 1772 about acquiring a "landed interest" in New York, for rich New Yorkers, and for various other "foreign noblemen," Tryon was interested in securing thousands of acres of prime real estate on the frontiers of his new government. Therefore he decided early in his term of office to take a trip up the Hudson River to look over these acres, and, as he had done in North Carolina, to get to know the land and peoples of the province of New York. In early July Tryon informed Hillsborough that he and Mrs. Tryon intended in the following week to set off on their adventure, his final aim being to meet a delegation of Mohawk and Oneida Indians at the home of Indian agent Sir William Johnson for the negotiation of a "considerable Indian purchase."[1]

Upon their arrival in Albany after an easy passage up the Hudson River, Tryon and his wife were greeted by the mayor, corporation, and "principal gentlemen of the city." He was also welcomed by the British army officers and garrison stationed there, at the order of General Haldimand, who, although no admirer of Tryon, acted with punctilious courtesy toward the Crown's chief civil magistrate in the province. Over the next few days Governor and Mrs. Tryon resided at the elegant home of Philip Schuyler, whom Tryon had come to know and like since his arrival in New York, while making the round of "elegant entertainments" laid on for them by the citizens of Albany. Then Tryon, leaving his wife as a guest of the Schuylers, and accompanied by his secretary, Edmund Fanning, and

Oliver DeLancey, proceeded on to Baron Johnson's domain in the Mohawk Valley, reviewing along the way three militia regiments and remarking upon the industriousness of the settlers and the fertility of the land. "I heartily wish," he mused ruefully, "the Eastern parts of the Province were as peaceably settled."²

On July 28 Tryon's conference with the Mohawks and Oneidas took place at Johnson Hall, the main result being that the governor secured for his rich clients about a million acres of land and for himself about 40,000 acres. "Vast Indian purchases have been made," Schuyler reported to William Duer; "Governor Tryon's fees, alone, will exceed £22,000; a good summer's work that." Indeed it was, and Tryon returned to Albany from the Mohawk Valley pleased at the outcome of his interview with the Indians, for he had not only enriched himself and his clients but also had made firm friends with the natives by promising to have the Assembly redress some of their complaints about unscrupulous white land grabbers. The Mohawks, he told Hillsborough, were firmly attached "to His Majesty's Interest," due largely to the genius and hard work of Sir William Johnson. After a short stay with Robert Livingston at Livingston Manor near Albany, Tryon and his wife returned to New York City in late August "after an absence of five weeks."³

When Dartmouth, the new secretary of state, received Tryon's news about Indian land purchases, he exploded in indignation that the Crown's chief executive in New York was again defying the king's instructions. In November Dartmouth wrote Tryon, beginning mildly enough with a word of approval about Tryon's fact-finding trip up the Hudson and Mohawk rivers. But then he blistered Tryon for continuing to allow private persons to purchase land from the Indians, despite the fact that such practices had "been repeatedly and justly complained of." Tryon was perfectly aware of the Board of Trade's rule, in effect since December 1761, forbidding governors to grant lands in New York "which may interfere with the Indians bordering thereon," and Dartmouth in no uncertain terms was refreshing his memory about the king's ruling. "I hope," Dartmouth concluded grimly, "no steps will have been taken to confirm to such purchasers the possession of those lands, until by a transmission of the deeds, the nature and extent of the purchases can be known, and the King's pleasure signified thereupon." Responding to Dartmouth's strictures in January 1773, Tryon profusely apologized for having inadvertently overstepped his authority in the matter of Indian purchases, but he went on to explain that he had not believed himself outside the bounds of his royal instructions. He then hastened to inform Dartmouth that "a number of his Majesty's subjects have already expended, as is estimated, near £5,000 curr. including purchases and surveys," to improve this land, which as Tryon slyly noted, "will be open to cultivation, and subject to the payment of a quit Rent to his Majesty." Hence, he hoped that the king would not make any demands about repudiating the deal, but if he did, "it will not be more my duty, than it is my sincere inclination, to yield the most implicit obedience to His Majesty's commands."[4]

Dartmouth answered Tryon's letter in March, declaring that he saw "no grounds to depart from the opinion" he had already formed on the matter. He agreed with Tryon that an argument could be made for bringing Indian lands under cultivation, but he specifically noted that the Crown's primary complaint about Tryon's deal was that (as in the case of the Vermont lands) he was allowing persons to work a deal to purchase more than a thousand acres at a time. Therefore, "I lament that I am not able to agree with you in thinking, that you were acting in conformity to [your] instructions," for Tryon's orders specifically forbade such grants. Glumly Tryon replied to Dartmouth that he had been following ancient local custom in allowing a multiparty land deal, and he pleaded with the secretary "to intercede with His Majesty that I may be left at liberty" to uphold the present transaction, for now "the authority and honour of this government"—i.e., of Tryon himself—was at stake. "Was I conscious of having erred, or offended," he said, "it would be my duty to be silent, and I should not presume to ask this Favor; but as my intentions were upright, and I was acting in the ordinary Course of the Landed Department, I confess it would give me very great uneasiness and concern to be reduced to the Necessity of dismissing those Petitioners & Purchasers without redress or compensation, and I conceive I cannot in honor dismiss them."[5]

Tryon took this opportunity to reiterate to Dartmouth views that he had already stated a year before to Hillsborough on the intimate relationship between governmental and social policy and land distribution. "I am sensible," he said, "that it frequently, and I believe, generally happens, that the purchasers [of land] eventually obtain a greater share" than their supposed limit of 1,000 acres. "But if this is an evil, it is hardly to be prevented. Men of property in a Country where the soil is of little value, must have it in their power to purchase large Tracts." For Tryon's part, this was a practice that should be encouraged rather than checked, for "the Subordination which arises from a Distinction in Rank and fortune, I have found from experience, to be friendly to Government and conducive to the strengthening the hands of the Crown, and perhaps it will prove the only counterpoise against a levelling and Republican spirit, which the popular constitutions of some Colonies, and the Temper of their Inhabitants . . . so naturally excite."[6]

Dartmouth continued to disagree with Tryon's overly liberal interpretation of his instructions and could only promise Tryon that he would attempt to have the Crown reimburse the land purchasers for any expenses they may have already incurred. In the meantime he wrote, "Sir, if I have expressed any thing in my letters to you upon that subject, which conveyed the most distant censure of the motives on which you acted, it was more than I either felt or intended to express, being fully satisfied, that your conduct did not proceed from any unworthy motives." Whatever the case, Tryon could explain himself to the secretary in person, as by this time Tryon had been ordered home for health reasons. In late 1773, in the expectation that the king would not allow him to return to New York after his leave of absence, Tryon mused, "The confirmations of these lands . . . will be the business of my successor in office."[7]

While Tryon dealt with land grants, both within New York and Vermont, he also grappled with clarifying where New York's boundary with neighboring provinces lay. To the north, he discovered, Canadian lieutenant governor H. T. Cramahé was asserting the right of French settlers to move into lands around Lake Champlain and was granting lands there accordingly. Tryon insisted to Hillsborough that New York's boundary with Canada was the St. Lawrence River, a claim that Hillsborough denied. In late 1771 Tryon and Cramahé agreed to survey a boundary line at 45 degrees latitude, from the St. Lawrence River on the east to the Connecticut River on the west. The work on that line proceeded slowly into mid-1773. At that point Tryon visited Quebec in an effort "to convert measures" for completing the partition line, and he reported hopefully to London that the survey would soon be finished. Nevertheless, the matter was not settled during the remainder of Tryon's tenure as governor.[8]

Regarding New York's boundary with Massachusetts, Tryon discovered in 1771 that the two provinces had been quarreling for two decades over where the line should be drawn. By 1767 all issues had been resolved except two: a dispute over a sixty-square-mile tract of land and whether Massachusetts would repudiate claims to lands as far west as the "South Sea" (Pacific Ocean), because such a claim might restrict New York's western boundary. In early 1772 Tryon, in order to break the deadlock, proposed to Thomas Hutchinson, governor of Massachusetts, that new commissioners, plus the two governors themselves, meet and resolve all difficulties. The Massachusetts General Court immediately accepted this idea, and the New York Assembly also finally agreed in March 1773. Thus the governors and commissioners of both colonies commenced deliberations at Hartford, Connecticut, on May 12.⁹ All parties at the boundary conference, but especially Tryon, manifested a sincere desire to settle the New York–Massachusetts boundary dispute, and therefore, a flexibility that had not always been present in earlier negotiations soon emerged. The New York commissioners quickly accepted Hutchinson's insistence upon retaining for his province the disputed territory and at the same time did not demand that he concede Massachusetts's claims to lands west of New York. Therefore on May 18 agreement was reached, and all the commissioners, plus Tryon and Hutchinson, signed it and sent it off to the Privy Council in London. There the agreement was confirmed on February 4, 1774. Although Tryon suggested to Hutchinson that a joint New York–Massachusetts survey team commence running the line in October, nothing was done about this proposal, and it was not until 1787 that the line was actually completed.¹⁰

Tryon's visit to Hartford afforded him an opportunity to see some of New England and get to know the people there. His journey, he reported to Dartmouth upon his return to New York, "was made very agreeable by the hospitable attention received from the Gentlemen of the Country and particularly from Govr. [Jonathan] Trumbull." He was likewise impressed with Governor Hutchinson, whom he found to be of "genuine worth, probity and decency." While on this trip, Tryon took advantage of an opportunity to purchase in Norwalk a "Collection of American [natural history] Curiosities," which collection John Adams later regretted had fallen into the hands of an Englishman.¹¹

Tryon's final boundary problem involved establishing, once and for all, just where the boundary between New York and northern New Jersey should run. At the time Tryon became governor, the two provinces had disputed this question for more than a century but by late 1770 had agreed upon a line that had just been surveyed. Over the next two years, the legislatures of the two provinces passed almost identical laws accepting the line, and Tryon visited Governor William Franklin of New Jersey in September 1773 to confirm these proceedings.¹² At that point, however, Tryon ran into a problem that almost wrecked the agreement. The Board of Trade, in examining issues relating to the boundary settlement, had asked that the minutes of the boundary commission be forwarded to London. But when Tryon requested that John Jay, clerk of the commission, deliver up these records, Jay declined to do so unless ordered by the Privy Council, which earlier had refused to compensate Jay and the other commissioners for their expenses. Tryon therefore quickly drew up a bill directing Jay to deliver up the documents, and when the New York Assembly met in January 1773, the measure was speedily enacted. In the face of this pressure from the leading men of his province, Jay relented and delivered the disputed papers to the governor, who immediately forwarded them to London with an explanation for the delay. Dartmouth, bemused by Jay's intransigence but not angry, sent the proceedings on to the Privy Council, which on September 1, 1773, accepted the New York–New Jersey boundary line as final.[13]

As Tryon smoothly handled the many problems relating to the governance of his province, he impressed many citizens and developed a reputation for probity, sobriety, and concern about advancing the interests of the New York ruling class (both Livingstons and DeLanceys) that eased the political operations of his administration. Considering that Tryon was governing in a period of heightened tensions between the mother country and America, and that the two political factions continued to snipe and carp at each other—sometimes still attempting to co-opt Tryon into one or the other camp—he had remarkable success year after year in pushing his legislative program through the Assembly. As Tryon told Hillsborough at the completion of the legislative session in the spring of 1773, "The Business had been carried on without any Occurrence sufficiently remarkable to merit Your Lordship's particular Attention," for it had been "with the greatest Tranquility and good Order."[14]

Despite his best efforts, however, Tryon did not manage to stay completely clear of the Livingston-DeLancey political bickering in the Assembly. During the session of 1772, he was embarrassed by the DeLanceys' exclusion of Judge Robert R. Livingston from his seat. When Livingston appealed to Tryon and Hillsborough for royal intervention in the matter, Tryon became convinced that Livingston was being unjustly denied his seat, and he argued privately to the speaker of the house that the judge should not be excluded. In fact, he dropped some broad hints that the king, upon hearing of this case, might look with serious disfavor upon the legislature. But when he could not move the speaker to intervene on his behalf, he saw, as he told Hillsborough later, that he "had no foundation" upon which to proceed further, for his only real weapon against the

DeLanceys was to dissolve the Assembly, an action that was much too drastic under the circumstances. "It is my ambition," he told Hillsborough, "to keep as clear as possible of the parties . . . subsisting in this province," for both the Livingston and the DeLancey factions were "affectionate & loyal subjects to His Majesty," and he did not want to antagonize either one.[15]

Tryon was sucked into another Livingston-DeLancey political dispute during the Assembly session of 1773, when the DeLanceys proposed a currency scheme with the design of either bullying Tryon into submission to their claque or destroying his administration so that a more complaisant gentleman, such as Lord Dunmore had been, might be appointed to the governorship of New York. According to William Smith, a Livingston partisan, "The DeLanceys," who were "certainly uneasy" under Tryon, prepared a bill "for a new Emission of Paper Money on pretence that the last [emission] of £120,000 was counterfeit." This popular measure, one likely to pass into law, was one which Tryon would be compelled by the Currency Act either to veto or accept and be exposed to a penalty of £1,000 sterling and disqualification for any office under the Crown. Tryon was rescued from the DeLanceys' plot by three men, William Smith, George Clinton, and Philip Schuyler, who proposed to the Assembly that the government, rather than emitting new currency, stamp "a Device upon the old Bills" to identify them as genuine. Early on the morning of February 5, before this bill was submitted to the legislators, "Clinton & Schuyler knocked Mr. Tryon up . . . & divulged the Scheme . . . but having been burnt before he would not promise to pass it." Nevertheless he saw no objection to the bill, and it certainly would save him from the embarrassment which the DeLanceys were cooking up for him. Therefore Smith and his friends put the question to the Assembly and it was adopted by a large majority, "to the Disgrace of the DeLancey Interest, who afterwards beg'd hard to sink the Minutes of this Days Transactions."[16]

Tryon's difficulties with the Livingston-DeLancey political bickering were not confined to Assembly politics. They spilled over into the judiciary as well. In late 1772 Tryon, at the prompting of Judge Robert R. Livingston and William Smith, agreed to propose to the Council a scheme thought up by the judge's son, Robert R. Livingston, and John Jay, to create the post of "presiding judge of the Common Pleas and Sessions." To fill the two positions created under this plan, the young Livingston and Jay immodestly suggested themselves as the most eligible candidates. When Tryon presented the plan to the Council, James DeLancey vehemently opposed it and finally persuaded a majority of councillors, only Smith and John Watts demurring, to vote against it. Thereupon Tryon dropped the entire idea, leading Smith to grumble, "Jay's friends as well as Livingston's are disgusted & consider Mr. Tryon as terrified or led by the DeLanceys." Tryon, wishing to redress the "factional scales" after this embarrassment to the Livingstons, only awaited an opportunity to "cross the DeLanceys," as Smith rather inelegantly put it. His chance came in the latter half of 1773, when Tryon offered to the young Livingston the recordership of New York City, even though he had earlier promised the position to Stephen DeLancey. Although Livingston was not eager to accept the post, his father and Tryon persuaded him, and on September 30 Tryon sent the patent "in secret," lest he arouse protest from the ever vigilant DeLanceys.[17]

Having placated the Livingstons, however, Tryon immediately proceeded to irk them by advocating that Thomas Jones, Jr., who was being replaced in the recorder's position by Livingston, be appointed to the Supreme Court in place of his father, Judge Thomas Jones, who was retiring. Livingstonians such as Smith disliked the young Jones because he was "ill natured & very unpopular," and Smith was sure that this appointment would confirm for "the Livingston Party or one half of the Province" that Tryon had become entirely a creature of the DeLanceys. Was not the governor "daily at Oliver's" for a visit? Had he not recently "made Stephen [DeLancey] Naval Officer in the Place of Charles Williams & . . . lately brought John Harris Cruger Oliver's Son in Law in the Place of his father Henry who resigned"? But Tryon was not to be deterred, and when he was questioned by Smith at a Council meeting about Jones's appointment, he "replied with some Emotion (with a Trembling Utterance as usual when Moved)" that he would have this man no matter what the Council decided. Hence Smith reluctantly relented in his opposition, and the Council voted for Jones to become a Supreme Court judge. Smith concluded gloomily, "Mr. Tryon's Adm. wears a new Face & he is upon the Point of clipping the Wings of his Power and tarnishing his Reputation."[18]

Had Smith been anything but a blind partisan of the Livingstons, he could have seen that Tryon was attempting only to "keep as clear as possible of the parties" while steering his own course. If confirmation of this fact was needed, Smith had only to reflect upon another judicial appointment of Tryon's that was being made almost at the same time he supposedly was giving all to the DeLanceys on a silver platter. In the summer of 1773, Tryon, confronted by the necessity to appoint three judges in newly organized Charlotte County, proposed to the Council the names of Philip Schuyler as first judge, and Philip Skene and William Duer. When Oliver DeLancey on the Council insisted that Skene must head the list, Tryon refused to humiliate Schuyler, and the list was passed as it stood—much to Smith's delight.[19] In addition, Tryon had close social contacts with the Livingstons, which Smith might have considered when he worried about Tryon's frequent visits with the DeLanceys. Tryon and his wife were constantly visiting the Livingstons, who delighted in their company. The governor, said Janet Livingston Montgomery, "was literally our affectionate father," and Mrs. Tryon, although a little eccentric, was a charming and delightful woman. Because Mrs. Tryon hated the official social duties attendant upon her position as the governor's lady, but which were "essential to the town," she made vivacious Janet Montgomery her substitute hostess on as many occasions as possible.[20]

Beginning in 1773, Tryon's problems with Livingston-DeLancey factional bickering were totally overshadowed by the deep political difficulties into which he was plunged by Parliament's Tea Act. In mid-October of that year, Smith wrote ominously, "A New Flame [of opposition to parliamentary taxation] is apparently kindling in America," for word had just arrived in New York that the East India Company had been empowered by law to reexport tea from England to America without paying customs duties there and that the company had chosen agents to sell its tea in each province. The problem for Americans was that the Townshend duty levied upon tea in American ports remained intact, and this new measure, by making the East India Company's tea inexpensive on the market, might entice Americans to purchase taxed tea and therefore dilute their long-standing opposition to Parliament's attempts to tax the colonists. As for New York, said Smith, 600 chests of tea were on the way to the city, and a "general Opposition" was being raised by Livingstons, DeLanceys, "Sons of Liberty" such as Isaac Sears, Alexander McDougall, and John Lamb, and "Dutch Smugglers" against the sale of taxed tea. Tea factors in New York were being held up "as another Species of Stamp Masters," and "I suppose we shall repeat All the Confusions of 1765 & 1766." Tryon reported these same problems to Dartmouth on November 3, but he assured London that "the peace of the Government will be preserved."[21]

Despite his brave words, Tryon's problem was that he must enforce the law and maintain the authority of the Crown by landing the tea, despite overwhelming opposition to this course of action by all classes of New

Yorkers, but especially by the Sons of Liberty. How he was to achieve this goal was a difficult matter, for he had practically no coercive power to enforce the law. He was perfectly aware that during the Stamp Act crisis of 1765, one of his predecessors in office, acting governor Colden, and General Thomas Gage, commander of British troops in America, had been unable effectively to use military power, even though it was available, to enforce an unpopular law. If anything, Tryon's own military position was weaker than Colden and Gage's had been, for although British regulars were still in the colony, acting commander in chief Frederick Haldimand had only recently dragged his feet about assisting Tryon with enforcement of land laws in Vermont, and the British government had upheld Haldimand's reluctance. While Tryon might believe that he was confronted with the very case of "absolute and unavoidable necessity" that Dartmouth in October had said was justification for use of redcoats, the governor believed as well that Dartmouth and (more to the point) Haldimand would be averse to his seeking support from the British army in his present crisis. Therefore he had no choice but to attempt enforcement of the Tea Act by subtler means.

While Tryon dealt with this tricky problem, the tea agents were being "persuaded" in early December by the Sons of Liberty to resign their positions. Thereupon the agents petitioned Tryon to take the tea under his protection, and he ordered Captain James Ayscough, commander of the sloop *Swan*, off Sandy Hook, to guard the tea ship upon its arrival, "until the Tea can be landed." That Tryon intended to bring the tea ashore, even if he had to threaten use of force (hollow though the threat might be), he made clear to his Council in late November. But when Tryon and the councillors hammered out a plan to land the tea, they decided to eschew bluster and to do so openly and without coercion. Once the tea was ashore, it would be stored in a safe place, either Fort George or the barracks, and the governor would make no attempt to sell the tea until the crisis was resolved to the satisfaction of all the townspeople. Tryon declared to the Council that "he would throw himself at that time into the Court of the Citizens," running "the risk of Brick Batts & Dirt," and he hoped that the councillors would stand by him. This moderate proposal seemed the wisest course of action (except to Smith, who was not impressed by it), for although the radicals abhorred the idea that the tea might be landed under any circumstances, most New Yorkers were not averse to this middle-of-the-road solution to their own and the governor's dilemma.[22]

Despite Tryon's wise attempts to defuse the tea crisis by appealing to New York's political moderates, events soon began to drift out of his control. The Sons of Liberty refused to accept Tryon's plan, only agreeing to guarantee the tea's safety if it remained on board ship in the harbor. McDougall even went so far as to propose to the radicals that they "prevent the Landing, and kill [the] Govr and all the Council." None of McDougall's compatriots were willing to go that far, but they did call for a rally at City Hall on December 17 as a show of mass support for their refusal to land the tea. Tryon himself inadvertently contributed to the success of this meeting. Fearing that it might become dangerous to public safety and order, he called his Council into emergency session for advice on what to do. After much discussion Tryon and the Council decided to dispatch the mayor and another official to the crowd with further assurances that Tryon would neither use force to land the tea nor sell any of the product before the present crisis had been resolved. The governor pleaded with the citizens through his emissaries to act moderately so as not to "disgrace their govr" or themselves "by any imprudent violent & intemperate behavior." The appeal miscarried when Mayor Whitehead Hicks in a speech to the crowd confined himself to a terse pledge that Tryon would not attempt to sell any tea and omitted to convey any of the governor's passionate appeal for moderation. At that point, John Lamb seized an opportunity to make his own pleas that Tryon be refused the populace's approval, and the crowd roared its assent. Lamb also proposed and had accepted a resolution that highly commended the "spirited and patriotic conduct" of persons in Boston and Philadelphia who were opposing the Tea Act.[23]

Tryon's attempt to woo moderate opinion in New York collapsed entirely on December 22, when word reached the city that Bostonians had thrown their tea into the harbor. At that point the governor conceded in conversations with a number of prominent citizens that he could not land the tea and was willing to give up trying. Nevertheless he must make it appear to the ministry in London that he had not reversed himself on this important matter. So he concocted a plan whereby the tea ship would be met by the recently retired tea agents at Sandy Hook and told to return to England after being provisioned at Tryon's expense. But the governor's face-saving charade fell through when Captain Ayscough, commander of the *Swan*, leaked word of this scheme to friends and it was printed in James Rivington's newspaper. Tryon, "in great Wrath," called Ayscough a "Blab Tongue" and suffered the embarrassment of public exposure for his retreat. Nevertheless he put his plan into execution, and everyone heaved a sigh of relief at having escaped a confrontation. In early 1774 Tryon admitted to Dartmouth that the tea could be brought ashore "only under the protection of the Point of the Bayonet, and Muzle of Canon, and even then I do not see how the consumption could be effected."[24] Because the tea ship *Nancy*, commanded by Captain Benjamin Lockyer, arrived only after Tryon had departed New York in April 1774, he did not have to find out; he left the unresolved tea crisis to his lieutenant governor, the aged Cadwallader Colden. One thing, however, was crystal clear to him: he could not compel Americans, even with the wisest of efforts, to accept his country's tax policies, and if Britain intended to force their reluctant acquiescence, massive military might must be employed. Quailing at this uncertain prospect, Tryon concluded some time during 1774 that the price was too high for both sides and that London ought to give up any notion of taxing Americans for revenue.

For Tryon, the momentary abating of political passions over the Tea Act did not mean that all his problems suddenly disappeared. Quite the contrary, for even in the midst of the tea crisis he and his family suffered a tremendous loss of personal property when the Governor's Mansion in Fort George was consumed by fire on the night of December 29, 1773. "So rapid was it's progress," Tryon reported to Dartmouth two days later, "that in a few moments after we were alarmed a thick cloud of fire and smoke pervaded the whole building." With utmost difficulty, his family and all the servants but one, "an unhappy Maid," managed to make their escape. But his daughter was "reduced to the sad extremity of leaping out of a Window of the Second Story," landing unhurt only because she fell into a snowbank. Practically everything that the Tryons owned in America was destroyed in this conflagration. All their furniture, clothes, personal possessions, and papers, as well as the memorabilia of a lifetime, were burned. Mrs. Tryon lost family jewels worth £2,000 sterling, and Tryon himself came out into the snow without shoes. Interestingly enough, Tryon's greatest feeling of loss on the night of the fire was for the great seal of the province, and he was delighted the next day when someone discovered it unharmed. Through all his trials, said Smith, "I never saw him more composed. . . . He was even attentive in the Midst of all the Confusion to Ceremony," and managed to quip, upon surveying the ruins of his home, "that he had rather this Sight, than the Burning of the Tea."[25]

After finding new quarters for his family and securing the immediate necessities of life, Tryon sat down to inventory his destroyed possessions in preparation for petitioning the king for a redress of his financial losses. This petition, which he sent Dartmouth, was twenty-three pages in length and reveals in a most amazing manner the magnificent and impressive array of furniture and other objects that the Tryons possessed. The total value of all these goods, Tryon told the secretary of state, was "upon a moderate Estimation . . . Six Thousand Pounds Sterling." When Dartmouth received this inventory, he passed it on to the king, who on February 5, 1774, ordered Dartmouth to expedite Tryon's petition for financial redress. But there the whole matter became mired in London's bureaucracy, and Tryon had to push it along after he arrived in England. The New York Assembly was more expeditious in its generosity to the governor, for during its session in early 1774 it appropriated £5,000 New York currency to help the governor recoup his losses.[26]

Even in the midst of the tea crisis, a matter of the gravest importance for Britain and America, and the fire that destroyed many of his worldly possessions, Tryon pursued the more mundane matter of completing a huge report for the king upon conditions in the province of New York. This document, the result of a decision by the ministry to have all the governors in America make wide and encompassing surveys of their respective colonies, covered twenty-one questions about diverse matters such as boundary, geographic features, form of constitution, manufactures, trade, size of militia forces, number and strength of Indians, amount and sources of revenue, and persons on the public payroll. Tryon enlisted the assistance of David Colden, James Duane, and other prominent citizens to amass and compose this report, which upon completion covered forty-five handwritten pages. In April 1774 he carried it with him to London for presentation to Dartmouth.[27]

In the spring of 1774, Tryon and his family began preparations for their long-anticipated return to England. By that time, the Tryons had been in America for ten years without a visit to the mother country. But the biggest factor in Tryon's decision to ask for an extended leave was his health. Although he was still a relatively young man at the age of forty-four, he had suffered ever since his "seasoning" in North Carolina from various recurrent agues. In 1772 he had been forced to take a health leave in Philadelphia, and a year later he complained to a correspondent that he had just recovered from "a most distressed state of health." Hence, he had asked for and had been granted a year's leave in England, but in October 1773, for various public and private reasons, he deferred his departure until the following spring. In February 1774 he suffered another debilitating bout of fever, but soon thereafter he had recovered sufficiently to travel across the Atlantic.[28]

As the time of his departure neared, Tryon was inundated with expressions of good wishes from New Yorkers, and he left the province (permanently, he believed) with his popularity at a very high level. The Assembly was first to offer him congratulations, voting in March an address glowing with esteem and respect for the governor. Next came a message from the Anglicans praising him for his "upright and disinterested administration" and wishing him a "speedy return." Then General Haldimand expressed his and the army's respects by sponsoring a great ball in Tryon's honor. These festivities being concluded, Tryon held a private meeting with Smith, who was convinced, as was the governor, that Tryon would be replaced "the instant" he arrived in England and that he would never see his friend again. Tryon thanked Smith for "useful Aid" on many occasions, then bade the entire Council farewell.[29]

The day of the Tryons' departure, April 7, 1774, was filled with ceremony and pathos, according to Smith. "The Clergy & Gentlemen of the Town" assembled to take leave of the governor and his lady at the house of William Alexander, Lord Stirling. Mrs. Tryon "wept much," and an "immense Crowd came down afterwards [to Murray's Wharf] with the Gov., who was deeply affected at the Salutations from the Windows." The Tryons then boarded the packet *Mercury*, bound for Falmouth, and the governor "wiped his Eyes, keeping his Hat off" as his ship slowly cleared its anchorage. As Tryon sailed down the harbor, he received artillery and flag salutes from ships and shore batteries, and at Sandy Hook, he took final leave of "a Number of Gent." who had followed him down to the sea in a sloop. The only sour note in these proceedings, Smith declared venomously, was that the DeLanceys "distinguished themselves in their Coolness towards the Govr. & sank into Contempt."[30]

After an uneventful voyage of seven weeks, Tryon and his family arrived safely at Falmouth on the Cornish coast. As quickly as could be arranged, they set out on a long coach ride to London, and when they reached the metropolis they immediately ensconced themselves in their comfortable Mayfair home off Hyde Park. After Tryon had paid his respects to members of the government and to friends long unseen, he and Mrs. Tryon were swept up in the social life of London. In addition to giving and attending numerous dinner parties and paying and receiving social calls, Tryon, ever the military man, attended infantry reviews in Richmond Park. He also made the required call upon Barrington, the secretary at war, just to remind him that Colonel Tryon was still available for military preferment, should conditions ever arise which called for Tryon to return to army duty.[31]

Immediately upon his arrival in London, Tryon learned that he still retained the confidence of the king and his advisers and that he was, after all, to be returned to New York as governor. Therefore for the remainder of his leave, Tryon's mind was at ease about his future employment, and he could devote his energies to recuperating from his illness and laying groundwork for a (hopefully) successful administration when he returned to America. Soon he was deeply involved in business relating to his governorships in both North Carolina and New York, appealing to the Crown for "some favor" for Edmund Fanning, who had accompanied him to England, because Fanning had made great sacrifices for the king during the Regulator problems in North Carolina and had recently been denied a position as surrogate and register of the Prerogative Court in New York. Despite Tryon's petition on Fanning's behalf, King George III was not forthcoming, and Fanning in the autumn of 1774 returned to New York a disappointed man.[32]

Tryon was also writing petitions on his own behalf, trying to expedite his earlier appeal for redress of losses in the disastrous fire that had destroyed the New York governor's mansion and all Tryons' belongings in America. Told by Dartmouth that he should work up an account of his losses for the Treasury, Tryon did so, only to be informed by Frederick Lord North, prime minister and First Lord of the Treasury, that he had not followed the proper procedure in drawing up his request. Thereupon Tryon tried again in the spring of 1775, this time adding to his claims unpaid expenses going back to his tenure as governor of North Carolina, which amounted to £13,000 sterling. When North received Tryon's new accounts, he neither denied their validity nor acted upon them, although he privately conceded that Tryon was one of the better royal governors in the king's service in America. Hence, all Tryon could do was wait in frustration for many years, actually until 1782, before he received any compensation. All the while he prayed that the ponderous Treasury bureaucracy would grind forth a decision before he was dead and buried.[33]

In the meantime, Tryon became enmeshed in another embarrassing business with the North Carolina Assembly, which was asking him to support a petition to the Crown denying Governor Martin's claim that Martin must assent to laws establishing courts of justice in order for them to be legal. As the assemblymen reminded Tryon, he had never made such claims when he served as governor of North Carolina, and as he was still popular there, the citizens wished him to lend his weight to their petition to the Crown. Tryon was flattered, of course, by the Assembly's praise and might have been willing to go along with their request on that basis alone. He also happened to believe that the assemblymen's interpretation of the North Carolina governor's powers was correct and that he ought to support the petition. But he was a friend of Governor Martin and did not wish to offend him. To solve his dilemma, Tryon wrote Dartmouth a letter, ostensibly asking for "guidance" on what to do in "so delicate an affair," but in fact couching his "explanatory" remarks in such a way as to make clear exactly where he stood.[34] At that point, to his relief, Tryon's involvement in the North Carolina Assembly's petition ended.

Tryon's plans since he had learned that he would be allowed a recuperative leave in England had been to spend much of this time at Bath, where all upper-class Britons in poor health gravitated to "take the waters." In July he and Mrs. Tryon proceeded to Bath for a two-month stay and during the remainder of their leave spent two more long periods there, as Tryon tried to overcome the debilitation of the fevers he had contracted in North Carolina. Neither his first round of treatments in the summer of 1774 nor his second the following winter completely restored him, although, as he told a friend, his health and spirits were "much improved." He took a third round of treatments in April 1775, even though he was being encouraged by Dartmouth to return to New York to deal with problems there. In fact, his delay might have resulted in his being superseded as governor. As he told Colden, "I was pressed to go out immediately; but my recovering health would not admit it." Confronted with Tryon's problem and his adamancy, Dartmouth, who had a high regard for his subordinate's abilities, reluctantly acceded to his insistence on extending his recuperative leave.[35]

Off and on between his visits to Bath, Tryon's attention was occupied primarily by two large political concerns that vexed the British government and himself: the Hampshire Grants land problems and the growing crisis in America over Britain's enforcement of the Tea Act. Because the Board of Trade was continuing to grapple with the Vermont land tenure crisis, a great deal of the governor's time and energy was engrossed with this issue. Asked by the Board to offer his thoughts on how to settle the problem, Tryon merely reiterated his earlier suggestion that the New Hampshire land titles be confirmed by New York for half fees. By being "generous" to the New Hampshire claimants, said Tryon, the British

Crown could "unite their interest with that of New York government" and woo them away from dependence upon their neighbors to the east. The board also asked him to comment further upon the validity of his grants of Mohawk Indian lands, and he restated his belief that the grants should be confirmed by the Crown in order to reinforce conservative land tenure policies in New York.[36]

Thus Tryon discharged his responsibility in the matter of land titles in New York, but the English governmental bureaucracy, with its usual snail-paced deliberations, had not come to any conclusions in the spring of 1775, when Tryon was preparing to return to America. On April 12 Tryon prodded Dartmouth to give him new royal instructions on land policy and was finally rewarded with word from Dartmouth about the state of the Board of Trade's thinking at that point. Regarding the Hampshire Grants, Dartmouth told Tryon, the board was still considering that matter, and the governor was to consider himself bound by the instructions he had already received. As for Tryon's grants of Indian lands to rich and powerful New Yorkers and others, the king had agreed to confirm these grants, as Tryon repeatedly had requested, but only if the petitioners persuaded New Yorkers to repudiate the "Association," an agreement among the citizens in protest of imperial tax policy, which was designed, according to Dartmouth, to obstruct "the lawfull importation and exportation of goods."[37]

By the time Tryon received these instructions, they were a dead letter, swallowed up, as were so many other matters, in tensions between the mother country and colonists over taxes. Shortly after Tryon had departed New York in April 1774 (as he learned by letter from Colden), the New Yorkers, in emulation of their brothers in Boston and elsewhere, had dumped a consignment of tea into the harbor. Hence, for the third time since 1765, English authorities were faced with the Americans' flat refusal to be taxed for revenue. Parliament, after having twice temporized on taxation, was in no mood in 1774 for more conciliation, and it passed the Coercive Acts, known in the colonies as the "Intolerable Acts," to bring Bostonians—but also by implication all Americans—to heel. These acts made the upper house of the Massachusetts legislature royal, moved the capital to Salem, closed the port of Boston until its citizens paid for the destroyed tea, restricted town meetings, made it easier for judges to select jurors friendly to Britain, provided for the requisition of private houses for army troops, and made it possible for public officials to be tried outside Massachusetts should they be accused of murder in the line of duty. Additionally, General Thomas Gage, British army commander in America, was made governor of the colony.[38]

As Tryon learned from Colden and Smith, these measures were vigorously protested by the colonists in a Continental Congress that met in the fall of 1774. The Congress agreed upon an Association whereby citizens agreed not to import or export goods to Britain, a Declaration of Rights demanding that Britain recognize certain American liberties, and a petition to the king and "people of Great Britain" asking for redress. The king and Parliament responded to these measures with a decision, made near the end of 1774, to refuse all further American petitions and to coerce the colonies into accepting parliamentary taxation. In New York the DeLancey moderates gained control of politics in late 1774, and despite the fact that the more radical Sons of Liberty tried to enforce the Association there, it was mostly ignored. The DeLancey-controlled Assembly, far from supporting other more radical colonies, broke with the other colonies and appealed on its own to England. But the Assembly's petition was ignored when it reached Parliament, even though Dartmouth earlier had encouraged Tryon to write Colden asking for such a statement and Tryon had passed the hint on to the lieutenant governor. As Dartmouth explained the rejection to Tryon, the king and Parliament were satisfied with most of the petition but found that it contained claims about a lack of authority by the "parent state" to tax colonists, "which made it impossible" to accept.[39]

Meanwhile, Tryon watched from his vantage point in England as Parliament extended its coercive policies from Massachusetts to New York and other colonies, and at the same time, amazingly enough, passed in February 1775 a Conciliatory Resolution, proposed by Lord North, which lifted parliamentary taxation for revenue from any colony that would agree to provide "satisfactorily" toward imperial defense and the upkeep of imperial officers. These policies, of course, were totally unacceptable to New Yorkers, even to moderates, and they only weakened the DeLancey position while strengthening that of the radicals. But the worst blow by far to the New York moderates was the news in April 1775 that British soldiers in Massachusetts had actually shot at fellow Americans. With one stroke the basis of the imperial quarrel had changed from economics to warfare. It was becoming more and more difficult for New Yorkers to maintain loyalty to the Crown.

Tryon was distressed by the deterioration of royal control in New York and even more so by the policy of coercion-concession adopted by king and Parliament. He freely admitted that New York contained some "hot heads" who were capable of "Rash conduct," but he also believed that these hotheads were a tiny minority that could be contained, if the English government would only make concessions on taxation to keep the essentially Royalist populace from falling into the clutches of the radicals. In early 1775, while sojourning at Bath, he wrote a candid and perceptive letter to Dartmouth, outlining what he believed the ministry's colonial policy ought to be. He flatly asserted that Americans would never accept parliamentary taxation for revenue in any form whatsoever, nor would they consume any British articles even if forced to receive them because they felt threatened by taxes. It was wrong policy, he mused, for the ministry to adopt half measures, holding out to the colonists an olive branch in one hand and a rod of chastisement in the other. Either Great Britain must give way to Americans on matters of taxes for revenue or exert extreme force with the full might of the army and navy to compel absolute colonial obedience. Because the armed forces could not be expanded quickly to the size necessary for the latter task, and because the process in any case would be enormously expensive, conciliation was the better choice. These points Tryon also urged at court.[40] But with neither ministry nor Crown did Tryon's views make the slightest impact, for by that time practically everyone in London had concluded that military coercion of the colonies was the only course of action left open to Great Britain. They would have done well to listen to the good advice that Governor Tryon was giving them.

CHAPTER EIGHT

The Collapse of Royal Authority

B y May 1775 Tryon's health had been restored to the point that he felt able to resume the burdens of his governorship in New York, although he still was not an entirely well man. He spent the last days of April terminating business in London, and on May 4 he and his family bade farewell to friends and acquaintances in London and journeyed by coach to Portsmouth. Three days later they went on board the ship *Juliana* to await favorable tidal and wind conditions for sailing. On May 9 they cleared the harbor and watched the Isle of Wight pass to starboard, as they once again sailed toward America. While at sea, the *Juliana* fell in with a ship from Maryland, the master of which apprised Tryon of political conditions in America since the skirmishing at Lexington and Concord. Hence, as he and his family arrived off Sandy Hook at the mouth of Lower New York Bay on June 25, he was aware that a new Continental Congress had formed, had organized a military force around Boston to oppose the British army, and had appointed George Washington of Virginia as Continental commander in chief.[1]

Tryon was surprised to learn from the New York City welcoming delegation which met him at Sandy Hook that General Washington was expected to arrive in town that very day. New Yorkers, faced with the necessity of giving both men official welcome, resolved their dilemma simply by laying on separate, and equally impressive, festivities. Tryon played his part in this political burlesque by agreeing with Fanning, who had come out to see him on board the *Juliana*, to wait until Washington's welcoming ceremonies were terminated before landing. At eight o'clock in the evening, Tryon and his party finally came ashore, and according to Councillor Smith, the governor was met at the ferry stairs "by a great Concourse" of citizens, including Mayor Whitehead Hicks and Colonel

John Lasher's Independent Battalion of Militia in their spanking new uniforms. Then Tryon and his wife paraded up Broadway, where they were wildly cheered by the people, thus leading Tryon to conclude correctly that he still was popular with the citizens of New York. Nevertheless, according to Smith, when Tryon reached the home of Hugh Wallace, where he and his family were to spend the night, "He appeared grave . . . & said little."[2] It is no wonder that he was sober, for those same crowds that had just welcomed him with such warmth, and those same militiamen that had just saluted him so smartly, had only hours earlier been welcoming and saluting with equal fervor a rebel general who represented for him all the radicalism, disrespect for established authority, and rebellion that he abhorred.

Only one day after his return to New York, Tryon's countenance fell further when he learned that the opponents of taxation were in such overwhelming ascendancy in his government that, as he wrote General Gage, "I . . . find the Lieutenant Governor has little authority to transfer to me." Hardly comforting was the fact that politically most New Yorkers in mid-1775 occupied a sort of middle ground of loyalty to the empire but also of support for the extralegal Provincial Congress, called to defend New Yorkers' political liberties until London "came to its senses." As an indication of the citizens' moderate political temper in June 1775, the Provincial Congress adopted a "Plan of Accommodation between Great Britain and America," which it sent to New York's delegates in the Continental Congress, urging extreme caution in the quarrel with England lest the "contest for liberty, fostered in [its] infancy by the virtuous and wise, become sources of power to wicked and designing men." Tryon attempted to encourage this moderation among New York opponents of imperial taxation, but as a royal governor, representing the might and authority of the king, he could only view the very existence of the Provincial Congress, moderate or no, as proof of rebellion. He thought his prime task, therefore, was to return New Yorkers to dependence upon constitutional government, consisting of himself, the Council, and the Assembly. Yet, as he told Dartmouth on July 4, his power was too enfeebled to attempt any coercive measures, and he dared not call the Assembly into session for fear that it would instantly reject Parliament's Coercive Acts. Already, New Yorkers were cooperating with the Continental Congress and would do nothing to damage the power of "the General confederacy." Moreover, New York's illegal Provincial Congress was raising 5,000 militiamen, and Continental army troops were said to have been ordered to the city to repel four British regiments that were rumored to be on the way to the colony.[3]

Having assessed the New York political scene close up, Tryon was more convinced than ever that the wisest course of action for the king and ministry in the present crisis was to yield to America on the question of taxing the colonies for revenue. "Oceans of blood may be spilt," Tryon said forcefully to Dartmouth on July 4, "but in my opinion America will never receive Parliamentary taxation. I do not meet with any of the inhabitants who shew the smallest inclination to draw the Sword in support of that principle, a Principle, I apprehend, the extremity of Calamity which threatens America will not induce her to accept." The great tragedy of England's policy was that it weakened the authority of "firm friends of government" while strengthening that of the radicals in the antitax coalition, whose "deeper designs" for a republican revolution were being helped along by London's adamant stance. Two days later, Tryon reinforced these arguments by telling Dartmouth that parliamentary taxation was the "heavy clog" that kept the vast majority of loyal, moderate Americans from vigorously supporting government. Despite the good sense of Tryon's views on taxation, they were ignored once again by London officials determined to use military force against recalcitrant colonists.[4]

Within days of his arrival in New York, Tryon was convinced that "the insolence of an inflamed Mob," led by Isaac Sears, might force him either to flee the colony or take refuge aboard a British ship in the harbor. Therefore he begged leave from Dartmouth to take advantage of either escape, should he be compelled to depart New York City. Since his "delicate state of . . . health" made it unlikely that he could long survive on shipboard salt provisions, his abandoning terra firma would probably guarantee that he would have to come home within four or five months. At the same time, he reported that the Provincial Congress had barred the mayor of New York from visiting him. In September Dartmouth gave Tryon permission to seek refuge on board a British ship if he thought fit, or to return home if absolutely necessary. But Dartmouth urged Tryon to remain at his post if at all possible and continue attempts at restoration of royal authority, which the ministry deemed at that time "not irrecoverable."[5]

Tryon's fears of Sears and the other radicals in early July seemed well founded, for he had just learned that Sears had recently returned from Congress in Philadelphia, ostensibly with orders to put him under arrest.

He felt helpless in the face of this threat, for as he told General Gage, even though he had not lost all his friends in New York and "the People" were still polite to him as the Crown's representative, "They dare not draw near to me." His concerns were exaggerated, for General Washington himself, as he departed New York for Boston in late June, had ordered Philip Schuyler, American commander of New York, to leave Tryon alone unless the governor attempted some overt action manifestly inimical to the dissidents' cause. Schuyler was manfully adhering to this policy by insisting that Sears drop any designs to seize Tryon "as rash and unjustifiable, and what the congress would not countenance." When Sears tried to change Schuyler's mind by asserting that some congressmen in Philadelphia liked the idea of kidnapping Tryon, Schuyler retorted that he had Washington's written orders on that subject, and Sears reluctantly acquiesced. Smith, who was privy to these arguments between Schuyler and Sears but sworn by Schuyler not to divulge them to Tryon, declared that he "never was more imbarrassed by any Secret than by this, which shews a dangerous Spirit in the People."[6]

Tryon was compelled in mid-1775 by political realities to disrupt many friendships with New Yorkers that he had formed since his arrival four years before. He believed, however, that no political quarrel could break his ties with Judge Livingston on the Supreme Court, for, he asserted, that gentleman would never resign his position because of present difficulties. But the judge soon made known that Tryon was completely wrong, and so Tryon, with vehement words of opprobrium toward his former friend, suspended him from office at the same time that the judge quit on his own. Tryon also angrily spurned General Schuyler, when the general attempted to call upon him and officially welcome him back to New York. According to a contemporary Tory historian, Thomas Jones, Schuyler "had the impudence to dress himself in the regimentals of rebellion," go to the governor's house on Broadway, and "send in word that '*General*' Schuyler would be glad to see him. The governor, with his usual spirit, returned for answer, *that he knew no such man.* No further attempts were ever after made for an interview."[7]

Although Dartmouth—whom Tryon now referred to as an "indecisive Minister"—still believed in July that Tryon might find an opening in New York for restoring royal government, Tryon himself was growing less sanguine by the day. On July 13 a mob burned a boat belonging to the British warship *Asia*, commanded by Captain George Vandeput, and although the mayor and aldermen had a new boat built to replace it, the new boat was also destroyed. That one was replaced as well, but the king's stores were regularly being looted, and Americans seemed more determined every day to resist parliamentary taxation. On August 7 Tryon ventured once again to urge upon Dartmouth the necessity for repeal of the duties on tea, "in compassion to the unhappy prejudices of opinion and wild delusion of His Majesty's American subjects." At the same time, he proposed that 5,000 or 6,000 regulars be sent to New York, to be supported by four regiments of Loyalist militia, which Tryon was now convinced he could raise in the colony, to destroy "the influences of committees and Congresses" and bring "the People . . . to a sense of duty and Allegiance." If these measures were not implemented, Tryon warned, America would declare independence within six months, despite the fact that at present a large majority of them were "utter enemies to such a principle."[8]

As August wore on, Tryon's position became more and more impossible as well as more and more frustrating. American friends of government, he growled to Dartmouth on the seventh, found themselves "between Scylla and Charybdis, that is the dread of Parliamentary taxation and the tyranny of their present masters." Seven days later, he wrote to Gage, "My Situation is singularly critical, left without any Ground to stand upon while the executive powers of Government in this colony are forced into other Channels." Tryon had become completely disillusioned with London's colonial tax policy, especially the ministry's notion that Americans would yield on the issue of paying taxes for revenue. Privately to Smith, that same day, Tryon criticized "the present Ministers" and their policies, calling North "haughty & self Sufficient" and complaining about "the Absurdity of the present Measures of Force." Expressing his belief—or hope—that the North ministry would fall as soon as the king realized that he was being deceived by it, Tryon was "very free in declaring what he had said in England to People about the Court agt. taxing America."[9]

Tryon also was angry at the Episcopal clergy of New York, for even that pillar of the establishment seemed to be crumbling in the face of adversity. In spite of all that Tryon had done for New York Anglicans since his arrival in 1771, their ministers were now grumbling at him for being too generous in granting charters to Presbyterian and Dutch congregations. Angrily, Tryon lashed out in a conversation with Councillor Henry White "agt. the Episcopal Clergy here" and confessed that he had been "misrepresented in England" by these same persons. He "lamented that the suspicion of High Church prevented his living as he wished with his Non

Episcopal Friends upon whom he had most Reason to rely." The major source of his problem, he mused to White, was the DeLancey faction on the Council, which did most of the carping upon these matters. But, he declared, he would continue to grant charters to dissenting churches whenever he thought such petitions were necessary, just, and prudent, no matter what the DeLancey partisans on the Council, or the grumbling Anglican clergymen of his province, said or thought.[10]

If Tryon believed in August 1775 that his lot as governor might improve any time soon, he was sadly disabused of that notion in very short order. On the twenty-third of the month, a radical mob forcefully began to remove eleven of twenty-one pieces of ordnance from the battery under Fort George and also broke into Tryon's home, most likely for the purpose of seizing the governor as a hostage. The day before, Tryon had received an anonymous note warning him of such a possibility and had taken himself and his family away from the city for a visit with friends on Long Island. Unfortunately for the citizens of New York City, the *Asia*, commanded by Captain Vandeput, anchored close ashore, and the captain ordered some muskets and cannon shot directed at the battery as a warning. When the crowd on shore continued to work feverishly to take away the cannon, Vandeput let loose a full broadside of thirty-two guns as a further warning to persons who would defy the authority of the Crown. Although a large number of New Yorkers fled their homes because of the *Asia*'s threatening gestures, they soon learned that Captain Vandeput intended no more hostilities and they slowly drifted back to the city over the next few days.[11]

Tryon was shaken by these events, but for the first time since his return to New York he saw an opportunity to turn politics to his advantage, and he shrewdly seized the chance. Leaving his wife and daughter in the country, where they remained for the rest of the summer, Tryon hurried back to town, where on August 25 he called a joint meeting of his Council, the city corporation, members of the Provincial Congress, and the New York City Committee of Safety. This was a curious meeting for Tryon, as he was not even supposed to admit that the last two political bodies existed. But he sensed that the time was ripe to wring concessions from the opponents of Crown policies, for they were as shaken as he by the recent ship's bombardment of New York City. He was correct. Members of the Provincial Congress, almost sheepish about their recent actions in defiance of Crown authority and forcefully reminded by the governor that any future similar episode might lead Captain Vandeput to destroy their city, agreed to leave royal cannon and stores alone, while continuing to supply provisions to British ships in the harbor. Tryon, for his part, agreed to let the eleven cannon that had been removed from the battery to the commons remain where they were under guard rather than be remounted in their former positions. But he pointedly refused the Congress's offer to provide him with an armed guard. Thus, he had practically immobilized the Provincial Congress, at least for the moment, while conceding very little on his own part.[12]

Doing the best he could politically in New York, Tryon was making another, almost desperate, appeal to Dartmouth for parliamentary concessions on colonial taxation. "Their dread of being taxed by Parliament," he said on September 5, "is the grand sinew of the league. No argument or address can persuade them that the British nation does not mean to exercise that principle. . . . They look upon themselves as mere tenants at will of all they possess." Therefore the government ought to announce "an intention, [even] if never meant to be carried into execution," of eliminating all parliamentary taxes, thereby cutting the ground from under the radicals, who would instantly be abandoned in their opposition by the vast majority of still-loyal American citizens. While this declaration might be entirely duplicitous, Tryon said (with no hint of bad conscience), that if it were "seconded by the powerful aid of government" and by a large grant of new powers and prerogatives for royal governors, so that they might in fact become viceroys and "take the preeminence of all other except the blood royal on every occasion not merely military," it would put American colonial government on a footing to function soundly and authoritatively far into the future.[13]

While anxiously hoping that his advice in favor of conciliation was having some effect in London, Tryon was becoming convinced that his personal safety in New York was precarious. Since his return in late June he had heard numerous rumors that Sears and his radical friends might defy Washington's orders and seize him as a hostage. In fact it seemed to him that they already had made one such attempt on August 23, and when on September 10 he received from Gage in Boston "Intelligence from no bad qtr" that he and every other royal governor and officer were soon to be seized, he credited it as true. His anxiety about his standing in the community was heightened on September 20, when he was compelled by Dartmouth to publish an order from the king threatening New Yorkers with bombardment by warships should they continue illegally to raise troops, construct fortifications, and pilfer royal stores. A few days later,

Tryon was convinced the end of his freedom had come when "the King's Stores in the Garrett of the Lower Barracks were carried away by armed Men," in direct violation of the Crown's recently published demands.[14] Tryon interpreted these events to be a deliberate provocation on the part of the Provincial Congress, designed to create an incident to cover his kidnapping. Feeling that he had little to lose by attempting a bluff, he peremptorily "demanded Restitution of the Magistrates," but as he told Smith, he did not expect any, and therefore at the same time he secretly ordered Captain Vandeput to fire "upon the Town" should satisfaction not be forthcoming—even though his enemies might be holding him prisoner in the city as a counterfoil to such a possibility. When Tryon finally learned that the looting had been done by drunken militiamen, and when the Provincial Congress, not wishing to pick a fight, obeyed Tryon's orders by restoring the stolen property, the governor subsided temporarily in his suspicions. Smith, however, was convinced that had the Congress known of Tryon's orders to Vandeput, it would have arrested the governor immediately and sent him as a "Prisoner to Hartford."[15]

Tryon was now convinced that he could not make a persuasive case to recalcitrant New Yorkers that they might be bombarded by warships while he lived among them. On October 10 he told Mayor Hicks that should he be kidnapped by "the Inhabitants" and not delivered "on Board the Fleet" immediately upon Vandeput's order, the captain was to "enforce the Demand" with his "whole Power." Mayor Hicks, horrified that Tryon could believe he was in danger of being seized, assured the governor that he could continue his residence among New Yorkers in perfect safety. Finally, Isaac Low, chairman of the New York Committee of Safety, also guaranteed Tryon's complete physical security. But the New Yorkers' pledges of protection were insufficient to mollify Tryon because he was not persuaded that the moderates making the guarantees had any control of radicals such as Sears. On October 19, having already sent his wife and daughter home to England, he removed himself and all the colony's public records to the *Halifax Packet*. Eleven days later he transferred his headquarters to the more roomy and comfortable *Duchess of Gordon*, where, subsisting upon fresh food provided by the fiat of the Provincial Congress, he spent the next few months devising every scheme he could think of to throw sand into the gears of the growing colonial rebellion.[16]

In November 1775 Tryon reluctantly accepted Britain's insistence upon a policy of military coercion against the colonies, not because he had changed his mind about the value of the program but simply because he realized that if he intended to retain his position as royal governor (and he did, never giving a second's thought to resigning in protest of ministerial policy), he had no choice. Still, he could not forbear musing to Dartmouth on the eleventh that Britain's abandoning any idea of collecting taxes for revenue in New York would vastly reduce the mother country's problems in returning the colony's citizens to the imperial fold. "I am confident," he said, "one thousand regulars here with such an olive branch would be equal to five in the present state of the contest." But concessions or no concessions, he believed that Britain ultimately would prevail against the rebels. Like many of his military colleagues at the outset of the American war, Tryon could not conceive that the British army and navy could not eventually overawe inept and undisciplined colonial militiamen. Moreover, by the end of 1775 he had persuaded himself that if Britain and America came to an all-out fight, and especially if the colonists declared their independence from the mother country, thousands of loyal Americans would flock to British arms and help restore royal authority in North America. Thus, with entirely too much optimism, he reported both to Dartmouth and to William Howe, newly appointed British commander in chief in North America, that the inhabitants of the lower New York counties were overwhelmingly loyal to the king and that once British soldiers arrived, he could guarantee 4,000 or 5,000 loyal militiamen would join the royal army. The only reason why New York seemed so totally under the sway of the dissidents was that the Loyalists were surrounded on all sides by enemies, and their spirits could not help but droop at the prospect of having to remain very long under control of a few rebel hotheads.[17] Almost overnight, Tryon seemed totally to have revised his viewpoint on Britain's ability to coerce Americans into acceptance of parliamentary taxation, and instead of continuing to play the part of an honest, realistic, and therefore pessimistic critic of ministerial plans for coercion, he had joined the Pollyannas who were giving decision makers in London bad advice about the nature of the American rebellion.

To counter the defenselessness of the Loyalists in the counties of Dutchess, Queens, Kings, Westchester, and Richmond, Tryon attempted in late 1775 to arm militia forces there. He asked General Howe to send him a senior officer, preferably Henry Clinton, 3,000 muskets, ammunition, and authority to mobilize provincial regiments against the rebels during the following winter. Should Howe allow him to embody the Loyalists, he could easily field two or three thousand men, who could do signal service not only in policing the province until regular troops arrived but also in operating with the regulars once they appeared. Replying to Tryon's appeals, Howe informed the governor in early 1776 that he was planning major operations in New York during the upcoming summer campaign but that at present his resources were so strained he could not provide Tryon with assistance. Therefore he ordered the governor not to mobilize Loyalist forces until the British army actually arrived. Tryon was disappointed at Howe's response, for he realized that the New York Loyalists were at the mercy of rebel troops, who were proceeding to disarm the king's friends in and around New York City with great enthusiasm. Continental forces under Colonel Nathaniel Heard made a sweep into Queens County in January, and Lord Stirling's New Jersey troops did the same on Staten Island and Long Island a month later.[18] But these attempts by supporters of the American Congress to overawe New York Loyalists were not completely successful, and many Tories only awaited the arrival of the British army to rise in indignation against their lawless persecutors.

Besides working with the Loyalists in the winter of 1775–76, Tryon was busy with numerous other projects to aid the royal cause in New York. He organized provisions' ships for General Howe's army in Boston and kept General Guy Carleton, commander of British forces in Canada, apprised of rebel efforts to send reinforcements to a Continental army operating there. He urged propaganda efforts against his enemies, especially the printing of the Reverend Charles Inglis's response to Thomas Paine's *Common Sense,* and he was unhappy when a mob burned all copies of Inglis's pamphlet printed in New York City. He made every effort to hire or bribe American gunsmiths to enter the employ of the British government with wage offers that many could not refuse. Three of New York's finest gunsmiths, Thomas Allen, John Woods, and William Tunx, joined the royal cause, and Tryon reported to Dartmouth on December 8, 1775, that only one New York arms maker had not accepted his generous offers.[19] Tryon also organized an extensive secret service network along the eastern seaboard of America. His headquarters on the *Duchess of Gordon* became a center for British communications and underground activities, unimpeded by any American naval threat. He communicated with a number of agents, such as EGRA (John Graham) in New York and James Brattle, valet of rebel Congressman James Duane, in Philadelphia, and he learned vital information from them. Brattle's unmasking as a spy and his narrow escape from rebel clutches became for Duane and other members of Congress a source of both embarrassment and unease in the spring of 1776. Tryon also instituted what John Jay referred to as a "very extraordinary oath," binding all persons returning to England to disclose nothing relating to American affairs except to the ministry. The Continental Congress found this requirement so disquieting that it appointed a committee to inquire into whether the governor actually had imposed so odious an oath.[20]

To create chaos in the financial operations of New York rebels, Tryon began printing and issuing huge quantities of counterfeit currency. He devised a number of ways to get the bogus money into circulation; one technique was to hand wads of it to Loyalist visitors as they departed the *Duchess of Gordon*. In early 1776 David Matthews, newly elected mayor of New York, was the recipient of "a bundle of paper," which he used to purchase rifles for use by Royalists on some future occasion. Both Matthews and gunsmith Gilbert Forbes were asked to explain themselves to an American Conspiracies Committee, and although both denied knowledge that the money was counterfeit, they were jailed under deep suspicion of "dangerous designs and treasonable conspiracies against the rights and liberties of the United States of America."[21]

In December 1775 Tryon suffered another outrage against the king's authority when 100 Connecticut men, led by Isaac Sears, rode into New York City and closed down the *Gazetteer*, James Rivington's Loyalist newspaper. "To the disgrace of the city," Tryon fumed to Dartmouth, these outlaws were unmolested in their depredations and were "suffered . . . to leave the Town when they were finished." Sears, mused Tryon, was "evidently a tool of the Continental Army, publickly declaring he acts regardless of Congresses and committees," and the governor predicted that it would "not be long before the assumed powers of the general congress will be transferred to their Army," à la the Cromwellian revolution in England.[22] A large number of reluctant American rebels harbored a similar fear that their growing protest against Britain might fall into the hands of its most radical proponents and become militarized.

Tryon soon retaliated against the rebels with a political maneuver designed to separate New York from the Continental Congress and restore the governor's authority. In a plan devised by Councillor Smith, Tryon proposed to the Provincial Congress, which seemed to be waning in popularity among the people, that it request a meeting of the Assembly, which Tryon had kept prorogued, to consider Lord North's conciliatory plans, which had been rejected by the Continental Congress in July. Had the Provincial Congress accepted this scheme, it would have practically guaranteed that the Assembly would accept North's conciliation and thereby break the unanimity of the colonies' opposition to the British prime minister's program. Other colonies might then follow the lead of New York, and Massachusetts might at last find itself isolated in protest against the mother country's laws. The plan was a "Piece of Finesse difficult to obviate," wrote John Jay to Alexander McDougall, and it almost succeeded. But the conservatives in the Provincial Congress overstepped themselves by wording their resolution to allow Tryon discretion in reporting to the king "the sense of the colony," and the measure was defeated. Smith bemoaned the fact that the proposal had been "incautiously framed," but by then the damage had been done.[23]

Tryon was undismayed by this setback, for he was now convinced that the radicals' cause was fast losing popularity in New York and that he and conservatives could regain control. Upon the advice of the shrewd Smith, Tryon in early 1776 dissolved the Assembly and called for new elections in February, believing that the voters would elect a majority of persons loyal to the empire and that the entire process of government disintegration could be reversed. Tryon's hope was that these elections might be held quietly and that the radicals would boycott them. However, the radicals became thoroughly alarmed at Tryon's scheme, widely assailing the elections as a Tory plot. Thus, Tryon's candidates were overwhelmed at the polls, and Tryon was compelled in some embarrassment to prorogue the new Assembly as he had the old.[24] The election only showed how impossible it was for Tryon, by any political artifice, to influence New York's politics at a time when all opponents of British imperial pretensions, radical, moderate, and conservative, simply could not be wedged apart in numbers sufficient to do damage to their cause.

Now fully aware that he could not regain political control of New York without the assistance of overwhelming military power, Tryon nevertheless continued to do all he could while awaiting such assistance to hearten friends of the king. In February his spirits rose when General Henry Clinton sailed into New York harbor on the frigate *Greyhound* for a visit while on the way to take command of British troops in the South. Clinton found that Tryon's life aboard the *Duchess of Gordon* was unpleasant and rather precarious, dependent as it was upon the insurgents on shore providing the governor's party with fresh provisions. Compounding Tryon's problems, General Charles Lee had just taken command of Continental forces in New York and had proceeded immediately to remove the artillery from Fort George, while British warships in the harbor, restricted in their navigation by ice floes, lay quietly offshore. In addition, Lee was disrupting, but not totally halting, the supplying of British vessels in the harbor.[25] Because of the ice, as Tryon later reported to Lord George Germain, newly appointed colonial secretary, Captain Hyde Parker, commander of the recently arrived warship *Phoenix* as well as all the North American station, was forced on February 17 to remove his vessels from New York harbor. He stationed his own ship "below the Narrows," and the *Asia*, commanded by Captain Vandeput, in the Hudson River above the city. Tryon, on the *Duchess of Gordon*, was forced to follow one or the other of these warships for his own protection, and chose to anchor, as General Lee reported to Washington on the nineteenth, under the stern of the *Asia*. From this new vantage point, Tryon publicized the Prohibitory Act, a law voted by Parliament the previous December that embargoed American trade, called for the seizure of all American ships, and defined colonial resistance as rebellion and treason. New Yorkers, upon learning of this measure, were stunned by its severity, and Tryon's own personal standing in the colony was certainly not enhanced by his publicizing the law.[26]

By mid-March Tryon's every gesture in New York was being held up to the most intense public scrutiny for evidence that he did not "trust" Americans. Only a short time before, said William Smith, Tryon had "escaped the Calumny of purchasing a Boat to cruize our rivers & seize Provisions to be sent to Boston." It was obvious that the citizens were in an excitable frame of mind regarding the motives and intentions of their royal governor. Nevertheless, on the sixteenth Tryon uncharacteristically risked his dwindling popularity, while also going against the advice of his Council, by publishing a proclamation that promised relief to Royalists in the near future. "Notwithstanding," he announced, that "prejudice, delusion, and faction, have hitherto among too many usurped the seat of reason and reflection," he had attempted to bring his opponents to their senses. Seeing that this hope was vain, he now could only offer "comfort [to] those who have been the object of oppression for their zealous attachment to our happy Constitution." Therefore he promised the "well-disposed subjects of this Government . . . every assistance and protection the state of *Great Britain* [could] afford them," and he cherished "every appearance of a disposition on their part to withstand the tyranny and misrule" of those who subverted legal government. He exhorted "all friends to good order and our justly admired Constitution, still to persevere in constancy," certain that in a few months they would be delivered of their "present oppressed, injured, and insulted condition."[27]

The consequences of Tryon's futile and bombastic proclamation, which appeared in New York's newspapers on March 21, were twofold: the destruction of whatever shreds of authority he still exercised in New York among rebels of every political stripe and the bringing down of even more opprobrium upon the heads of his friends on shore, who unlike himself were not on a safe British ship. A huge, unruly crowd immediately reacted by parading the governor's effigy through the streets with a derogatory placard around its neck reading "William Tryon, late Governor of this Province, but now a professed rebel and traitor to its dearest rights and privileges." When the mob reached the commons, it hanged Tryon's effigy on a mock gallows, while rebel leaders made speeches against Tryon, and then the effigy was cut down and kicked around until it disintegrated. The Loyalists thereafter were compelled to exercise even greater circumspection in their speech and actions, and one bitterly complained of Tryon's "weak and ill-judged action," declaring, "O Lucifer, once the son of morn, now fallen!"[28]

In early April Tryon, who already was isolated from New Yorkers both by distance and politics, became even more cut off from his government. At that time he learned that General Washington and his "Cambridge Army" were soon to be "let loose . . . on this devoted colony" by Howe's withdrawal to Halifax. "My Feelings on this occasion," he groaned to Germain, "are not to be expressed, and I look forward with increased anxiety for the Time when the continental army shall be opposed by a Body of the King's Forces sufficient to give them an entire Overthrow." Washington had already sent orders to New York that "All Communications between the Ships and the Shore" were to be severed, so Tryon had been compelled on April 7 to fall "down the River to the Phoenix," below the Narrows, where British shore-raiding parties were keeping alive persons aboard the king's ships by stealing water and provisions until Howe's army arrived. In the meantime, Tryon, upon the advice of his Council, dissolved the Assembly, which had never met. That the Council could make such a recommendation, Tryon gloomily told Germain, was "a strong evidence of the little attention that is now paid even towards preserving the Form of a legal and constitutional Representation of the people."[29]

After Washington arrived at New York on April 13, Tryon became involved in a convoluted scheme, known as the "Hickey Conspiracy," or

"Tryon's Plot," to kidnap the American general and hold him as a hostage to end the war. The cabal was discovered when two Continental soldiers, Thomas Hickey and Michael Lynch, were arrested for passing forged bank notes and after being jailed tried to enlist a fellow prisoner in a Loyalist military force that was being raised within the Continental army. This corps, 700 men in all, was being paid for by Tryon through the conduit of Mayor David Matthews. Notified by the prisoner, the Provincial Congress commenced an investigation of the plot and learned that some members of Washington's headquarters guard, Hickey included, were members of the Loyalist corps. The scheme being exposed, it immediately collapsed, and the major conspirators within reach of the Provincial Congress, Mayor Matthews not excepted, were arrested. Hickey was court-martialed, convicted of mutiny and sedition, and hanged. Governor Tryon could only look on in impotent fury as another of his attempts to weaken the rebel cause fell into ruin.[30]

To his intense delight, on June 26 Tryon welcomed General Howe to New York. The general, who preceded his army by four days, arrived on the *Greyhound* and immediately held a secret conference with the governor on board the ship. Howe received from Tryon and other "fast friends to Government" a great deal of information "on the state of the Rebels, who are numerous and very advantageously posted," and he commenced to formulate plans for an assault on the Continental army. Tryon's advice to Howe was to land immediately upon Long Island with British forces that arrived from Halifax on June 29 and assault the Americans, without awaiting a fleet and reinforcements from England under the command of his brother, Admiral Richard Lord Howe. But General James Robertson dissuaded Howe from his plan at the last moment, and the commander in chief thereupon determined to encamp on Staten Island to await the buildup of his army.[31] Tryon's very first action as a military adviser to the British commander in chief manifested a characteristic that would typify his thinking throughout the conflict: a desire to charge ahead in order to seize the initiative, even if it meant taking great risks. In the same way, Howe's rebuff was typical of how most of Tryon's suggestions were received by his commanding officers, who were charged with the responsibility of attempting to quell the rebellion by judicious applications of military power and who had no desire to take any risks at all if they could possibly be avoided.

As a professional soldier with the rank of colonel in the British army, Tryon wholeheartedly supported General Howe's military efforts after he

General William Howe, by J. Chapman. Howe, Tryon's first commander in chief in the American war, listened politely to Tryon's military advice but rarely implemented it. Although Tryon at first thought highly of Howe's abilities, he later concluded that Howe did not have the killer instinct necessary for successful army command. (Courtesy of the William L. Clements Library, University of Michigan)

arrived in New York. But one aspect of Howe's authority, having to do with civil government, discomfited him. Under provisions of the Prohibitory Act, Howe and his brother, Admiral Lord Howe, were given authority as peace commissioners to suspend civil government anywhere in America until they should decide that the area was "at the peace of his Majesty." They had promptly applied these provisions in Tryon's government, discontinuing practically all civil functions and throwing Tryon's office into limbo. In place of the civilian governor's office, the Howes instituted the office of commandant of New York City, which they activated in September after the rebels evacuated the town. Tryon was offered this position but refused it on the ground that "he could not see the propriety of the civil government of the Colony and the military command of its capital being vested in the same person."[32] Therefore the office was filled by General James Robertson, and Tryon was reconfirmed as governor, but with practically no powers, as the Howes did not lift martial law at that time.

Tryon disliked this blurring of civil-military distinctions, for he felt that it was poor constitutional practice and also unwise from a practical standpoint to allow military officers to rule civilians. These strictures applied especially in colonial America, where everyone—including Loyalists—were suspicious of military power and wanted it carefully controlled by civilian officials. In fact, part of Tryon's motive in his long squabble with London about the governor taking precedence over military men in America was his urge to see civilian government in command of the military. Uneasily, Tryon wrote Germain in September, "It is the opinion of both His Majesty's commissioners for restoring peace to the Colonies that I should postpone any executive Acts of Government, until the Province is more liberated from the control of the Rebels. I therefore have kept the executive powers of Civil Government dormant, leaving every thing to the direction of the military." Yet, he did not want anyone to become used to this arrangement. As Ambrose Serle, Admiral Lord Howe's secretary, noted after Tryon discussed his concerns with Serle, "Tryon didn't want to postpone his civic duty for even a day," and when Tryon was petitioned by prominent New Yorkers on October 16 for a restoration of civil government, the governor informed Germain that he was drawing up a list of civil officers in preparation for the reestablishment of regular administration. After Britain's military fortunes were reversed at Trenton and Princeton in the winter of 1776–77, the restoration never took place. Perhaps because Tryon over the next few years became more preoccupied with advancing his military career than with exercising his duties and responsibilities as a governor, he never pressed the matter further. Forced to live under martial law, many New York neutralists, and perhaps even some persons who were loyal at heart, joined the ranks of the rebellion because they abhorred the ham-fisted manner in which the British pushed them around during the occupation.[33]

In early July 1776, amidst army and naval officers in fancy uniforms, some of them old acquaintances such as Henry Clinton, Tryon shifted most of his attention away from his now-dormant civilian status toward cooperating with Howe in military coercion of American rebels. In fact, Tryon had hoped that General Howe would bring from the king a regular military commission for the governor to serve as an officer under the commander in chief. Since no such commission was forthcoming, Tryon swallowed his disappointment and promised Germain on July 8 to do everything within his power "to promote his majesty's service." True to his word, he immediately began organizing Loyalist militiamen from counties surrounding New York City, although he sometimes ran into difficulties, as he told Germain in November, because of "the vicinity of the Rebels and the uncertainty of the Royal Army giving them continued support." By the end of the year, he had enrolled about 1,800 New Yorkers, predominantly from Richmond, Queens, and Westchester counties, and Staten and Long islands, in a brigade led by General Oliver DeLancey, a battalion commanded by Colonel Edmund Fanning, and a corps of provincials officered by Major Robert Rogers. Additionally, Tryon gave encouragement to Colonel Charles Lord Rawdon, Colonel Montfort Browne, Colonel Beverly Robinson, Lieutenant Colonel Banastre Tarleton, and Lieutenant Colonel John Graves Simcoe in their attempts to recruit Loyalist volunteers from New York for various military units. Germain praised Tryon highly for these efforts, remarking upon his "Zeal & Attachment to the King's service" and promising that once the colonies had been brought to heel, Tryon would be amply rewarded for his devotion to duty.[34]

Although in one way Tryon's efforts at organizing these Loyalist militiamen were impressive, in another way they were not, for a few months earlier he had practically guaranteed the British ministry that some 5,000 of the king's friends would flock to the colors upon Howe's arrival. The disparity between his promise and performance showed that in one respect at least, Tryon was not serving his English masters well during the initial phases of the American war and that having accepted the Crown's policy of military coercion, he has swung from realistic pessimism about Britain's chances of successfully coercing the rebels to unrealistic optimism. In August he reported to Germain the New Yorkers' promulgation the month before of the American Declaration of Independence, which had been accompanied by a mob's destruction of a statue of the king and the king's arms in City Hall, the shutting up of all the established churches, and the seizure by rebels of all royal officers such as mayors, judges, councillors, and magistrates. However, he had decided that this event was not particularly significant, for as he confidently asserted to Germain, the war would be successfully concluded within one year, and the vast majority of New Yorkers, who remained loyal to the Crown, would return to the fold once the hotheaded rebel minority had been suppressed.[35] This was a theme to which Tryon reverted over and over again during the next few months in his letters to London, and he left the ministry with an inaccurate impression of the overall political temper of his colony. Certainly his intention was not deliberately to delude the king and his councillors, for his earlier realistic reports about the mood of Americans regarding parliamentary taxation had shown no reticence about telling unpleasant truths. The problem was that he now tended to view things too optimistically, and he would continue to do so during the initial months of the war.

Meanwhile, Tryon continued to serve General Howe as an important source of military advice and information, and he remained a part of the commander's inner circle of confidants during military operations in New York over the next few months. As Ambrose Serle's diary recorded, Tryon was constantly dancing attendance at Howe's headquarters upon both official and social occasions. He was with General Howe in September, during military operations on Long Island that culminated on the fifteenth in a pitched battle with General Washington's rebel army. Later that month, he accompanied Howe in the British invasion of Manhattan at Kip's Bay, where, according to American surgeon James Thacher, he took part in an entertainment given Howe by Quakers Mr. and Mrs. Robert Murray, which supposedly slowed the British advance across Manhattan and allowed Washington's army to escape entrapment in New York City. On the twenty-first, while visiting the home of Councillor William Axtell in Flatbush "for the recovery of my health and strength," he was a horrified witness to a fire in New York City that consumed one-fourth of the metropolis. He reported to Germain his "conjecture that Mr. Washington was privy to this villainous act"; but at least the remainder of the city was habitable, and Tryon, after an absence of nine months, ensconced himself in the capital of the province upon the departure of the Continental forces.[36]

As the war over the next few weeks swept northward to White Plains and then westward across New Jersey, Tryon remained in New York City, conducting what little business was left to him as governor, while General Robertson as commandant actually exercised authority. He spent a considerable amount of time administering loyalty oaths to New Yorkers who flocked to receive pardons from the king, and by February 1777 he and his subordinates had sworn 5,600 inhabitants to royal allegiance.[37] Facing extraordinary public expenses attendant upon these and other matters, Tryon was compelled to draw bills upon the Treasury for thousands of pounds. His own salary proving inadequate, he appealed to Germain in 1776 for an increase of £1,000 sterling per year, enlisting Ambrose Serle to point out to the ministry "the Difficulties of his present Situation, his private Circumstances, and the unavoidable Expenses of Hospitality & c. to which he is particularly exposed at this Time." The "hospitality," of course, was the lavish entertainment of numerous generals, admirals, and other officers who had arrived in the colony during the previous six months. His appeal was successful.[38] In addition, he appointed Robert Bayard as judge of the vice admiralty court to be reopened in New York so that British naval prizes could be legally condemned, but he did not receive authorization from Germain officially to empower the court until October 1777.[39] He also had time to think about the future prospects for British authority in the American colonies, and his reflections were not pleasant.

CHAPTER NINE

Soldiering against Republicanism

As the year 1776 drew to a close, Governor Tryon was unhappy with the war's progress, and he had abandoned completely his earlier prediction that the rebellion would be suppressed within a year. He was particularly mortified, as he told Germain, by the Hessian defeat at Trenton, an event that had given him "more real chagrin, than any other circumstance this war." The moment had been critical, the rebel officers were desperate for a victory to restore "their sinking cause," and a trouncing at Trenton would have been their hiatus. But now their spirits were restored, they probably would be able to raise another army in 1777, and the war would drag on for at least one more campaign. The only comfort Tryon drew from these events was that "the Rebels . . . with all their arts" had been unable "to seduce the Hessian Prisoners from their allegiance to their Prince and duty to His Majesty."[1]

Tryon was now convinced that General Howe was not prosecuting the war with the savagery and vigor that he ought. Only a harsh war of brutal depredation against rebel leaders in America, he had come to believe, would ever bring the rebellion to an end, and the longer British leaders evaded this truth, the longer unnecessary bloodshed would continue. Like many of his British contemporaries, Tryon assumed at the commencement of the war that the rebellion was being perpetrated by a tiny minority of hotheads, who held the essentially Loyalist population in thrall. In Tryon's mind, merciless warfare against these leaders, as distinct from the citizenry as was possible in warfare, was actually humane and just in the long run, because it was designed first to reduce the overall fighting and bloodshed, and second to liberate helpless Americans from the grasp of wicked "Committee Men." Hence the war must be taken to these civilian leaders in all its horror and viciousness, otherwise they would never give up their delusions and cease their oppressions. Certainly any number of defeats for their armies in conventional battles would not persuade them. In this viewpoint, his thinking ran diametrically counter to other British army officers, the "conciliators," best represented by Henry Clinton, who maintained that British soldiers, rather than making war upon rebel civilian leaders, must "gain the hearts & subdue the Minds of America." Clearly Tryon was numbered among those British officers, such as Major General James Grant and Colonel Charles O'Hara, who were "hard-liners."[2]

Given this way of thinking, Tryon could not but believe that the Howes in the dying days of the campaign of 1776 had suddenly become conciliators. They had issued a proclamation to the rebels demanding that the Continental army disperse and the Congress renounce its powers, in return for which any rebel could come forward within sixty days and, upon his oath that he would in the future be an obedient citizen, receive the king's pardon. Tryon was flabbergasted at the Howes' pronouncement, and he immediately wrote Germain to declare his "prejudice . . . against so much lenity to rebels." Privately, Germain concurred with Tryon, quoting the governor's letter to William Knox, his undersecretary, and declaring, "This sentimental manner of making war will, I fear, not have the desired effect." Publicly, however, Germain supported his peace commissioners, only suggesting that perhaps they went too far in their generosity to rebels.[3]

Except for his comments to Germain, Tryon kept his failing confidence in the Howes to himself during the winter of 1776–77, so that he could continue to be included in British military operations. In early 1777 he provided General Howe with 500 select Loyalist militiamen for the defense of New York City, as the general's regulars were posted in other, more strategic locations. As Howe's planning for the campaign of 1777 proceeded, Tryon sought to make a place for himself by petitioning the general for a temporary major generalship and command of the provincial forces, consisting of Oliver DeLancey's New Yorkers, and the battalions of David Fanning, Montfort Browne, and William Bayard. His request was approved. In actual fact, Tryon did not much like this arrangement, for as he told Knox in April 1777, his temporary rank placed him "behind all the Majors General in this army though I am an older colonel than any of them." However, "at this crisis a passe droit does not weigh so strongly with me as an opportunity given me to lend a hand to beat down this Republican Revolt." Perhaps Tryon's zeal for the cause was as powerful as he claimed, but at least part of his reason for not attempting to secure a regular commission was Germain's earlier notice to him that provincial officers were not "to expect Rank in the army" while they served or half pay when they were reduced. Whatever the circumstances, Tryon, with the king's approval and Germain's blessing, was promoted major general of the provincials in the spring of 1777, and as Howe's plans matured, Tryon learned what his role was to be in the upcoming drama. On April 2 Howe outlined to Germain his final campaign plan for 1777, in which he proposed to lead 11,000 troops against Philadelphia by sea, while leaving garrisons of 4,700 in New York City and 2,400 in Rhode Island. In addition, 3,000 provincial troops under General Tryon would operate "upon the Hudson's River or . . . enter Connecticut as circumstances may point out." Meanwhile, General John Burgoyne, who intended to drive southward from Canada toward Albany, would be left free, as he desired, to fend for himself against American forces in upstate New York.[4]

On April 20, 1777, Tryon was given the honor of opening the campaign by leading a raid upon Danbury, Connecticut, with 1,800 troops, assisted by Sir William Erskine and Brigadier General James Agnew. The purpose of this foray, as Howe told Germain, was "to destroy a large magazine of provisions and military stores formed by the enemy" at that place. Embarking in transports on the twenty-first, Tryon's forces a day later sailed eastward on Long Island Sound under escort of two frigates toward Norwalk, Connecticut. On April 25 Tryon landed his forces on the eastern side of the Saugatuck River at Cedar Point and marched without opposition through that night and the following day toward Danbury by way of Redding Ridge and Bethel. He reached Danbury in the late afternoon, and although the village was garrisoned with about 150 Continental soldiers, these troops wisely retreated after firing only a few shots at Tryon's troops from a distance. Except for seven "Daring Rascals" who blazed down on the general's forces from a house as they entered Danbury, the British took the place and its military depot without any difficulty. Although it was now almost dark and Tryon's men had been on the march for a night and a day without sleep or adequate rations, the commander put his men to collecting Continental stores for torching. Throughout the night of the twenty-sixth, the British soldiers destroyed enormous quantities of military supplies as well as—without Tryon making any attempt to stop them—considerable private property of the more prominent rebels in the town.[5]

This work completed on the morning of April 27, Tryon ordered his exhausted men out of Danbury on a march toward the coast by the way of Ridgefield and Wilton. Soon he and his officers received intelligence that rebel forces were collecting under Generals Benedict Arnold, David Wooster, and Gold Silliman to oppose their progress. Sure enough, at a place about five miles from Danbury, they got into a fire fight in their rear with about 200 men under Wooster's command, and Wooster was killed. Although this shooting did little harm to the Britons, they soon were in for much worse, for as they drew near Ridgefield, they discovered Generals Arnold and Silliman posted on the hills and in the village with about 500 men blocking their advance from behind a barricade of wagons, earth, and stones. Tryon, not having led troops in battle since his fight with the Regulators six years before, had the good sense at this point to turn over tactical command of his troops to Erskine, who proceeded to deal smartly with the Americans. Immediately, he attacked Ridgefield and gained possession of it; then he sent flanking parties out on both sides of Arnold's position. According to royal engineer Archibald Robertson, who was with the expedition, this maneuver, designed to entrap the enemy, would have worked had the two parties advanced at the same time, but because they did not, "We only Dispersed them and drove them off." Arnold himself came close to being killed, escaping only by the narrowest of margins. The British troops now being almost too tired to walk, Tryon encamped in and near Ridgefield for the night. Blessedly, his army's repose was not interrupted by the rebels during the night.[6]

The following day, with Erskine still in command of military operations, Tryon reflected apprehensively upon the many miles his army must march to reach the coast, for he knew that the entire distance was going to be contested by the Americans. It was. The aroused inhabitants of Connecticut, flocking to the British line of march, fired upon their enemies from houses, walls, and fences along the route, but with little effect. Meanwhile, Tryon's forces had to circumvent two enemy roadblocks that Arnold had thrown in the way of their progress. Finally they reached Compo Hill, from which they could discern their ships about five miles away "and the Rebels drawn up about 2 miles in front to oppose our Passing a Bridge over Sauketuck [Saugatuck] River." But Erskine simply skirted the bridge, crossed the river at a ford, and led 400 men in a bayonet charge that broke Arnold's ranks, and Tryon's army embarked "without a Shot being fired." By May 1 Tryon and his weary forces were safely back in New York City, having suffered about 20 to 30 killed and 60 to 70 wounded during the entire time they were in Connecticut.[7]

The day after his return to British headquarters, General Tryon wrote Germain informing him that he was sending information to London by General Sir William Moore about the success of his recent expedition. While modest about his own accomplishments, he was unstinting in his generous and wholehearted commendation of Sir William Erskine. His obligations to Erskine, Tryon declared, were "beyond the measure of praise on the occasion; without him I should have been much embarrassed if nothing worse, and with his aid I met no difficulties." A month later, Tryon added to his kind words about his colleague, asserting that Erskine's "Military abilities [are] so superior to my own, that were I allowed to make a request to His Majesty in his behalf, it should be that he might succeed to the command of a Regiment before me, as much as I wish for that honour myself." Tryon's admiration for Erskine did not abate over time, for in 1779 he told his friend William Smith that Erskine "was the first General [in the British Army] without Exception."[8]

Tryon's success at Danbury was significant, for the Americans had lost thousands of barrels of pork and flour, 60 hogsheads of rum and 20 of wine, 1,000 tents, 5,000 pairs of shoes, and many other items that the hard-pressed rebels could not easily replace. Yet, for his efforts Tryon received not a word of commendation from General Howe, or even recognition that his raid had done any good at all. In fact, the commander in chief's letter to Germain describing the expedition was so worded as to suggest that Tryon somehow had been lax in his duty in not having procured wagons and teams in Connecticut to drag the tons of supplies back to the seacoast intact! Germain, upon receiving Howe's letter, was so shocked at its tone that he wrote William Knox, "The General's silence [on Tryon's merits] is remarkable, but I should hope he is not dissatisfied with [his] conduct." Then he suggested to Knox, "I do not see why you might not say something civil to Tryon, as he commanded a successful expedition."[9]

Tryon was disgusted at Howe's lack of appreciation for his efforts. In fact, the commander in chief's apparent coolness toward him only reinforced in his mind a notion that had been growing for the past few months. Writing to Germain on May 5, he earnestly solicited leave to return to England, as he had lost all but a "Shadow" of his government and had no consolation "in any thing relative thereto." Already the previous April he had hinted to Germain that he wanted to give up his governorship and had attempted to connive for himself upon his potential departure "the same provision . . . as has been made by Government for Governor Hutchinson" of Massachusetts, which was an annual pension of £1,000 sterling and a baronetcy. Replying to these solicitations, Germain assured Tryon that "I should find a particular pleasure in forwarding any proposition of yours of a tendency to promote your happiness and advantage." But Tryon's public service to that point had been so important to the king's affairs that Germain could not consider recommending to His Majesty that Tryon be allowed to resign "until peace is restored, & the Constitution has resumed its legal form and authority."[10]

Reluctantly, Tryon gave in for the moment to Germain's soothing assurances that he was indispensable in his role as governor of New York (although in early October he reverted to the same old theme by grumbling to Germain, "The incidents that have occurred to me since my return to this Country, my present situation, and the state of my family affairs, all powerfully invite me to return home"). It was not until July 1777 that Tryon finally unburdened himself to the colonial secretary about what was really bothering him. The basic problem, after all, was not Howe's attitude toward him, for in fact Tryon now knew that in spite of Howe's recent seeming lack of enthusiasm for his handling of the Danbury raid, the commander in chief actually thought he was a "Zealous" officer of some merit.[11] Actually, he was dissatisfied with his rank as major general of provincials, despite his recent protestations of willingness to forgo personal position in order to destroy American republicanism. The previous May, he had proposed to Dartmouth, Lord Privy Seal in the Cabinet, that he be allowed to sell his captaincy in the First Foot Guards, which he had purchased in 1751, to Francis Lord Rawdon and secure from the king the command of a regiment. On July 8 he wrote Dartmouth another letter, composed by Ambrose Serle, thanking the king for promoting him to his present rank as a provincial officer but noting that by this designation "I find myself not only placed after all the Major Generals in America, though of later standing in the army, but must also be under all such as may hereafter be appointed here, or come out under the King's Brevet." Because Dartmouth must "perceive the mortifications" that Tryon suffered under this arrangement, surely he would bring the matter to the king's attention for adjustment.[12] When Dartmouth did not, Tryon for the moment reluctantly swallowed his pride and retained his command of the provincials, but he was only biding his time until he sensed a more opportune time than the middle of a military campaign to reopen the issue of rank.

While Tryon dealt with the impact of the Danbury raid upon his reputation within the British army and in London, the rebels were excoriating him in satirical verse. In a particularly effective example of this style, entitled "Expedition to Danbury," a patriot versifier put these words in Tryon's mouth:

> In cunning and canting, deceit and disguise,
> In cheating a friend, and inventing of lies,
> I think I'm a match for the best of my species,
> But in this undertaking, I feel all in pieces;
> So I'll fall to the rear, for I'd rather go last;—
> *Come, march on, my boys*, let me see you all past;
> For his Majesty's service (so says my commission)
> Requires that I *bring up* the whole expedition.

This satire, which was published widely in American newspapers in the summer of 1777, was indicative of the low estate into which Tryon's name had fallen with Americans by this time, and in fact for the rest of his life.[13]

Meanwhile, in early July Tryon had settled into a life of quiet military routine, commanding provincial forces, about 1,800 strong, at Kings Bridge, just north of Manhattan on the Harlem River. Howe, according to plan, was soon to depart with his army for Philadelphia, and Tryon's commanding officer was now Henry Clinton, an old friend with whom he got along famously. On July 8 Clinton solicited his advice on what improvements might be made in the town's defenses, and Tryon proposed posting more armed patrol boats on the Hudson River and establishing an ammunition factory at Fort Knyphausen. Other than this assignment, Tryon during the summer and half the autumn was not required to perform any military duty more onerous than filing periodic reports at headquarters.[14]

On August 22 Tryon's peaceful military routine was shattered when General Washington attacked Clinton's lines around New York in three places to probe the strength of the city's defenses. While General Samuel Holden Parsons and 700 men assaulted General Oliver DeLancey's positions on Long Island, rebel troops from New Jersey advanced upon General John Campbell's posts on Staten Island and a Continental force of about 600 men made an appearance near Tryon's foreposts at Kings Bridge. Clinton, correctly concluding that the Kings Bridge attack was a feint, left Tryon to fend for himself and made immediate provision for dealing with the other two attacks. Hence, Tryon upon his own authority formed his provincials and advanced against the rebels, who after some sharp skirmishing retired in good order. The two main assaults, meantime, had been thrown back by Campbell and DeLancey without need for Clinton to reinforce either one. Thus, Washington's attacks failed, and Clinton was led to remark that the rebel general was a "blockhead."[15]

For Tryon, Washington's attacks, which were a break in the seemingly endless routine of administering his encamped provincials, soon faded into memory and he characteristically began to suffer intense fits of boredom with army garrison life. Seeking ways to alleviate his ennui, he began devising projects to fill his time and, hopefully, to contribute to the war effort. One was organizing a troop of Westchester County light horsemen under command of Colonel James DeLancey for operations in the so-called Neutral Ground between British and American lines north of Kings Bridge. This was the unit that later became famous, or infamous, among both British and American forces as "DeLancey's Cowboys."[16] Another was a proposal to Clinton in late September that he lead an expedition of 2,710 men into Westchester County for purposes of clearing rebels from that strategic place and securing forage and provisions for the army. With Clinton's approval, Tryon commenced organizing this force, but the expedition was never launched. As Tryon learned not long thereafter, Clinton was only using Tryon's preparations as a cover for planning a much more ambitious military operation, the seizure of the Highland forts above New York City in an attempt to take rebel pressure off General Burgoyne, who was now beleaguered by General Horatio Gates's forces in upstate New York.[17]

When Clinton's operations commenced on October 3, Tryon and his provincials found themselves caught up in the largest military operation they had ever seen. That day, Clinton transported 1,100 troops, the provincials included, to Spuyten Devil Creek and the following day ferried them on to Tarrytown. Other contingents of British soldiers arrived at Tarrytown on the same day, and over the next two days Clinton moved a force of 3,000 men by stages to Stony Point. On October 5 he maneuvered his troops into position to attack Forts Montgomery and Clinton, with Tryon taking position with his command, the Royal Fusiliers and the Hessian regiment of Trumbach, to guard Clinton's line of communications with the fleet. The following day, October 6, at about two o'clock in the afternoon, Clinton attacked Forts Montgomery and Clinton. The fighting lasted for about three hours, with the Americans putting up a spirited defense and refusing Clinton's demand that they surrender. During the battle, Tryon and his men were hurrying, upon

Clinton's orders, to join General John Vaughan before Fort Clinton, in case their assistance was needed in the final assault. At dusk, both forts were stormed successfully, and Tryon arrived at Fort Clinton just "in time to join in the cry of Victory." Early the following day, General Clinton embarked Tryon's forces, under escort of Sir James Wallace's warships, to assault Fort Constitution, opposite West Point; but when Tryon reached his destination he found the fort abandoned and showing every sign of having been hastily evacuated by the enemy garrison.[18]

As Fort Constitution had so easily fallen into his hands, Tryon on October 8 was ordered by Clinton to march his forces, augmented by the addition of Captain Andreas Emmerich's chasseurs, fifty *Jägers*, and two cannon, to destroy a rebel supply depot named Continental Village, located about four miles southeast of his present encampment. He proceeded to his destination without incident and spent the day burning barracks, storehouses, and wagons loaded with military supplies. His haul was huge because, as Clinton observed, Continental Village was the only supply depot that the rebels possessed in the Highlands. His work of destruction complete, Tryon marched back to Fort Montgomery and was welcomed by Clinton at army headquarters there.[19]

Tryon rejoined a commander who was bemused at having just received word from Burgoyne that American general Gates was about to force his surrender and that he awaited Clinton's orders. With justification Clinton spurned this attempt on the part of the previously cocky Burgoyne to shift blame for his impending disaster. Clinton believed that his seizure of the Highland forts, given his limitations of manpower and knowledge of Washington's intentions, was all he could do to assist his brother officer. At the same time, he was too conscientious to ignore Burgoyne's dilemma, so he cast about for a way within available means to give further assistance. It happened that Tryon had a plan. Move the bulk of British forces upriver to effect a junction, he suggested, allowing half the troops to travel part of the distance on the limited number of available transports, while the other half marched; then alternate the arrangement. In this way, the army could proceed by forced marches and relieve Burgoyne's men before a disaster occurred. Should Clinton's forces arrive after Burgoyne had been compelled to retreat to Fort Ticonderoga, nothing would have been lost, for the troops could simply return to New York City in the same way they had proceeded northward. Clinton rejected Tryon's plan as too audacious, which it certainly was, but he was not surprised to receive such a proposal from an officer who he was beginning to believe was more than slightly imprudent.[20] Tryon, for his part, was not surprised that Clinton had rejected his plan, for he was becoming convinced that Clinton, like Howe, was too cautious militarily and not to be trusted as a commander. Over the next few years the views of Tryon and Clinton toward each other hardened into certainty and led to mutual animosity.

Tryon did not have a role in the operation that Clinton finally decided upon to assist Burgoyne. The commander ordered General Vaughan with 2,000 soldiers to push up the Hudson River and aid the beleaguered general in any way he could. But as Vaughan sailed northward, he saw that the banks were bristling with rebel militiamen and that the exercise was futile. So when Clinton received a request from General Howe in Pennsylvania for a reinforcement of 4,000 men, he recalled Vaughan, who, as he returned down the Hudson River, burned Esopus and ruined Forts Clinton and Montgomery, then fell back to New York City. Before long, General Tryon, back at his old post at Kings Bridge and now in command of both provincial and Hessian troops, received the discouraging news that Burgoyne had surrendered his army to Gates at Saratoga on October 17.[21] The only apparently happy results for the British army in the entire campaign of 1777 were Howe's triumphs over Washington in Pennsylvania and the capture of Philadelphia, which the king's forces now occupied.

Despite Howe's victories, however, Tryon was by no means optimistic about the future of the American war in the autumn of 1777, and he had ceased predicting when the rebels would be forced to capitulate. He still believed that Britain could restore royal authority and crush the republican rebellion, but only if the king's generals would conduct what he now called "desolation warfare" against the property of rebel civilian leaders. By practicing what he preached, Tryon began to define this type of conflict in Westchester County and the lower Hudson River valley shortly after he returned to Kings Bridge from the Highlands. In late October and early November he unleashed Loyalist guerrilla groups such as De-Lancey's Cowboys and Captain Emmerich's regulars to conduct terror raids outside British lines upon rebel officials, or "committeemen," as Tryon contemptuously called them. In one of these raids, Tryon's troops burned parts of Tarrytown and in another the home and outbuildings of Colonel Ann Hawks Hays at Haverstraw, New Jersey.[22]

Immediately Tryon's "desolation warfare" evoked a powerful reaction among American revolutionaries, and General Samuel Holden Parsons taxed him for deliberately targeting prominent rebel civilian leaders for military action. Tryon responded, "Much as I abhor every principle of inhumanity or ungenerous conduct, I should, were I in more authority, burn every Committee Man's house within my reach, as I deem, those Agents the wretched instruments, of the continued calamities of this Country." In fact, he predicted, "Before the end of the next campaign, they will be torn to pieces by their own Countrymen whom they have forcibly dragged, in opposition to their principles and duty . . . to take up arms against their lawful Soveraign." Parsons, infuriated by Tryon's stance, compared his views to those of Nero, Caligula, and Judas Iscariot and condemned them as "Machiavellian Maxims." Meanwhile, some of Parsons's compatriots were retaliating by burning the home of General Oliver DeLancey and, according to one British soldier, "using his Wife and Daughter extremely ill."[23]

In December Tryon reopened his campaign to resign the governorship of New York. "I can now hardly be said," he mused to Germain, "to sit within the shade of my Government," and once more he declared his desire to leave the worthless office, sell his captaincy in the Foot Guards, and secure command of a regiment. Four months later, while recovering from a severe case of gout, he made the same solicitation but received from Germain in answer to both his letters only the cryptic remark that he would soon be hearing from Secretary at War Lord Barrington concerning his request for promotion. Nothing whatsoever was said about his petition to be rid of the governorship. Meanwhile, Tryon was maneuvering with General Howe to secure a regular British army commission for the campaign of 1778. Near the end of 1777, and thus the end of that year's fighting, Tryon had informed Howe that his commission as major general of the provincial troops had lapsed. He awaited Howe's orders for his next "command and destination in my British Rank, next to Major General Robertson." Howe, of course, refused to give Tryon such rank because it could come only from the king, offering him instead the same rank and command he had held in 1777.[24]

Tryon rejected Howe's proffer, grumbling to Ambrose Serle that he was "being slighted" by the commander in chief, and he again threatened to go home to England. Instead, however, he referred the entire matter of rank and command to Germain, with Howe's blessing, begging that his petition for a major generalship in the regular army and the colonelcy of a regiment be referred to the king. In early May, Barrington took the matter to His Majesty, who immediately granted Tryon's requests (with the caveat that his rank of major general was "for America only") and antedated his rank to January 1, 1776, so that he enjoyed more seniority in the army. His colonelcy was for the Seventieth Regiment. Hence, at long last he had achieved a position that was more precious to him than any colonial governorship could ever be. That point, of course, was ominous for Germain, who had hoped that Tryon would settle down in the now-hollow office of governor and not embarrass the North ministry by re-signing under circumstances that might be construed by the rebels as a weakening of British will in New York. To be sure, Tryon was to give more trouble over that matter in the future, but for the moment, he was de-lighted that General Clinton, who had recently superseded Howe in Phila-delphia as commander in chief in North America, had placed him in charge of all British troops on Long Island during Clinton's absence from New York.[25]

Although military matters were uppermost in Tryon's mind in 1778, he still was governor of New York and must exercise the truncated functions of that office. One of these that he particularly enjoyed was issuing letters of marque to privateers for predations on American shipping. In late March he announced to loyal New Yorkers his intention of issuing such letters as soon as he received permission from the Lords of Admiralty, and many enthusiastically commenced to fit out vessels for such service. Three weeks later, he received a request from Admiral Lord Howe to delay this process until the king could be informed of the impact that it would have on manning naval vessels, and Tryon agreed. But with Admiral James Gambier lending his weight to the idea, the Admiralty overrode Lord Howe's protests in August and granted Tryon the authority to issue letters of marque. The success of New York privateers over the next few months was one of Tryon's greatest joys in the entire American war. By March 1779, 150 vessels worth more than £600,000 sterling had been brought into New York harbor, thus confirming for Tryon that he had not been in error to suggest "the important utility of that depradatory commerce." But when Tryon sought support from British admirals for his policy, he did not always get complete cooperation. Lord Howe was only lukewarm in his assistance, and Sir George Collier refused any aid at all. Admirals Gambier and Marriot Arbuthnot, however, were entirely supportive and won Tryon's grateful thanks. As the American war spread and Britain began to fight first France in 1778 and then Spain a year later, the ministry granted Tryon power to issue letters of marque against those nations' ships as well.[26]

In April 1778 Tryon received from Germain copies of a resolution that

Lord North had laid before Parliament on February 17, which rescinded the laws that had led Americans to rebellion and renounced Britain's right to tax the colonies. It was unanimously adopted. With North's resolution came drafts of bills that had been prepared "in pursuance of it, and presented and read in the house." It was the king's will, Germain told Tryon, that these draft laws be copied and dispersed widely, so that Americans could quickly become aware of their contents and, presumably, cease hostilities and rejoin the empire. As Tryon read Germain's letter and the draft bills, he experienced a number of emotions, none particularly pleasant. Although it was not his nature to be cynical or sarcastic, he could hardly help feeling both after reading North's resolutions, as the ministry at this late date was finally accepting his recommendations of three years before not to tax the colonists. But he now had the sinking feeling that North's attempts at conciliation were too little too late; France had allied herself with the rebellious colonies and Britain found herself locked in a desperate worldwide conflict with her ancient foe. Moreover, Americans in early 1778 showed not the slightest sign that they would accept any terms from Britain short of independence—an attitude, in fact, that predated the French alliance. Finally, as Tryon recognized to his mortification, the form of the British proposals left them open to rebel ridicule, for as they stood they were not laws and had no force as such. It appeared that Lord North was in such haste to put his resolutions before the American people that he had sent out to the colonies only drafts of laws. Although everyone understood that they would almost automatically be ratified by Parliament eventually, at present they had not been.

In spite of his qualms, Tryon, ever the good soldier for the king, obeyed orders and began publicizing the proposals. On April 17 he forwarded copies to Governor Jonathan Trumbull of Connecticut, recommending that he distribute them to the inhabitants of his colony, and the same day wrote General Washington, asking that the Continental commander in chief circulate the resolutions in the American army. Trumbull spurned the proposals, pointing out that they were not official and that even if they were, they offered nothing to entice Americans back to the empire. He then went on to list all the barbarous and inhumane ways that Britons, such as Tryon himself, had mauled the people of his poor state and destroyed irrecoverably any feeling of loyalty toward the mother country. Then he suggested that in future Tryon send all diplomatic proposals to Congress, rather than to state governors, lest Tryon arouse suspicion that he was more interested in dividing Americans than in advancing the cause of peace.[27]

Tryon's response from Washington, and through Washington from the Continental Congress, was equally sterile and humiliating. The rebel commander in chief informed him on the twenty-fourth that he had sent North's resolutions to the army, confident that his soldiers' fidelity to the United States would not be shaken by them. Then he turned the tables on Tryon by requesting that Tryon promulgate a recent resolution of Congress among persons who were "objects of its operation," offering pardons to anyone who had warred against the United States but would surrender before June 10. At the same time, Washington wrote Governor William Livingston of New Jersey that he had "some difficulty" deciding whether Tryon's "impertinence, or his folly" were more obvious in his request. Tryon swallowed hard when he received the rebel general's letter, but he manfully proceeded to comply with the counterproposal. In the meantime, American newspapers, such as the *New Jersey Gazette*, seethed with indignation against Tryon for his attempts to "corrupt" Americans with his "nonsensical" propositions, and congressmen worked themselves into a white-hot fury against Tryon's machinations against republicanism. It was not surprising, therefore, that Tryon in May had even less success in getting Americans' attention when the official acts of Parliament ratifying North's proposals arrived in New York. As he had suspected all along, the entire exercise was a fruitless waste of time.[28]

While Tryon conducted business as governor in the year 1778, he also acted in his military capacity as commander of British forces on Long Island. In late June General Clinton returned to New York City after fighting his way across New Jersey from Philadelphia. During the following month he resolved to send Tryon eastward on Long Island at the head of 1,000 Loyalist volunteers to "secure the peacable behaviour of the disaffected inhabitants in that quarter, secure cattle for the army, and be in a position either to reinforce British troops in Rhode Island or make a descent upon the Connecticut coast, as need arose." In late July Tryon marched out of New York City with his troops, and over the next few days encamped at Mattituck and other towns "on the North side of the Island," all the time collecting "fat Cattle," administering oaths of loyalty to the inhabitants, and threatening those who refused the oath with forced removal "with their families and furniture to Connecticut." As Tryon later told Germain, "Not one of the whole chose the latter, even the hottest Rebels said, my proposal was generous, and took the oath." In

Sir Henry Clinton, by J. Smart. When Clinton replaced Howe as commander of the British army in America, Tryon was delighted, for he and Clinton were firm friends. However, Tryon became disillusioned with Clinton's conduct of operations, and their relationship became strained. (Courtesy of the William L. Clements Library, University of Michigan)

mid-August Tryon posted his men at Huntington, where he guarded the coast against enemy foraging raids from Connecticut.[29]

Later in August, Tryon became involved in Clinton's preparations to send reinforcements to Rhode Island, after American general John Sullivan attacked General Robert Pigot there. Admiral Lord Howe also responded to this enemy threat, sailing out with his fleet to engage French admiral Jean Baptiste Comte d'Estaing and thus open the waters of Long

Island Sound to Clinton's relieving transports. After the two fleets were caught in a storm and d'Estaing was forced to take his ships to Boston for repairs, Sullivan abandoned his attacks upon Pigot, just as Clinton arrived off Rhode Island with 4,000 troops. Tryon's part in these operations was to march his men back to Mattituck in preparation for embarkation for Rhode Island should the need arise. It did not, and he returned to New York City on September 4. Later in the month he made a quick "second excursion" eastward on Long Island, this time all the way to Montauck Point, swearing more citizens to "oaths of peaceable behaviour to His Majesty's Government."[30]

The British relief of Rhode Island and Tryon's Long Island ventures put a period to the campaign of 1778. As Tryon surveyed General Clinton's military activities during that short season of martial operations, he discerned neither genius nor the slightest indication that the new commander in chief intended to modify Howe's pusillanimous precepts upon humanitarian warfare. For that reason, Tryon during the summer had lost even more confidence in his friend's military abilities, and the relationship of these erstwhile bosom companions began to show strains. In early September Tryon ventured to lecture Germain on strategy, by implication criticizing Clinton's plans. "British forces on the Continent," he declared, "were never in so good a condition as at present to reconcile America to the dependency on Great Britain." From their bases in New York and Rhode Island, they ought to lash out with "such vigorous and hostile depredations on the continent as would oblige America to call aloud" for peace. In fact, by this late date in the war, only by such vicious warfare could Britain attain victory. However, should the army be weakened by sending detachments hither and yon for other purposes, as Clinton seemed prepared to do, thus forcing the British "to remain defensive on the Continent, I apprehend, American dependency on great Britain will be precarious indeed."[31]

These remarks, besides showing Tryon's growing ambivalence toward Clinton's abilities, indicate another point, that Tryon had added a major modification to his earlier views on desolation warfare. Until now he had always distinguished between rebel leaders and Americans in general when he advocated harsh warfare against his foes. The former, not the latter, had heretofore been the focus of his enmity because he had believed the population at large to be as much innocent victims of their leaders' malice as were Loyalists and Britons. But now he had decided that a significant proportion of Americans were also infected with rebellion and must be brought to heel by the same ruthless measures previously intended for their leaders. He expressed his new policy to Smith on September 5, 1778; "Forgive all that is past," he said, "and tell them that they shall have no quarter for Time to come." The seriousness with which he viewed his new plan was underscored in December, when he suggested to Germain that Indians and Canadians be unleashed upon America's frontiers, "unrestrained, excepting to Women and children." Tryon was also urging these ideas upon General Clinton, pleading with him in October 1778 for the command of a force of either 3,000 men, to conduct "menacing Descents on the Sound in Connecticut," or of 8,000 men to attack Danbury, while Clinton himself directed an assault upon the Highland forts. Clinton laughed at these proposals, said Tryon later to Smith, believing them to be "frantic." Instead, Clinton told Tryon that he was "satisfied with his Campaigne," and he ordered Tryon to join General Wilhelm Von Knyphausen's command "above King's Bridge." At the same time, Clinton flatly rejected any idea of a predatory war, leading Tryon to snap to Smith, "I see that he has narrow Views."[32]

But Tryon, ever the enthusiast for any new idea, would not give up urging Clinton to take the war to American civilians in late 1778. On November 15 he proposed that he be allowed to "take a Party" to Tarrytown "for the Seizure of the Stores there." Clinton refused his suggestion, declaring that he had no intention of "carrying a Torch thro' the Country, for he apprehended Mr. Tryon's Designs were to burn the Villages." The only proper plan of military operations, Clinton said, was to seize the Highland forts by conventional warfare with the bulk of his army, while smaller detachments made diversionary lodgments on the coast of Connecticut to draw General Washington's attention in that direction—but not with any aim to loot and pillage civilians. Tryon, disgusted at another rebuff from Clinton, fumed to Smith that Clinton "was imbarrassed by the Contraction of his Mind." Smith, however, had considerable sympathy for Clinton's views, asserting that Tryon was rushing "forward with a Contempt of Prudence." He "wants to be a Heroe," mused Smith, and refuses therefore to take into account the ideas of others who had much to lose if a risky venture failed. Smith also agreed with Clinton regarding Tryon's ideas about desolation warfare, thinking them "Odious."[33] With opposition to his schemes cropping up all about him in late 1778, Tryon for the moment belayed his enthusiasm for predatory warfare and bided his time. But he had by no means given up the idea.

Throughout 1778, as he conducted military operations on Long Island and attempted to fire Clinton's enthusiasm for warfare against civilians, Tryon renewed his appeals to Germain to be allowed to resign the governorship of New York. Now he was adding two new arguments to his usual repertoire. First, he must return to England because of his health, as during the past few months he had suffered recurring bouts of his old malady, the fevers contracted in North Carolina. Second, he needed to see to the education of his daughter, Margaret, who was seventeen years old and totally in the care of his wife, an "incompetent" when it came to such matters. Actually, his "fevers" were as much the product of his conflict with Clinton as they were of disease. As for his sudden solicitude for Margaret's education, it was merely an excuse; he knew he could depend upon his capable wife to oversee her course of instruction with full confidence. In July he reminded Germain that the peace commissioners sent out by the ministry to woo Americans back to loyalty had power to appoint a new governor. Therefore he wanted them to replace him and allow him to return home because, as he said, "I can no longer be serviceable in my civil line." He was also petitioning the king to allow him to exchange his governorship for a military position that would return him the same salary that he received in his civil office. When Germain replied with an exhortation that Tryon remain in America until "peace is made, or all hope [of subduing the rebels] is lost," Tryon reluctantly agreed to stay in New York "a certain time longer" in "zealous obedience" to his sovereign's wishes. But his heart was not in it.[34]

Tryon was not a happy man in the winter of 1778–79, for it seemed to him that he would never rid himself of the worthless office of the governorship. But just when things looked their worst, he received from Germain in the spring of 1779 the welcome news that the king had lifted his burden, granting him leave to return to England for restoration of his health as soon as his replacement, General James Robertson, who had gone back to England in 1778, could return to New York. But regarding Tryon's request to exchange his civil office for a military one with the same pay, Germain could make no commitments. Perhaps upon his arrival in London, Tryon could convince the king that such a dispensation was just and proper. Tryon replied that these arrangements suited him fine, except that now the burden of civil government was about to be eased, he suddenly felt vigorous enough to remain in America as a soldier during the following campaign. Also, he quickly forgot his daughter's education. No matter how "warm & sanguine my wishes to re-visit my native country & family," he declared, "I have not formed the least idea, in the present momentous period of the war," to walk away from "what may very possibly be a decisive Campaign." Neither the king nor Germain objected to this plan, as the governor had to await Robertson's arrival in any case (and it was not at all certain when that gentleman would depart for his new post). Tryon therefore was granted leave to remain in America during the next few months.[35]

CHAPTER TEN

The Fruits of Desolation Warfare

The reason General Tryon suddenly decided that he would like to take part in one more season of campaigning, despite his gloomy begging to be allowed to return home only a short time before, was his wish to implement his theories of desolation warfare. So strong was this desire that he now convinced himself that he would be able to work with General Clinton, despite their differences, and that Clinton would somehow relent and give him a chance to conduct independent operations as a part of the campaign of 1779. The previous November, Clinton had ordered 3,500 men southward from New York to join Augustine Prevost for military maneuvers against Savannah, Georgia, and although Tryon thought this dispersal of Clinton's strength a mistake, he was pleased when Clinton offered him command of the expedition. But he could not avail himself of this opportunity due to fears of reawakening his dormant fevers, so the command was given to Lieutenant Colonel Archibald Campbell. In February 1779, when Clinton contemplated sending an even larger reinforcement to the South (which he finally did not dispatch), he once more asked Tryon to take charge and was once more turned down, for the same reason. At the end of the month, Tryon was delighted when Clinton gave him command of a less health-threatening but also less important expedition to West Greenwich, a town on the Connecticut seacoast more popularly known as Horseneck, for the purpose of destroying rebel stores.[1]

On the morning of February 25, Tryon left Kings Bridge at the head of five regiments plus Emmerich's chasseurs and a detachment of royal artillery to carry out his assigned task. Proceeding fifty miles to West Greenwich without incident, he arrived there on the following morning. As he entered the town, his troops were fired upon by American militiamen under command of General Israel Putnam, but soon he put the enemy to flight. He then seized and disabled three artillery pieces and directed the Seventeenth Regiment to proceed on to Greenwich and destroy some salt pans and three small vessels in the harbor. Shortly after this detachment rejoined him at two o'clock in the afternoon, Tryon received intelligence that an enemy force of 1,000 militiamen was collecting in the neighborhood, and therefore he commenced his return march to New York City. Throughout the afternoon he pushed his troops forward, crossing many rugged defiles, while all the time enemy skirmishers fired upon the rear of his column. But at dusk, as he crossed the border into New York, the Connecticut militia ceased its pursuit, and Tryon ordered his men to fall out and rest. Next day he completed his march back to British lines at Kings Bridge, arriving without further incident.[2]

Not long after his raid on West Greenwich, Tryon's short-lived spell of good relations with General Clinton came to an abrupt halt, and the two men recommenced their carping at one another. The trouble began when Clinton lost his temper over Tryon's personnel losses on the Horseneck expedition, accusing Tryon of "adventuring" and claiming that two killed and nine wounded were excessively high casualties. Clinton was also upset that Tryon, as governor, was issuing proclamations of pardon to rebels without his advice or approval. Commenting upon Clinton's behavior, Smith remarked, "What Marks of a narrow-minded Jealousy! What can be expected from such a Character? What does he attempt? Nothing, and therefore is impatient at Tryon's Spirit and Activity." For his part, Tryon declared his astonishment at Clinton's "Torpor" and began to rant about all that he could accomplish on the Connecticut coast if he were given command of 3,000 men. When Clinton finally did decide to act in late May, by launching an expedition against Stony and Verplanck's points on the Hudson River, he refused to take Tryon with him. "The Governor," said Smith, "is vastly mortified by being left at Home."[3]

During Clinton's absence, Tryon improved his time by reflecting upon his terroristic military strategy, and by late June he had come up with a new idea. When his commander in chief returned, Tryon proposed that Loyalist soldiers, who were organizing themselves under the name Associated Loyalists, be officially sanctioned under command of William Franklin, royal governor of New Jersey, to raid the Connecticut coast in guerrilla-type hit-and-run operations. According to Tryon's thinking, these troops would be given the right to keep all "the plunder they take, which is to be only from rebels," and although he did not say so, he thought they should also be allowed to wreak vengeance upon rebel civilians. When

Tryon told Smith about this scheme, the latter was appalled at the idea and would have nothing to do with it. When he suggested it to Clinton, the commander in chief rejected it on grounds that "the Nature of such a Service" was too horrible for him to contemplate.[4]

Finally, in July 1779 Tryon was given the opportunity to test his theories of desolation warfare on a fairly large scale. At that time, Clinton drew up a plan of operations in which Tryon, assisted by Sir George Collier's fleet, would conduct raids along the Connecticut coast specifically designed to draw General Washington's army eastward out of the Highlands. Once the Continental forces were dislodged from their strong defensive positions, Clinton would occupy the American camp at Middlebrook, New Jersey, destroy rebel supply depots at Trenton and Easton, and force Washington to march back and defend these positions. Thereupon, the rebel commander would be brought to a general action, his army smashed, and the rebellion crushed. It is not clear what admonitions Clinton gave Tryon about how he was to conduct himself during those raids, but given Clinton's abhorrence of warfare against civilians it seems likely that he warned Tryon against such attacks. Afterward, Clinton certainly insisted that Tryon's destructiveness was contrary to both his opinions and his orders. "I have been a *buccaneer* already too long," he declared; "I detest that sort of War." However, his written instructions to Tryon on the Connecticut operation neither confirm nor repudiate his assertions; they were entirely silent upon the matter. As for Tryon, he "admitted the first but denied the last." The commander in chief, he said, "knew his Opinion to be for burning, and on one Occasion when he [Tryon] ask'd for Orders to burn, Sir Henry replied, 'I know you will if I don't forbid it.'" But he had not forbidden burning, and Tryon took the silence to mean that desolation warfare had been approved, at least tacitly. William Smith concluded that "Sir Henry wished the Conflagrations, and yet not to be answerable for them."[5]

Whatever the case, General Tryon on July 3 departed New York City with 2,600 men, under protection of Collier's warships, for the Connecticut adventure. His first division, under Brigadier General George Garth, was comprised of the Fifty-fourth Regiment, the light infantry companies of the Guards, the Fusiliers, and a detachment of *Jägers*, while his own division was made up of the Hessian Landgrave regiment, the Royal Welch Fusiliers, and the King's American Regiment. Early on the fifth, the fleet anchored in New Haven harbor off the town of West Haven, and the two divisions landed. General Garth, with light opposition from some militiamen, seized New Haven under orders from Tryon to burn the place, but instead he only destroyed public stores, some vessels in the harbor, and a few pieces of ordnance. Then he seized six field pieces and an armed privateer for use by the British forces. Meanwhile, Tryon had captured East Haven with minimal resistance from a few rebel militiamen. By that time night was fast approaching, and both divisions settled in for some much-needed rest.[6]

The following afternoon, Tryon, rejoined by Garth at East Haven, reembarked his troops and sailed with Collier eastward toward Fairfield. Landing there on the eighth, Tryon occupied the village without much opposition from the Americans; the inhabitants had fled and the militia had shown little stomach for a fight with British regulars. The soldiers then proceeded to plunder private houses of any goods that struck their fancy and to set fire to 83 dwellings, 2 churches, 54 barns, 47 storehouses, 2 schoolhouses, the courthouse, and the jail—ostensibly, as Tryon later said, in retaliation for his troops having been fired upon by Americans from some of those buildings. After another night on shore in an armed camp, Tryon and his booty-laden troopers returned to their ships and sailed across Long Island Sound to Huntington, New York. There he allowed his command two days to rest and resupply for further adventures, and on July 11 he sailed out to do more damage to rebel civilians' property in Connecticut.[7]

That evening, Tryon's forces anchored in the Bay of Norwalk, and at nine o'clock commenced landing, the commander's division on the east side of Norwalk harbor and Garth's on the west. As these operations were not finished until three o'clock the following morning, the soldiers rested until daybreak, then effected a junction, under fire from fifty enemy militiamen, at about eight o'clock on the twelfth. Tryon thereupon ordered Garth to clear the enemy from his front, which the brigadier easily did with the Fusiliers and the Guards light infantry, and Tryon proceeded to take possession of Norwalk village. His soldiers again were set to the task of destruction, burning most of the village and stealing more than $50,000 worth of rebel private property. Many salt pans, whaleboats, magazines, stores, and small vessels in the harbor were destroyed or confiscated. This work done, Tryon returned to his ships, sailed again to Huntington, and commenced refitting for further raids before receiving orders from Clinton to cease operations and return to New York City. On July 14 Tryon reported to his commander in chief that casualties incurred during all his operations since the third were 26 killed, 90 wounded, and 32 missing.[8]

Strategically, Tryon's raids on the Connecticut coast were a dismal failure. On July 9 Clinton, in order to take advantage of Washington's expected dash eastward with his forces to fend off Tryon, massed his army at Mamaroneck and Byram's Bridge, south of White Plains. But Washington did not dash. Writing to Governor Trumbull, who was putting intense pressure on him to save Connecticut's seacoast towns from Tryon's marauding, Washington on July 12 was solicitous of Trumbull's feelings but insisted that he must guard the Hudson River. Seeing through Clinton's plan, he mused that Tryon was bait to lure him eastward. In fact, on the night of July 15–16, Americans turned the tables on Clinton, for at that time Anthony Wayne captured Stony Point on the Hudson River, at least in part because Clinton had reduced the garrison there and at Verplanck's Point to provide Tryon with adequate forces for his Connecticut raids. "What a Blunder to leave a Weak Garrison to be taken," Smith moaned, "which not only discredits the King's Arms but will prevent Connecticut from quarreling with Washington for not coming to their Relief!"[9]

As he must have anticipated, Tryon unleashed a storm of protest and indignation against himself by conducting his predatory raids on Connecticut's seacoast towns. Americans led the way, with Washington contemptuously dismissing "the intrepid and Magnanimous Tryon" as a soldier who made war on "Women and Children" in order to add "fresh lustre to [British] Arms and dignity to [his] King." Silas Deane condemned Tryon's "atrocious" acts of "barbarity," claiming they were "almost beyond description," and he was echoed by a score of other Americans, great and humble, who condemned Tryon's warfare upon citizens instead of armies.[10] Many of Tryon's British compatriots joined the rebels in castigating their comrade for prosecuting desolation warfare. John Pownall in London mused to Dartmouth, "What could have induced our friend Tryon to countenance or rather command the wanton severitys, to use no harsher expression, of which the innocent inhabitants of Fairfield . . . so loudly complain?" As for General Clinton, he was indignant at Tryon for acting "contrary to his . . . Orders" and demanded that his subordinate submit a written report justifying "the burning as well as he can." Tryon, coolly insisting to Clinton that the commander in chief was attempting to change his orders after the fact, willingly agreed to produce such an apologia, and he turned to his old friend Smith for assistance in its composition.[11]

On July 20 Tryon in a dignified letter made his case to Clinton and the world for having burned Fairfield and Norwalk. Admitting regret that two churches had been destroyed inadvertently in Fairfield, he nevertheless insisted that the rebels had brought this desolation upon themselves by unjustly defying the sovereignty of their king. Having illegally unleashed the terror of war upon others, they now wished to avoid "decisive actions" with the British, preserving their own property intact and forcing Britain to spend herself into impotent penury. "I wish," he said unrepentantly, "to detect this delusion . . . if possible without injury to the loyalists," and he concluded that he apprehended "no mischief to the public from the irritation of a few in rebellion if a general terror and despondency can be awakened among a people already divided . . . and easily impressible."[12] With these remarks Tryon, who long had prided himself on his ability to sense the mood of Americans and who had succeeded so admirably in 1775, showed that he was losing touch with the revolutionaries. His terroristic coercion was doomed to failure, for the whole idea was based upon a false premise about the colonial mentality. His burning raids, instead of inculcating "terror and despondency" among "easily impressible" rebels, only confirmed them in their belief that Britain was irremediably evil and made them ten times more determined to throw off "English tyranny." Tryon, basically a humane and intelligent man, who by his own lights had the best interests of America at heart, had allowed the frustrations of the American war to blind him to the realities of coercive warfare, both in terms of human decency and practical political consequences.

If Tryon's desolation warfare impressed almost no one on either side of the conflict in America—except some Loyalists and military "hard liners"—it was found acceptable by the king and ministry. On November 4 Germain gave approbation to Tryon's conduct, despite his full knowledge that Clinton thought such warfare madness and grist for the mills of opposition politicians in the House of Commons. Clinton, refusing to conciliate Tryon simply because he had the ear of Germain, continued to distrust his subordinate and to refuse him any significant military command for the remainder of Tryon's tenure in America. "Tryon," said Clinton to Smith, "is clear enough, but I cannot make him obey Orders. He will always expose himself to Risks." Tryon, for his part, continued to think ill of Clinton, declaring to Smith in August, "His Station is too vast for his Capacity," and in September, "His Mind is manifestly imbarrassed," and in October, "His Procrastinating disposition . . . leaves everything to to Morrow." Although Tryon did write Clinton in November to declare his "strong affectionate friendship," the two men were never again close. Even though Tryon had lost confidence in Clinton as commander in chief, he was not pleased when Charles Lord Cornwallis, who recently arrived from England, was touted for a time by a war-weary Clinton as a potential new commander in chief. Tryon believed Cornwallis only "a Man of Modest Form," too constricted by "establish'd Rules upon General Theory" ever to "prosecute the War with Reference to the Nature of the Country."[13]

In December Tryon was pleased when General Clinton removed himself from New York for a time by taking command of British troops in the South. During his absence, Clinton gave Knyphausen overall command of British and Hessian forces in New York City, and Knyphausen with Clinton's approval appointed Tryon to command only British troops. Soon, Smith reported, Tryon was being fawned over by Britons seeking to curry his favor, and Roger Morris was even addressing him as "the *Commander in Chief*." But Tryon did not allow this empty flattery to go to his head, knowing as he did who actually controlled things while Clinton was away. Instead, he launched with his usual vigor into the business of administering his command and of entertaining. In early December Baron and Mrs. Wilhelm Von Riedesel arrived in New York, where the baron, who had been captured at Saratoga in 1777, hoped to arrange his exchange. Tryon was living at his headquarters on Long Island at the time, and he gave the Riedesels use of his home on Manhattan during their stay. Over the next few months, Tryon became friendly with this couple, and when he departed for England in 1780 he gave Mrs. Riedesel the furnishings of his house as a gift.[14]

Problems with the weather plagued Tryon during the winter of 1779–80, for he and his British comrades were experiencing some of the severest temperatures ever known in America. Biting winds out of the Arctic brought four feet of snow, frozen harbors around New York, and temperatures fifty degrees below what Britons were accustomed to in their milder homeland. On a number of occasions, firewood ran low in the military camps and the city, and Tryon suffered the cold along with everyone else. All he could do personally was provide as much free firewood for the poor as he could procure. Fortunately, the weather was not so harsh as to produce any major calamities in his command, but in mid-January 1780 it did freeze the waters around New York City sufficiently to allow American general William Alexander Lord Stirling to carry out an ineffectual raid across the ice against Staten Island.[15]

In the early months of 1780, Tryon was kept busy reading intelligence reports forwarded to him by William Smith, who had been appointed upon Tryon's recommendation intelligence chief for the British high command. The burden of this information was that the revolution was about to collapse, that Washington's army was teetering on the edge of disbanding, and that American merchants despised rebel leaders. Tryon, without taking much of this intelligence seriously, passed on what he considered most important to Germain. On January 17 he ordered six blockhouses constructed on the Hudson River in preparation "for an Ascent . . . in the Spring." In February he was asked by General William Phillips, who had been taken captive at Saratoga in 1777, to arrange a prisoner exchange, but he had to refuse, for Clinton, before his departure southward, had specifically ordered Tryon not to get involved in that business. When General James Pattison asked him on February 22 for permission to organize militia forces for defense of New York, he gave his hearty assent and support.[16]

Tryon was stricken with a serious case of fever in early March and was forced to his bed for a month. During his recuperation, he was able at last to welcome General Robertson, his successor as governor, to his new post and to give up the burdens of civil office entirely. However, now that he was free to depart America for England, he had second thoughts about abandoning his military responsibilities, especially with another campaign season about to open. He was still disgusted with Clinton's leadership of the British army and in fact had recently been offended again. Not only had Clinton just informed him that Robertson would immediately take precedence over him in military rank, but also the commander in chief had withheld thanks from him for his services during the previous winter. Although Tryon thought about contesting Clinton's ruling on Robertson, he was dissuaded by Smith from doing so. "He acquiesces," said Smith, "but is amazingly hurt." The commander in chief, Tryon told Smith, was "wild and inconsiderate." Despite Clinton's latest slight, Tryon was "gloomy at the Thought" of having "his Leave to go Home," and when six months later he finally did depart for England, he confessed to Smith on his last day in America a "Reluctance . . . to leave this Country." Smith, believing Tryon needed to get away from the heartbreak of watching the disintegration of all he had worked for in public life over the last sixteen years, wisely declared, "He will be the happier for it, at least for a Time."[17]

While he lay sick in bed, Tryon reflected upon many things besides his inevitable departure for home and his anger at Clinton. General Robertson, he told Smith, had asked him for no information since he had taken office regarding the business of New York's government. General Knyphausen was neglectful of planning summer operations for the British army. Governor Franklin of New Jersey was too "fond of low Company" and did not pay attention to the king's business. Listening to this litany of complaints, Smith with the condescension of a warm friend, mused, "I allow Scope to the Mortifications all Men feel in a Loss of Office." One thing that Smith was pleased with, however, was that the general now had become "heartily reconciled to moderate Measures" in the war against the rebels and seemed penitential about his operations against Connecticut in the previous year. Tryon only thought "himself lucky in having the King's Approbation" as a shield against the malice of his foes. His one profound regret in all the American business was the ministry's "coming so tardily into liberal Sentiments. They would not hear him when in England for suggesting the Cessation of the taxing Claims." Although he was still "a flaming Loyalist," he was no longer ardent for "the Violence of the Sword" as the only, or even the likely, mode for ending the rebellion.[18]

General Tryon was fully recovered from his illness by early May, and he decided to delay his departure from America until some time late in 1780. Rumors were circulating that Knyphausen was planning an expedition into New Jersey against rebels whose grip supposedly was weakening upon the mass of citizens, and if the tales were true, Tryon wanted to join him. During the previous February, Tryon had received intelligence from a spy in New Jersey, known only as AZ, encouraging a massive British show of force in that province in the near future. Tryon had passed this information on to Knyphausen and Germain, with suggestions that active British military operations might raise the flagging spirits of New York Loyalists. On May 22 Tryon volunteered his services to Knyphausen but was told that at present "only little Parties" were to be sent out. Even rumors of war, however, were enough to rouse Tryon's fighting blood, and when in early June Knyphausen asked him to join, as a volunteer without field command, a large excursion planned to depart Staten Island on the sixth, Tryon immediately accepted.[19]

After assembling a force of 5,000 men under Generals Edward Mathew and Thomas Sterling, Knyphausen, with Tryon accompanying him, landed his forces at Elizabethtown. Washington was too weak to oppose this British force directly, so he met it with large militia units, which by the pertinacity of their opposition instantly disabused Tryon and his colleagues of all the "intelligence" they had received about Americans being disaffected from the republican cause. Nevertheless, the militia were easily swept aside, and Knyphausen drove forward through Connecticut Farms, which he put to the torch. As the British forces approached Springfield, they were once again opposed by militiamen, as well as Continental army detachments, even though British agents had told Tryon earlier that Washington's army was "mutinous." Knyphausen now saw that "the information upon which the expedition had been undertaken" was false, and he marched back to Elizabethtown and prepared to ferry his forces to Staten Island. After some thought, however, he decided to remain in New Jersey "for the credit of the British arms," so his forces entrenched themselves and sat down to await his further orders. Tryon, who thus far had taken no active part in the fighting in New Jersey, also encamped and bided his time until Knyphausen decided what more to do.[20]

After a tedious wait of two weeks, Tryon got his chance for more action when on June 23 Knyphausen marched back toward Springfield, harassed in his advance by rebel militiamen. As he neared the town, Knyphausen divided his forces, sending Mathew with half his men to the right on Vauxhall road with orders to turn the Americans left, himself taking the other half of his army, with Tryon in attendance, directly toward Springfield against the enemy forces of Nathanael Greene. While Mathew smashed through rebel troops at Vauxhall Bridge, Knyphausen attacked the main rebel force and compelled it to withdraw to a stronger position northwest of Springfield. Thereupon, Knyphausen, realizing that "every mile of future march" into New Jersey "would be no less obstinately resisted" than the last few, began his withdrawal to Elizabethtown after burning most of Springfield. During their retreat, the British troops were harassed on their flanks by American militiamen, but they got back to Elizabethtown in good order. General Tryon, according to a later comment by William Smith, "was very active [during all these maneuvers] and much in Danger," but Smith had learned this information from others, as "Tryon is modest himself" and "did not lisp a Syllable of that Nature."[21]

When Knyphausen evacuated New Jersey on the evening of June 23, Tryon returned to New York and became "Hors de Combat," as Smith put it. In fact, although Tryon did not know it at the time, he had taken part in his last military campaigning and combat. General Clinton, having just returned to the city from successful operations in South Carolina, gave no indication of employing Tryon further for the summer. According to Smith, the commander in chief made this point abundantly clear when he sent Mathew up the Hudson River "with a Command," even though Tryon was senior in rank. "What is the Language of this Conduct but that he prefers Mathew to Tryon for Service here?" Smith concluded. So Tryon returned to the command of his old provincial units and Hessians at Kings Bridge, where he spent the next two months in peace and quiet, except for once having to break camp and march southward on Manhattan because Washington appeared, incorrectly as it turned out, to be massing troops at Tappan for an assault on British lines.[22]

By September 1780 Tryon could think of no more excuses to linger in America, and he prepared for a final departure for the British Isles. After many farewells to friends and acquaintances, but especially to his close comrade, William Smith, Tryon on September 2 boarded a British transport, part of a "Large Fleet returning to Europe," in company with Generals Mathew and Pattison, Lieutenant Colonel William Faucitt, Lord and Lady William Cathcart, and many other notables. Two days later, Tryon's ship "fell down the harbor" with the fleet, and by nightfall the general had lost sight of the country where he had made whatever reputation he now or ever would possess as a public figure. His arrival home was certainly a partial compensation for what he had left behind, for he was welcomed by his wife and daughter, whom he had not seen for almost five years, and by his many relatives, friends, and intimates in London.[23]

Settling with his family into their comfortable home on Upper Grosvenor Street, Tryon in late 1780 commenced a new phase of an already varied life, that of a rich, leisured gentleman with time to pursue his interests without having to earn his bread. Although he had been compelled to spend some of his wife's fortune of £30,000 in America, most of his estate had remained intact during his years as a colonial governor and general. Moreover, after years of appeals to the Treasury for recompense of his American expenses and his losses when the New York Governor's Mansion burned in 1773, Tryon received £8,000 from public funds in 1782. Also, he was awarded £5,511 2s. 5d. for extraordinary expenses incurred while serving as royal governor of New York during the American war. A year later, he asked for even more money, £4,294 5s. 9d., as compensation for landed property that he lost in North Carolina and New York when the legislatures of those two states attained his estates. The Treasury, however, was not willing to award him these monies, and so his vast landholding of 18,640 acres, plus building lots and houses in Hillsborough, New Bern, and New York City, were lost. Nevertheless, by 1786 his income from all his other assets was £2,300 per year, enough to provide himself, his wife, and daughter with a sumptuous, elegant standard of living.[24]

One of the first things Tryon did after arriving in London was reacquaint himself with surviving members of his family. Always proud of his family's lineage, he was inordinately fond of showing visitors to his London home a portrait of Robert Devereux, earl of Essex, from whom his mother's family was descended. In 1781 Tryon unpacked this picture, which had belonged to his father and had been in storage for years, and hung it in a prominent place. Both his brothers, the Reverend Dr. Charles Tryon and Robert Tryon, were many years dead, but Charles's widow and natural daughter still survived, as did Tryon's three sisters, Mary, Sophia, and Ann. Mary, one of Queen Charlotte's maids of honor, was a lively lady in company and passed on to Tryon juicy tidbits of court gossip—such as the story that the king was so distressed in 1782 at the way the American war was going that he was often "up all Night walking his Room, & without laying off his Cloaths." Tryon and his wife entertained all these relatives in their home whenever possible, but Mary, who lived at St. James's Palace, found it difficult to work her schedule around the queen's and often of an evening had to accompany Her Majesty to Drury Lane Theatre.[25]

Tryon had one other family member, his illegitimate daughter, Elizabeth, whom he did not invite to Upper Grosvenor Street despite his "strong Affection" for her. Elizabeth, who had "a grateful Simplicity" that appealed to Tryon's "Pride & Liberality," had made an unhappy marriage with a butcher named James Saunders, separated from him, and moved back to her mother's home at Stony Stratford, Northampton, with her two sons and a daughter. In 1785 Elizabeth was attempting to make the separation permanent, and Tryon, to assist her in these proceedings, enlisted the aid of William Smith, who had come to London as a Loyalist refugee. Elizabeth Saunders, meantime, was lodged at her father's expense on Red Lion Street. After considerable negotiating, Smith got James Saunders to accept an arrangement whereby Tryon paid him £20 per year for life, the first ten years' payments to be advanced in a lump sum of £200, in return for which he bonded himself never to bother his wife and family again. Smith was impressed by Tryon's love and concern for Elizabeth Saunders; "His heart," said Smith, "is in this Business & it raises my Opinion of [him]." Tryon, in appreciation for Smith's assistance in this matter, paid him £100 and presented him with a beautifully wrought silver cream and sugar set, valued at £10 19s. 7d.[26]

Smith was also much impressed with the young woman. "She has plain Sense and an amiable Temper," he said, "and is neat & upon the whole comely. . . . With a good Education [she] had been a fine Woman." Even as things stood, she was "infinitely more like him [her father] than Miss

[Margaret] Tryon, & the better Person of the Two." The legitimate Miss Tryon, who in Smith's eyes suffered in comparison with her half sister, was of marriageable age and heiress to a fortune, but she seemed unlucky in love. Since her arrival in London, she had been courted by a nobleman with an annual income of £6,000, but she had refused his offer of marriage because he was sixteen years her elder. Later she became enamored of Mr. George Villars, member of Parliament and youngest son of Thomas Villars, earl of Clarendon, with whom she became acquainted when members of the Villars family came to dine at Tryon's home. Young Villars, however, did not reciprocate her affection, and in fact was slightful of and inattentive toward her, perhaps because he knew that his mother, Lady Clarendon, disliked the liaison. Tryon was of two minds about Margaret's attachment to Villars, worried on the one hand that his daughter was being hurt by a snobbish young cad but believing on the other hand that a marriage between a Villars and a Tryon "could not be better for himself" from a practical and economic standpoint. The relationship finally was broken off, and when Miss Margaret Tryon died prematurely in 1791, she was still unmarried and residing in the Tryon family household.[27]

Tryon and his wife were lavish entertainers on the London social scene during the 1780s, inviting scores of rich and highborn guests to dinner parties large and small in their elegant Mayfair home. Besides Smith, who seemed almost to live with the Tryons because he was so often their dinner guest, and the Villars, whom Tryon cultivated for a number of reasons other than his daughter's love for young George Villars, Tryon and his wife welcomed many famous and influential persons to dine with them. Among these were high-ranking military officers such as Lord Jeffery Amherst, Generals John Forbes and Edward Mathew, Sir Guy Carleton, and Colonel Thomas Carleton, his brother. Also in attendance were H. T. Cramahé, former lieutenant governor of Canada, Sir George Howard, Sir Charles Gould, Mrs. Tryon's cousin Fountain Elwin, and a host of other men and women of rank and position in the British imperial establishment. Naturally these ladies and gentlemen reciprocated the Tryons' hospitality, and thus the general and his wife were constantly visiting friends' homes, both in London and in the country round about, especially Bath, Yarmouth, Tunbridge Wells, Norfolk, and Suffolk. In 1783 Tryon was particularly pleased by a visit from his old friends Baron and Mrs. Riedesel, who stopped in London for a time on their way home to Germany from America.[28]

As a former royal governor of two American provinces, Tryon had personal acquaintances to cultivate and affairs to see to in London Court and government circles, while Mrs. Tryon did the best she could to amuse herself with other diversions. He often attended the king's levees, wherein fifty or sixty persons crowded themselves into a receiving room at St. James's Palace and awaited their chance to kiss the monarch's hand and have a few words with him. On one occasion Tryon was present when John Wilkes, who many years ago had quarreled with the king, attended court for the first time since the falling out and was greeted by the royal personage without incident. Everyone, including Tryon, used these occasions to gauge the mien of George III and try to determine from that and from court gossip which way the political winds were blowing. The king's levees were always great social affairs, allowing all in attendance to rub elbows and hobnob with the richest and most important men in the empire. Tryon also faithfully attended other, lesser levees, given by important government officers such as the younger William Pitt.[29]

During his retirement, Tryon took an almost obsessive interest in the fate of persons mighty and inconsequential who in one way or another had suffered personal loss from the American Revolution and the resultant British war against the rebels. From his comfortable position in London, he followed first the course of the conflict in its last agonies and second the parliamentary and diplomatic maneuvering in 1782–83 that finally led to Britain's granting independence and recognition to the United States of America. These events, so glorious to the triumphant American republicans, were from Tryon's viewpoint unmitigated disasters, resulting in destitution and often homelessness for many thousands of Loyalist colonials who had remained true to king and empire to the bitter end. Consequently, he did everything within his power for the remainder of his life to requite the sufferings of these unfortunates. Mostly his efforts took the form of recommending to the British Commissioners for American Claims and other London officials those whom he felt merited assistance from the Crown for past services. Some of these persons were John Edge Tomlinson and John Hamilton, New Bern merchants; Henry Eustace McCulloh and Lewis Henry DeRosset, former members of the North Carolina Council; Mrs. Margaret Murray, widow of Councillor James Murray; Arthur Benning, a North Carolina militia officer; William Williams, a New Yorker who had been fined £1,100 New York currency by a rebel jury in 1780; and Colonel Fanning, Lieutenant Colonel Emmerich, and Montfort Browne, all of whom had served under Tryon in the war.[30]

Tryon also put an enormous amount of time and effort into soliciting compensation for his old friend Smith, whom he privately advised and openly promoted to friends in government from 1781 to 1786 as a gentleman worthy of attention and financial recompense. Even before Smith came to England in 1783, he had corresponded with Tryon from New York at great length about various issues, but especially about his attempts to have Vermont annexed to Canada and thus snatched from the clutches of American republicans. Although Tryon liked Smith's efforts and intervened with Shelburne in London to urge the notions of his "confidential friend" upon the ministry, nothing came of them. In the end, Tryon was delighted that Smith received from the British government a monetary reward—although not the £66,999 sterling he had requested—as well as appointment to be chief justice of Quebec and Lower Canada. When Smith departed England for his new post, Tryon said good-bye to a man who had been one of his closest confidants and friends for more than a decade.[31]

Despite his retirement in 1780 from wartime service as a major general in the American conflict, Tryon, still a military man at heart, continued to direct the affairs of his Seventieth Regiment, which was stationed in the colonies. He attended to matters of promotion and supply, and in 1783 he gave directions to William Fawcett, regimental adjutant general, to bring the Seventieth Regiment home for disbandment. The year before, Tryon had been promoted lieutenant general in the British army, and in 1784, at the behest of the king, he became colonel of the Twenty-ninth Regiment upon the death of General William Evelyn. That regiment was in Canada, and Tryon wrote Governor Haldimand asking for information about its physical condition and officers. He also ordered Lieutenant John Enys of the Twenty-ninth Regiment, who then resided in England, "to join the Regt. in America." During the remainder of his life, he kept in touch with the affairs of his regiment, mostly by naming young officers who had promise or connections to vacancies in the officers' ranks.[32]

In late 1787 Tryon, although still a relatively young man at the age of 58, felt twinges of mortality as a result of some unspecified illness and proceeded to draw up his will. In this document he made generous provision for his daughter Margaret, his three sisters, Mary, Sophia, and Ann, and his close friends Edmund Fanning, Fountain Elwin, and Robert Palmer. Less handsomely he remembered Mary Stanton, the mother of his illegitimate daughter, as well as Elizabeth, the daughter, and her younger son, William Saunders. But he left the bulk of his estate to his "ever affectionate wife," Margaret Wake Tryon, and to her heirs. That business completed, he composed himself in his elegant town house on Upper Grosvenor Street for his approaching death, which came on January 27, 1788. Shortly thereafter, he was entombed at St. Mary's Church, Twickenham, Middlesex, by an Anglican priest who committed his soul to eternity with the solemn and awe-inspiring words of the church's burial liturgy.[33]

Within days of his demise, Tryon's obituary appeared in *Gentleman's Magazine*, relating in bombastic fashion his political and military career in America. First, said his eulogist, Tryon had suppressed "rising seeds of revolt in North Carolina" and had come to be seen by the Carolinians as a "friend and protector, whose jurisprudence breathed as much of paternal tenderness, as of legislative authority." Then, having accomplished these prodigies in the South, Tryon had moved on to New York, where he found open to him "a wider field of action" for his "superior powers of wisdom and philanthropy." These he had "unceasingly exerted for the real welfare of the colonists," exercising munificence even to the least of his charges and earning "the heartfelt gratitude . . . [of] every branch of the community." Therefore, "the name of *Tryon* [will be] revered across the Atlantic while virtue and sensibility remain," as it also would among his private circle of family and friends, where he had diffused "honor and happiness in an extensive circle."[34]

Had the writer of Tryon's obituary confined himself to analyzing the man's career up to the outbreak of the American rebellion, his comments would not have been far off the mark. Until that time, William Tryon did indeed bask in considerable popularity among all ranks of people in North Carolina and New York, despite the fact that the Regulators in western North Carolina and some settlers in the Hampshire Grants found him exceptionable. Colonists seemed to admire Governor Tryon's insistence upon promoting the king's interests, even though his devotion to duty sometimes put him at odds with their own interests, especially during the Stamp Act and tea crises. The secret of Tryon's success during those extremely difficult times was that he understood American thinking on basic constitutional issues such as taxation, finance, and trade policy. He knew how far he could push Crown interests before inviting outright rebellion and endangering the very interests he was trying to protect. Hence, when he sensed that he was near that breaking point, he would relent, even if in the process he sometimes violated the letter of his royal instructions. This was the principle Tryon had attempted to implement with his paper money policies in North Carolina, his land grant policies in both North Carolina and New York, and his pleas to king and ministry in 1775 to give up their insistence on taxing Americans for revenue. Had his wise and flexible administrative programs been given a more sympathetic hearing in London, there may never have been such widespread rebellion among the colonists in the mid-1770s. Instead, the British government insisted upon stubborn adherence to parliamentary laws and then coercion, and Tryon, out of devotion to the Crown, reluctantly went along (only later becoming too optimistic about Britain's chances). Therefore, he saw his popularity among Americans plummet in short order.

It was Tryon's career as a soldier, however, that finally gave his reputation a fatal blow in the colonies. In that role, Tryon was far less sensitive to American moods than he had been as governor and also far less successful—although ironically he prided himself more on his supposed skills as an army officer than as a politician. He was not gifted in either tactical or strategic thinking. His forte seemed to be the impetuous thrust for the jugular, without giving due consideration to the intricacies of logistics and communications. Forever railing that Generals Howe and Clinton were too cautious, he seemed to overcompensate in the direction of rashness. His greatest military failing was his insistence on the necessity for terroristic warfare against rebel civilians in order to break their will and force them to yield. Not only did such warfare make him, and Britons in general, appear moral monsters to Americans, but it also suggested to them that the king's military men were strategic cretins. The British army's plundering confirmed for rebels and neutrals alike that they had no place in an empire whose sovereign allowed such practices. Near the end of his military career, Tryon finally recognized this fact and repudiated the use of desolation warfare. Thus, he saved himself from having that failed idea forever on his record as his final word on how the British should prosecute the American war. But his change of heart came too late to redeem him in the eyes of aggrieved Americans, who came out of the war believing that he ranked not much higher than the most hated despots of history in terms of brutality toward foes. Therefore they tried to excise his name from American memory and from geographic features such as Fort Tryon in New York and two Tryon counties. Despite his eulogist's prediction, William Tryon was not remembered with reverence "across the Atlantic."

In the last analysis, Tryon's career as a faithful supporter of Crown prerogatives in America during the decline of the British Empire in the

1760s and 1770s underscores how impossible it was for Britain to maintain control over America, no matter how talented her representatives on the scene, if ministries and monarch refused to make timely concessions on crucial questions of the colonies' relationship with the mother country. For Tryon, indeed, was a talented colonial administrator, who throughout those unsettled times gave careful, perceptive, intelligent attention to forwarding the king's interests under difficult and sometimes hazardous circumstances. In comparison with other important royal executives— Thomas Hutchinson of Massachusetts, William Franklin of New Jersey, Lord Dunmore of Virginia, Lords Charles Greville Montagu and William Campbell of South Carolina—who shared with him problems of imperial collapse, Tryon ranks second only to Hutchinson in terms of ability and accomplishment. And it is instructive to know that Hutchinson suffered the same fate that Tryon did.[35] Tryon's frustrations as a military man only confirmed his earlier understanding that the American will was adamantly set against the "injustices" of British tax policies and would never be budged by military coercion or anything else. Tryon, basically an intelligent and humane man, who by his own lights had the best interests of the colonists at heart, became, like thousands of others in those times of upheaval, a pawn of forces entirely beyond his control.

Notes

Abbreviations Used in the Notes

Add. MSS., BL	Additions to the Manuscripts, British Library
ADM [series/volume]	Correspondence with Admiralty, Public Record Office
BL	British Library
CO [class/volume]	Colonial Office Papers, Public Record Office
HCA [class/volume]	High Court of Admiralty Papers, Public Record Office
HL	Houghton Library, Harvard University
HSP	Historical Society of Pennsylvania
MHS	Massachusetts Historical Society
NYHS	New-York Historical Society
NYPL	New York Public Library
PRO [series/volume]	Public Record Office
PRO, AO [class/volume]	Audit Office Papers, Public Record Office
PRO, T [class/volume]	Treasury Papers, Public Record Office
RSA	Royal Society of Arts
SPG	Society for the Propagation of the Gospel in Foreign Parts
WLCL	William L. Clements Library, University of Michigan
WO [class/volume]	War Office Papers, Public Record Office

Chapter One

1. Thomas Jones, *History of New York*, 1:164; Charles Inglis to William Johnson, August 19, 1771, O'Callaghan, *Documentary History*, 4:457.

2. Lewis Morris, Jr., to Lewis Morris, September 14, 1776, *Letters to General Lewis Morris*, 446; John Vardill to William Eden, April 11, 1778, Stevens, *Facsimiles of Manuscripts*, 4:438.

3. Powell, *Correspondence of William Tryon*, 2:897; *Northamptonshire Notes and Queries*, 236; Morant, *County of Essex* 2:251; Pevsner, *Buildings of En-*

gland: Northamptonshire, 130–31; Arnett, *From England to North Carolina*, 73–75.

4. Powell, *Correspondence of William Tryon*, 2:897, 900–901; Arnett, *From England to North Carolina*, 73–75, 82–83.

5. Powell, *Correspondence of William Tryon*, 2:898–99; Fries et al., *Records of the Moravians*, 1:353.

6. William Tryon to William Knox, April 21, 1777, CO 5/1108; Tryon to Sewallis Shirley, July 26, 1765, Powell, *Correspondence of William Tryon*, 1:136; William Smith, *Historical Memoirs 1763 to 1778*, 1:147; Dill, *Tryon*, 6; Bargar, "Tryon's House," 306–9; North, *Eighteenth Century Gentleman* and *Library of William Tryon*. There is a description of Norbury Park in Nairn and Pevsner, *Buildings of England: Surrey*, 388–89, but according to the authors it was constructed in 1774 for William Lane. Apparently this estate was not Tryon's Norbury Park.

7. Lord Botetourt to Lord Hillsborough, February 22, 1770, CO 5/1348; Lord Barrington to Thomas Gage, December 4, 1771, Peckham, *Sources of American Independence*, 1:98; Lorenzo Sabine, *Biographical Sketches of Loyalists*, 2:364.

8. Saunders, *Colonial Records*, 8:xxxix; Hastings and Holden, *Public Papers of George Clinton* 1:95–96; Raper, *North Carolina*, 65; Dunbar, "Royal Governors," 250.

9. Ann Hulton to Mrs. Lightbody, January 31, 1774, Hulton, *Letters of a Loyalist Lady*, 70–72; Tryon to Jonathan Trumbull, September 16, 1773, Trumbull Papers, III, 70, Connecticut State Library; Petition of ladies of New York City to Tryon, January 30, 1773, Simon Gratz Autograph Collection, HSP; Tryon to Lord Dartmouth, February 4, 1773, CO 5/1104; *New York Mercury*, March 3, 1773; Upton, *Diary and Selected Papers*, 2:95; Commager and Morris, *The Spirit of 'Seventy Six*, 1:335–36; Wertenbaker, *Father Knickerbocker Rebels*, 30–31.

10. Saunders, *Colonial Records*, 8:xxxix; Leonard Woods Labaree, "William Tryon," 26; McIlwraith, *Sir Frederick Haldimand*, 89.

11. William Smith, *Historical Memoirs 1763 to 1778*, 1:117, 267.

12. Tryon to Shirley, July 26, 1765, Powell, *Correspondence of William Tryon*, 1:142; Seccombe, "William Tryon," 1203; Willcox, *Portrait of a General*, 22, 69.

13. *Gentleman's Magazine and Historical Chronicle* 27 (1757): 577; Will of William Tryon, November 21, 1787, Powell, *Correspondence of William Tryon*, 2:888–92.

14. Ann Blair to Martha Braxton, August 1769, Blair Papers, Earl Greg Swem Library, College of William and Mary; Janet L. Montgomery, "Memoirs," Livingston Family Papers, III, 142, NYPL; Upton, *Diary and Selected Papers*, 2:95, 97–98, 1211–22; Dill, *Tryon*, 9; Dangerfield, *Robert R. Livingston*, 50.

15. Corbett, *Seven Years' War*, 1:264–66.

16. Tryon to [Henry Clinton], September 12, 1758, Clinton Papers, WLCL; Corbett, *Seven Years' War*, 1:292–301.

17. Tryon to ——, September 16, 1758, Clinton Papers, WLCL.

18. Tryon to Hillsborough, July 8, 1769, CO 5/312.

19. Tryon to Hillsborough, October 15 and 16, 1764, and to Halifax, October 15, 1764, Tryon Letter Book, 2–3, 5–6, HL; Warrant appointing Tryon lieutenant

governor of North Carolina, April 26, 1764, CO 324/51; Halifax to Arthur Dobbs, May 12, 1764, CO 5/310; *Journals of Commissioners for Trade,* 12:44–45.

20. Tryon to Shirley, July 26, 1765, Powell, *Correspondence of William Tryon,* 1:136; John Pownall to Tryon, July 24, 1764, CO 5/325; *Journals of Commissioners for Trade,* 12:78; Bargar, "Tryon's House," 306–9.

21. Tryon to Richard Hughes, April 24, 1765, CO 5/299; *North-Carolina Magazine,* August 10, September 28, and November 2, 1764.

22. Tryon to Board of Trade, October 15, 1764, CO 5/299; Tryon to Halifax, October 15, 1764, and to Hillsborough, October 16, 1765, Tryon Letter Book, 2–6, HL; Tryon to Shirley, July 26, 1765, Powell, *Correspondence of William Tryon,* 1:141–42; *Journals of Commissioners for Trade,* 12:130; South, " 'Russellborough,' " 361–62.

23. Tryon to Messrs. Drummond, bankers, October 31, 1764, and to Hillsborough, October 16, 1764, Tryon Letter Book, 5–6, HL.

24. Saunders, *Colonial Records,* 6:1078; Powell, *Correspondence of William Tryon,* 1:18–19; *North-Carolina Magazine,* November 2, 1764.

25. Tryon to Shirley, July 16, 1765, Powell, *Correspondence of William Tryon,* 1:136–42; Dill, *Tryon,* 10–11.

26. Tryon to Shirley, July 26, 1765, Powell, *Correspondence of William Tryon,* 1:136–42.

27. Ibid.; *North-Carolina Magazine,* December 28, 1764, January 4, 1765.

28. Tryon to Shirley, July 26, 1765, Powell, *Correspondence of William Tryon,* 1:136–42; Dill, *Tryon,* 13–15.

29. Justina Dobbs to Alice Marsden, March 8, 1765, Tryon to Shirley, July 26, 1765, Powell, *Correspondence of William Tryon,* 1:38, 136–42; Fries et al., *Records of the Moravians,* 1:301.

30. Tryon to Board of Trade, April 1, 1765, CO 5/299; Tryon to Halifax, April 2, 1765, CO 5/310; Proclamation, April 3, 1765, Powell, *Correspondence of William Tryon,* 1:56.

31. Tryon to Board of Trade, April 1, 1765, CO 5/299; Tryon to Halifax, April 2, 1765, CO 5/310; *Journals of Commissioners for Trade,* 12:185; Clarke, *Arthur Dobbs,* 199; Marshall DeLancey Haywood, *Tryon,* 46–52; Raper, *North Carolina,* 82–83.

32. Halifax to Board of Trade, June 26, 1765, CO 5/199; Jno. Larpent to Tryon, July 10, 1765, CO 324/41; Board of Trade to George III, December 24, 1765, CO 5/305; Royal instructions to William Tryon, December 24, 1765, CO 5/325; George III to clerk of the signet, January 16, 1766, Powell, *Correspondence of William Tryon,* 1:222–23; Treasury orders for Tryon's salary, March 23, 1766, PRO, T 53/50.

Chapter Two

1. Tryon to the justices, n.d., Powell, *Correspondence of William Tryon,* 2:1–2.
2. William Hunter to Tryon, March 2, 1765, Powell, *Correspondence of Wil-*

liam Tryon, 1:36–37; Sosin, *Agents and Merchants*, 16; Jack P. Greene, *Quest for Power*, 416–20.

3. Tryon to Board of Trade, June 24, 1765, Tryon Letter Book, 18, HL.

4. Tryon to Board of Trade, August 15, 1765, CO 5/299; Board of Trade to Tryon, November 29, 1765, CO 5/305; Assembly to Tryon, November 6, 1766, Tryon to Assembly, November 10, 1766, CO 5/351; Lord Hyde to Dartmouth, August 13, 1765, *Manuscripts of Dartmouth*, 2:17; Jack P. Greene, *Quest for Power*, 416–20.

5. Tryon to Hillsborough, February 25 and March 31, 1769, CO 5/328; Tryon to Council and Assembly, October 23, 1769, CO 5/313; Council to Tryon, October 30, 1769, Assembly to Tryon, October 30, 1769, Saunders, *Colonial Records*, 8:91–92, 113–15; Hillsborough to Tryon, June 7, 1769, Tryon to Hillsborough, November 22, 1769, CO 5/313.

6. Legal papers relating to the murder of Thomas Whitehurst, March 18–May 22, 1765, Constantine John Phipps to Tryon, April 8, 1765, Tryon to Phipps, April 9, 1765, Tryon to Board of Trade, June 24, 1765, February 1, 1766, CO 5/299; Tryon to Lord Colville, April 22, 1765, and to Francis Fauquier, May 20, 1765, Tryon Letter Book, 13–15, HL; *Journals of Commissioners for Trade*, 12:213, 214.

7. Tryon to Earl of Shelburne, July 18, 1767, Kings Manuscripts, vol. 206, f. 102, BL; Lefler and Newsome, *North Carolina*, 145; Marshall DeLancey Haywood, *Tryon*, 53.

8. Tryon to Henry Eustace McCulloh, April 6, 1765, McCulloh to Tryon, April 25, 1767, Powell, *Correspondence of William Tryon*, 1:57, 66–82; Proclamation of Tryon, May 18, 1765, McCulloh to Tryon, November 29, 1766, Marmaduke Jones to Tryon, May 15, 1767, CO 5/350; Tryon to Board of Trade, April 28, 1767, and to Shelburne, October 31, 1767, CO 5/311; Dill, *Tryon*, 98.

9. Tryon to Lord Hyde, December 8, 1764, and to William Bull, July 16, 1765, Tryon Letter Book, 7–10, 20, HL; Tryon to Assembly, May 3, 1765, Assembly to Tryon, November 29, 1766, CO 5/351; John Ashe (for Assembly) to Council, May 15, 1765, CO 5/352; Tryon to Board of Trade, August 11, 1765, CO 5/299; Tingley, "Postal Service"; Crittenden, "Means of Communication," 374; Marshall DeLancey Haywood, *Tryon*, 14–15; Lefler and Powell, *Colonial North Carolina*, 173.

10. Tryon to Benjamin Barons, January 3, February 17, May 3, and June 17, 1766, to Peter Timothy, February 20, 1767, and to Peter DeLancey, April 24, 1767, March 22, 1768, January 10, 1769, Tryon Letter Book, 31–32, 41–43, 75–76, 81, 110–12, 118, 205–6, 234, HL; Tryon to Shelburne, March 7, 1768, CO 5/300; Tryon to Hillsborough, December 15, 1768, January 10 and September 5, 1769, CO 5/312; Tryon to Assembly, January 16, 1771, Powell, *Correspondence of William Tryon*, 2:569; Watson, "Ferry in Colonial North Carolina," 257.

11. Tryon to SPG, July 31, 1765, Fulham Papers, VI, 304–5, Lambeth Palace Library; Worseley, "Catholicism in Antebellum North Carolina," 400; Lefler and Powell, *Colonial North Carolina*, 199; Lefler and Newsome, *North Carolina*, 125.

12. Tryon to Daniel Burton (secretary, SPG), July 18, 1767, Tryon Letter Book,

180, HL; Warrant for church silver, July 9, 1765, the Reverend John Burnett to Burton, August 22, 1767, Powell, *Correspondence of William Tryon,* 1:118, 572; Lee, *Lower Cape Fear,* 215, and "Old Brunswick," 238.

13. Tryon to bishop of London, October 6, 1766, Tryon Letter Book, 98–99, HL; Tryon to bishop of London, October 9, 1768, Fulham Papers, XXIII, 60, Lambeth Palace Library; Edward Jones to Tryon, March 29 and April 28, 1769, Tryon to Burton, July 22, 1770, Powell, *Correspondence of William Tryon* 2:318–19, 332, 481.

14. Tryon to Assembly, May 3, 1765, CO 5/351; Lemmon, "Protestant Episcopal Diocese," 432; Conkin, "Church Establishment," 2; Jack P. Greene, *Quest for Power,* 352–53.

15. Tryon to Assembly, May 5, 1765, Assembly to Tryon, May 6, 1765, CO 5/351; Council to Tryon, May 6, 1765, the Reverend Andrew Morton to SPG, January 9, 1767, Powell, *Correspondence of William Tryon,* 1:86–87, 401; Tryon to Board of Trade, August 11, 1765, CO 5/299; Clark, *State Records,* 23:660–62; Cross, *Anglican Episcopate,* 243; Conkin, "Church Establishment," 5; Jack P. Greene, *Quest for Power,* 352–53.

16. Tryon to Burton, April 30, 1767, Tryon Letter Book, 131–32, HL; Board of Trade to Tryon, November 29, 1765, CO 5/305; Board of Trade to George III, July 13, 1767, CO 5/325; Shelburne to Tryon, August 7, 1767, CO 5/328; Tryon to Board of Trade, February 1, 1768, CO 5/311; Tryon to Hillsborough, January 10, 1769, CO 5/312.

17. James Murray to Tryon, July 3, 1765, James Murray Papers, MHS; Tryon to Burton, October 1, 1766, Tryon Letter Book, 95–96, HL; Tryon to bishop of London, April 30, 1767, Fulham Papers, VI, 322–23, Lambeth Palace Library.

18. Tryon to bishop of London, October 6, 1766, and to Burton, April 30, 1767, Tryon Letter Book, 98–99, 131–32, HL; Jack P. Greene, *Quest for Power,* 352–53.

19. Tryon to Burton, March 20, 1769, Tryon Letter Book, 243–47, HL; Petition of inhabitants of Rowan County to Tryon, [1769], Vestry of St. James's Parish, Wilmington, to Tryon, May 11, 1770, Powell, *Correspondence of William Tryon,* 2:415, 458; Lee, *Lower Cape Fear,* 220; Conkin, "Church Establishment," 11; Lemmon, "Protestant Episcopal Diocese," 432–33.

20. Tryon to Shelburne, January 31, 1767, Shelburne Papers, WLCL; Marriage permit for Thomas Wilson and Catherane Levinson, January 22, 1767, Tryon to German families, January 1, 1771, Powell, *Correspondence of William Tryon,* 1:407–8, 2:600–601; Fries et al., *Records of the Moravians,* 1:353–56, 462–67; Marshall DeLancey Haywood, *Tryon,* 20–22.

21. Tryon to Burton, March 20, 1769, Tryon Letter Book, 243–47, HL; Tryon to Assembly, January 1 and 25, 1771, Powell, *Correspondence of William Tryon,* 2:570, 582.

22. Andrew Morton to SPG, August 25, 1766, Saunders, *Colonial Records,* 7:252–53; Mecklenburg Presbyterians to Tryon, [1769], Powell, *Correspondence of William Tryon,* 2:281–83; Presbyterian ministers to Tryon, August 23, 1768, CO 5/312; Durward T. Stokes, "Henry Patillo," 381–82; Conkin, "Church Establishment," 14.

23. Theodorus Swaine Drage to bishop of London, November 23, 1769, Fulham Papers, VI, 332–33, Lambeth Palace Library; Tryon to St. Luke's vestry, Rowan County, November 11, 1769, Petitions of Rowan County Anglicans, [December 1769] and [July 1770], Drage to Tryon, March 13 and May 29, 1770, Powell, *Correspondence of William Tryon*, 2:408, 415, 432–33, 460–67, 471; Conkin, "Church Establishment," 15–16.

24. Tryon to Drage, July 9, 1770, Powell, *Correspondence of William Tryon*, 2:476–77.

25. Tryon to Assembly, May 1, 1765, CO 5/351; Royal Instructions, December 24, 1765, CO 5/325; Tryon to Board of Trade, December 3, 1766, CO 5/300; Tryon to SPG, July 31, 1765, Fulham Papers, VI, 304–5, Lambeth Palace Library; John Ashe to Tryon, May 13, 1765, Inhabitants of New Bern and Craven County to Tryon, May 16, 1765, Powell, *Correspondence of William Tryon* 1:93, 96–97; Raper, *Church and Private Schools*, 25; Conkin, "Church Establishment," 20; Marshall DeLancey Haywood, *Tryon*, 23.

26. Tryon to Assembly, December 5, 1770, and to Hillsborough, March 11, 1771, CO 5/314; Tryon to Hillsborough, November 6, 1771, CO 5/1102; Act to establish Queen's College, January 15, 1771, Powell, *Correspondence of William Tryon*, 2:564–67; Fries et al., *Records of the Moravians*, 1:338–41; Connor, "Higher Education," 4–5; Conkin, "Church Establishment," 21; Lefler and Powell, *Colonial North Carolina*, 211–13; Lefler and Newsome, *North Carolina*, 135.

27. Tryon to Gage, May 19, 1765, Gage Papers, WLCL; Tryon to Shirley, July 26, 1765, Powell, *Correspondence of William Tryon*, 1:136–42; Bartram, *Diary*, 18; South, " 'Russellborough,' " 360–72.

28. Tryon to Shirley, July 26, 1765, Powell, *Correspondence of William Tryon*, 1:136–42; Tryon to Henry Seymour Conway, November 5 and December 26, 1765, CO 5/310; Tryon to Board of Trade, February 1, 1766, CO 5/299; Murray to Tryon, May 5 and 31, 1766, Murray Papers, MHS.

29. Tryon to Shelburne, July 21, 1767, Kings Manuscripts, vol. 206, ff. 237–38, BL; Watson, "Ordinaries," 70; Lefler and Powell, *Colonial North Carolina*, 115–16.

30. Tryon to Richard Hughes, April 24, 1765, CO 5/299; Hughes to Tryon, August 27, 1765, CO 5/300; Tryon to Board of Trade, February 2, 1767, Kings Manuscripts, vol. 206, f. 15, BL; Tryon to Edward Bridgen, July 8, 1767, Guard Books, XII, no. 93, 20–23, RSA; Hudson and Lockhurst, *Royal Society of Arts*, 147–48; Lefler and Powell, *Colonial North Carolina*, 165.

31. Tryon to Shirley, July 26, 1765, Powell, *Correspondence of William Tryon*, 1:136–42; Tryon to Board of Trade, April 30, 1766, CO 5/199; Tryon to Board of Trade, August 2, 1766, CO 5/310; Proclamations of corn embargo, March 26 and June 9, 1766, CO 5/299; Fries et al., *Records of the Moravians*, 1:339–41, 353–54; Paul, "Colonial Beaufort," 114–25; Lee, *Lower Cape Fear*, 176–78.

32. Board of Trade to Tryon, August 1, 1766, CO 5/327; Shelburne to Tryon, December 11, 1766, January 13, 1767, Tryon to Shelburne, June 29, 1767, CO 5/310; Tryon to Board of Trade, January 30, 1767, and to Shelburne, July 16, 1767, Kings Manuscripts, vol. 206, ff. 13–14, 95, BL; Tryon to Treasury, March

28, 1767, PRO, T 1/461; Robert Palmer to Tryon, May 4, 1767, CO 5/112; Tryon to Board of Trade, July 8, 1767, CO 5/300; Tryon to Shelburne, March 15, 1768, CO 5/311; Board of Trade to Tryon, September 30, 1766, Powell, *Correspondence of William Tryon*, 1:350.

33. John Rutherfurd to Tryon, May 6, 1767, CO 5/111; Tryon to Shelburne, July 18, 1767, Kings Manuscripts, vol. 206, f. 102, BL.

34. Rutherfurd to Tryon, January 19, 1769, Samuel Strudwick to Tryon, May 20, 1769, Tryon to Hillsborough, May 27 and July 3, 1769, CO 5/311; Rutherfurd to Tryon, April 9, 1770, Tryon to Hillsborough, April 13, 1770, CO 5/313; Tryon to Hillsborough, March 9, 1771, Hillsborough to Josiah Martin, June 5, 1771, CO 5/314; Tryon to Hillsborough, January 1 and February 2, 1770, Tryon Letter Book, 279–80, HL; Rutherfurd to Tryon, December 13, 1769, Powell, *Correspondence of William Tryon*, 2:420–21.

35. Tryon to Gage, May 18, 1765, Gage Papers, WLCL; Tryon to Welbore Ellis, May 26, 1765, to Barrington, June 29, 1766, and to Marquis of Granby, August 1, 1766, Tryon Letter Book, 15–16, 84, 87–88, HL; Tryon to Board of Trade, April 30, 1766, CO 5/299; Tryon to Board of Trade, August 1, 1766, CO 5/310; Howe's commission as commandant of Fort Johnston, July 14, 1766, Powell, *Correspondence of William Tryon*, 1:325.

36. Board of Trade to Tryon, September 25, 1765, CO 324/17; Assembly to Tryon, November 22, 1766, December 29, 1767, CO 5/351; Tryon to Assembly, October 7, 1767, Tryon to Shelburne, December 11, 1767, CO 5/311; Tryon to Shelburne, March 7, 1768, CO 5/300; Assembly to Tryon, November 23, 1768, CO 5/353; Tryon to Hillsborough, January 10, 1769, CO 5/312; Tryon to Gage, December 13, 1767, Gage Papers, WLCL; Tryon to Barrington, April 11, 1767, Tryon Letter Book, 126, HL; Tryon to Assembly, November 20, 1766, Powell, *Correspondence of William Tryon*, 1:368; Merrens and Paschal, "Map-Maker's View," 272–73.

37. Tryon to Hillsborough, April 24, 1769, CO 5/312; Tryon to Assembly, October 23, 1769, Tryon to Hillsborough, January 1, 1770, Hillsborough to Tryon, April 14, 1770, CO 5/213; Assembly to Tryon, October 30, 1769, Powell, *Correspondence of William Tryon*, 2:390.

38. Hillsborough to Tryon, September 28, November 15, and December 11, 1770, January 22, 1771, CO 5/241; Tryon to Assembly, December 5, 1770, Assembly to Tryon, December 10, 1770, Tryon to Robert Howe, January 28, 1771, Tryon to Hillsborough, March 13, 1771, CO 5/314; Tryon to Gage, April 26, 1771, Gage Papers, WLCL; Tryon to Assembly, January 26, 1771, *Journal of the House of Assembly*, 70; Powell, *Correspondence of William Tryon*, 2:571, 576.

39. Letters patent appointing Tryon vice admiral of North Carolina, July 13, 1765, HCA 50/12; Tryon to Board of Trade, February 1, 1766, CO 5/299; Tryon to Shelburne, June 29, 1767, Decree of vice admiralty court, January 21, 1767, Marmaduke Jones to Tryon, February 10, 1767, Tryon to Gabriel Cathcart, February 16, 1767, Patrick Gordon to Tryon, February 23, 1767, Tryon to Board of Trade, March 28, 1767, CO 5/310; Tryon to Shelburne, July 5, 1767, Tryon Letter Book, 164–65, HL.

40. Tryon to Shelburne, February 2, 1767, Shelburne Papers, WLCL; Saunders, *Colonial Records*, 7:358, 422.

Chapter Three

1. Douglas, *English Historical Documents*, 9:655–56; High, "Henry McCulloh," 24; C. Robert Haywood, "Stamp Act," 317; Lee, "Days of Defiance," 188–89; Butler, *Coming of the Revolution*, 14–15; Lee, *Lower Cape Fear*, 243–44; Lefler and Powell, *Colonial North Carolina*, 243.

2. Tryon to Assembly, May 3, 1765, CO 5/310; Higginbotham, "James Iredell's Efforts," 134; Spindel, "Law and Disorder," 5–6.

3. *North-Carolina Gazette*, November 20, 1765; Butler, *Coming of the Revolution*, 18; Lee, *Lower Cape Fear*, 245, and "Days of Defiance," 193; C. Robert Haywood, "Stamp Act," 332.

4. Tryon to Henry Seymour Conway, December 26, 1765, William Huston's resignation, November 16, 1765, CO 5/310; *North-Carolina Gazette*, November 20 and 27, 1765; Morgan and Morgan, *Stamp Act Crisis*, 181–82; Gipson, *British Empire*, 10:317–18; Raper, *North Carolina*, 235; Jack P. Greene, *Quest for Power*, 368; Spindel, "Law and Disorder," 10.

5. Address of Brunswick, New Hanover, and Bladen County gentlemen to Tryon, November 18, 1765, CO 5/310; Morgan and Morgan, *Stamp Act Crisis*, 164–165; Raper, *North Carolina*, 235–36; Lefler and Powell, *Colonial North Carolina*, 247.

6. Tryon to Conway, December 26, 1765, CO 5/310; Tryon's proclamations, December 20, 1765, January 6, 1766, CO 5/350; *Maryland Gazette*, February 20, 1766; Samuel Johnston to Thomas Barker, January 9, 1766, Powell, *Correspondence of William Tryon*, 1:218–20.

7. *Maryland Gazette*, February 20 and March 16, 1766; Johnston to Barker, January 9, 1766, Powell, *Correspondence of William Tryon*, 1:218–20; Gipson, *British Empire*, 10:318–19; Spindel, "Law and Disorder," 11.

8. Tryon to Board of Trade, February 1, 1766, CO 5/299; Jacob Lobb to William Dry, January 14, 1766, Dry to Robert Jones, January 16, 1776, Jones to Dry, February 3, 1766, CO 5/310; Jensen, *Founding of a Nation*, 137; Lee, *Lower Cape Fear*, 247, and "Days of Defiance," 197; Spindel, "Law and Disorder," 12.

9. Tryon to Conway, February 25, 1766, "Association against the Stamp Act," February 18, 1766, CO 5/310; Citizens to Dry, February 15, 1766, Powell, *Correspondence of William Tryon*, 1:238; *North-Carolina Gazette*, February 26, 1766; Edmund S. Morgan, *Prologue to Revolution*, 117; Gipson, *British Empire*, 10:347; Jensen, *Founding of a Nation*, 137; Lee, *Lower Cape Fear*, 247, and "Days of Defiance," 197–98; C. Robert Haywood, "Stamp Act," 335.

10. John Ashe, Thomas Lloyd, and Alexander Lillington to Tryon, February 19, 1766, Tryon to Constantine John Phipps, February 19, 1766, Tryon to Conway, February 25, 1766, CO 5/310.

11. Tryon to the commander of the *Viper* or the *Diligence*, February 20, 1766, Phipps to Tryon, February 20, 1766, CO 5/310.

12. Tryon to Conway, February 25, 1766, CO 5/310; Tryon to John Dalrymple, February 10, 1766, ADM 1/2052; Lobb to Dalrymple, February 20, 1766, Tryon Letter Book, 59, HL.

13. Tryon to Conway, February 25, 1766, Lobb to Dry, February 20, 1766, CO 5/310; *North-Carolina Gazette*, February 26, 1766; Lee, *Lower Cape Fear*, 249, and "Days of Defiance, 199–200; Butler, *Coming of the Revolution*, 23; C. Robert Haywood, "Stamp Act," 335–36.

14. Tryon to Conway, February 25, 1766, CO 5/310; *North-Carolina Gazette*, February 12, 1766; Lee, *Lower Cape Fear*, 149–50, and "Days of Defiance," 200–201; Lefler and Powell, *Colonial North Carolina*, 248–49; Morgan and Morgan, *Stamp Act Crisis*, 164–65.

15. Tryon to Conway, February 25 and March 3, 1766, and to Lobb, February 23, 1766, Lobb to Tryon, February 24, 1766, CO 5/310; Tryon to Board of Trade, April 30, 1766, CO 5/199.

16. Tryon to Conway, April 28, 1766, CO 5/310; Council Journals, February 26, 1766, 355–58, HL; Jack P. Greene, *Quest for Power*, 294; Dill, *Tryon*, 75–78.

17. Tryon to Conway, March 3, 1766, CO 5/310; Tryon to Board of Trade, April 30, 1766, CO 5/199.

18. Lobb to Tryon, February 22, 1766, Tryon to Moses John DeRosset, February 24, 1766, DeRosset to Tryon, February 28, 1766, Tryon to Conway, March 3, 1766, CO 5/310.

19. Conway to Tryon, March 1 and 31, 1766, CO 5/66; Board of Treasury to Tryon, May 5, 1766, PRO, T 27/29; Tryon to Board of Treasury, April 5, 1766, PRO, T 1/455; Tryon to Board of Trade, April 6, 1766, William Houston to Tryon, April 21, 1766, CO 5/299; Tryon to Francis Fauquier, March 3, 1766, Tryon Letter Book, 94, HL. Tryon returned the stamped paper on February 3, 1767 (Tryon to Board of Treasury, February 3, 1767, Tryon Letter Book, 117–18, HL).

20. Proclamation of Tryon, May 25, 1766, CO 5/299; Corporation of Wilmington to Tryon, June 26 and July 28, 1766, Tryon to Corporation of Wilmington, June 26 and August 2, 1766, CO 5/310.

21. John Pownal (secretary, Board of Trade) to Tryon, July 2, 1764, CO 5/325; Skaggs, *Boundary Disputes*, 74; Lefler and Newsome, *North Carolina*, 149–59.

22. Tryon to Board of Trade, October 15, 1764, January 27, 1765, CO 5/299; Tryon to Hillsborough, October 27, 1768, CO 5/312; Tryon to William Bull, February 14, 1765, and to Charles Greville Montagu, April 16, 1767, Tryon Letter Book, 11, 127, HL; Saunders, *Colonial Records*, 9:xix; Skaggs, *Boundary Disputes*, 78; Lefler and Powell, *Colonial North Carolina*, 95–96.

23. Montagu to Tryon, December 6, 1768, Saunders, *Colonial Records*, 8:563; Tryon to Montagu, December 11, 1768, and to Hillsborough, December 12, 1768, CO 5/311; Assembly to Tryon, January 24, 1771, Powell, *Correspondence of William Tryon*, 2:581; Council Journal entry, January 24, 1771, Council Journals, 518, HL; Skaggs, *Boundary Disputes*, 78–85.

24. Tryon to Gage, May 19, 1765, Gage Papers, WLCL; Board of Trade to Tryon, September 12, 1765, CO 5/306; Tryon to Board of Trade, August 2, 1766, CO 5/310; Tryon to Assembly, November 4 and 11, 1766, Assembly to Tryon,

November 29, 1766, CO 5/351; Tryon to Samuel Wyley, April 5, 1766, February 17, 1767, and to Sir William Johnson, June 15, 1766, Tryon Letter Book, 67, 79–80, 119–20, HL; Petition of Tuscarora chiefs to Tryon, [July 1766], Tryon to Assembly, November 27, 1766, Powell, *Correspondence of William Tryon*, 1:321–24, 381–82.

25. "Plan for the Future Management of Indian Affairs," July 10, 1764, O'Callaghan, *Documents Relative to Colonial New York*, 7:637–41; Tryon to John Stuart, February 16, 1767, CO 5/310; Shelburne to Tryon, September 13, 1767, CO 5/222; Proclamation of George III, July 16, 1767, CO 5/350; Stuart to Tryon, September 15, 1768, CO 5/69; Tryon to Stuart, July 21, 1767, March 28, 1769, Tryon Letter Book, 178, 249–50, HL; Proclamation of Tryon, July 16, 1767, Powell, *Correspondence of William Tryon*, 1:557–58; Alden, *John Stuart*, 240–50.

26. Stuart to Tryon, February 5 and May 28, 1766, Tryon to Stuart, April 9, May 5, and June 17, 1766, CO 5/66; Tryon to Stuart, July 30 and August 31, 1766, Tryon Letter Book, 84–86, 94–95, HL; Richard G. Stone, Jr., "Tryon," 40–47; De Vorsey, *Indian Boundary*, 94–100; Alden, *John Stuart*, 219–20; Gipson, *British Empire*, 11:442.

27. Assembly to Tryon, November 29, 1766, CO 5/351; Stuart to Tryon, March 2, March 31, and May 14, 1767, Tryon to Stuart, May 20, 1767, and to Alexander Cameron, May 23, 1767, Tryon's orders to the escort, May 19 and June 1, 1767, CO 5/310; *South Carolina Gazette*, June 12, 1767; De Vorsey, *Indian Boundary*, 100–101.

28. Tryon's talk to Cherokees, June 1, 1767, Cherokee's reply, June 2, 1767, Journal of Tryon's escort, June 13, 1767, CO 5/310; Tryon to John Mitchell, June 2, 1767, Tryon Letter Book, 140–41, HL; Alden, *John Stuart*, 221; Richard G. Stone, Jr., "Tryon," 49–51.

29. Tryon to Shelburne, July 8 and 15, 1767, Journals kept by commissioners, June 4–18, 1767, CO 5/310; Expenses of running dividing line, n.d., CO 5/311; Tryon to Shelburne, July 14, 1767, Shelburne Papers, WLCL; Alden, *John Stuart*, 221; Gipson, *British Empire*, 11:442; De Vorsey, *Indian Boundary*, 102–9.

Chapter Four

1. On the capital, see Powell, *Correspondence of William Tryon*, 1:xxi; Richard G. Stone, Jr., "Tryon," 55–57; and Dill, *Tryon*, 103–10. On north-south sectional tensions, see Ekirch, *"Poor Carolina,"* 150–52.

2. Tryon to Board of Trade, April 1, 1765, CO 5/299; Tryon to Board of Trade, December 3, 1766, CO 5/300; Tryon to Shelburne, January 31, 1767, CO 5/310; Clark, *State Records*, 23:664–65; Jack P. Greene, *Quest for Power*, 263.

3. Agreement between Tryon and John Hawks, January 9, 1767, Powell, *Correspondence of William Tryon*, 1:399–401; Tryon to ——, February 13, 1767, Gratz Autograph Collection, HSP; Shelburne to Tryon, June 20, 1767, Tryon to Shelburne, March 7, 1768, CO 5/311; Assembly to Tryon, January 6, 1768, CO 5/351; Tryon to Hillsborough, January 12, 1769, Hillsborough to Tryon, March

24, 1769, CO 5/312; Tryon to Hillsborough, January 8 and June 7, 1770, CO 5/313; Dill, *Tryon*, 111–16; Richard G. Stone, Jr., "Tryon," 58–61.

4. Tryon to Hillsborough, January 1, 1770, CO 5/313; Tryon to Assembly, December 5, 1770, and to Council, June 29, 1771, CO 5/314; Tryon to Samuel Cornell, May 10, 1769, and to Assembly, January 4, 7, and 21, 1771, Assembly to Tryon, n.d., Powell, *Correspondence of William Tryon*, 2:333–34, 559, 560, 574, 586; Assembly to Tryon, January 26, 1771, *Journal of the House of Assembly*, 71.

5. *Virginia Gazette*, November 7, 1771; Assembly to Tryon, December 10, 1770, CO 5/314; Richard G. Stone, Jr., "Tryon," 64.

6. Tryon's commission to Samuel Swann, June 26, 1765, Powell, *Correspondence of William Tryon*, 1:115; Tryon to Board of Trade, August 15, 1765, CO 5/299; Tryon to Shelburne, January 31 and July 4, 1767, CO 5/310; Tryon to Shelburne, March 7, 1767, CO 5/300; Assembly journals, November 6 and 10, 1766, Council journals, November 20 and 25–27 and December 1, 1766, January 4 and 15, 1768, Saunders, *Colonial Records*, 7:312–14, 324, 327–28, 330–31, 337, 348–49, 356, 430–31, 443, 597–99, 622–23; Jack P. Greene, "North Carolina Lower House," 51.

7. Proclamation of Tryon, June 25, 1766, CO 5/299; Tryon to Shelburne, July 4, 1767, CO 5/310; Tryon to Shelburne, March 7, 1768, CO 5/300; Tryon to Assembly, November 4, 1766, CO 5/351; Tryon to Council and Assembly, December 7, 1767, CO 5/311; Parker, *History of Taxation*, 91–92; Kay, "Provincial Taxes," 444–49; Julian P. Boyd, "Sheriff in Colonial North Carolina," 167–68; Watson, "Appointment of Sheriffs," 391–93.

8. Tryon to Assembly, December 7, 1767, CO 5/311; Tryon to Hillsborough, November 30, 1769, CO 5/313; Assembly to Tryon, December 10, 1770, CO 5/314; Tryon to Assembly, October 31 and November 6, 1769, December 5 and 14, 1770, Powell, *Correspondence of William Tryon*, 2:392–95, 407, 548; Jack P. Greene, *Quest for Power*, 76–80; Kay, "Provincial Taxes," 449–51.

9. Proclamation of Tryon, November 28, 1768, CO 5/350; Assembly to Tryon, December 10, 1770, January 26, 1771, Richard Henderson to Tryon, March 18, 1771, CO 5/314; Tryon's examination of Samuel Robert Hall and James Mansfield, August 14 and 24, 1770, Powell, *Correspondence of William Tryon*, 2:490–97; Scott, "Counterfeiting," 475–76; Weir, "Currency Act," 183–84, 187; Raper, *North Carolina*, 143.

10. Tryon to Shelburne, January 31, 1767, Assembly to Tryon, enclosing petition to king, January 16, 1768, Tryon to Board of Trade, February 2, 1768, CO 5/310; Pasquotank County inhabitants to Tryon, November 20, 1766, Powell, *Correspondence of William Tryon*, 1:369–70; Assembly journals, December 11, 1767, January 16, 1768, Saunders, *Colonial Records*, 7:570, 681; *Journals of Commissioners for Trade*, 13:29.

11. Tryon to Drummond and Company, February 2, 1768, Tryon Letter Book, 191–92, HL; Hillsborough to Tryon, April 16 and August 13, 1768, Tryon to Hillsborough, June 16, 1768, CO 5/311; Jack P. Greene, *Quest for Power*, 391–92; Weir, "Currency Act," 189–91.

12. Tryon to Assembly, November 7, 1768, CO 5/112; Assembly to Tryon, December 2, 1768, Tryon to Assembly, December 5, 1768, CO 5/353; Tryon to

Hillsborough, January 10 and February 10, 1769, Hillsborough to Tryon, March 1, 1769, CO 5/312; Tryon to Hillsborough, February 25 and 27, 1769, CO 5/328; Jack P. Greene, *Quest for Power*, 392; Weir, "Currency Act," 191.

13. Hillsborough to Tryon, June 7, 1769, CO 5/312; Tryon to Council and Assembly, October 23, 1769, CO 5/315; Council and Assembly to Tryon, October 30, 1769, *North-Carolina Gazette*, November 10, 1769; Tryon to Hillsborough, January 1, July 2, and October 3, 1770, CO 5/313; Assembly to Tryon, January 25, 1771, Tryon to Assembly, January 26, 1771, CO 5/314; Weir, "Currency Act," 192–93.

14. Tryon to Shelburne, March 7, 1767, CO 5/300; Shelburne to Tryon, June 20, 1767, "View of the Polity of . . . North Carolina," June 29, 1767, CO 5/310; Tryon to Council, December 7, 1767, Council to Tryon, December 10, 1767, CO 5/311; Jack P. Greene, *Quest for Power*, 341.

15. Board of Trade to Tryon, December 12, 1770, CO 5/325; Assembly to Tryon, December 21, 1773, Powell, *Correspondence of William Tryon*, 2:849–50; Taylor, "Foreign Attachment Law," 20–22; Jack P. Greene, *Quest for Power*, 420–24.

16. Tryon to Assembly, November 15, 1766, CO 5/351; Harry Gordon to Tryon, January 5, 1767, CO 5/328; Tryon to Shelburne, March 28, 1767, Shelburne to Tryon, June 20, 1767, CO 5/310; Tryon to Shelburne, December 11, 1767, CO 5/311; Shelburne to Captain Winn, September 2, 1767, Redington and Roberts, *Home Office Papers*, 4:155; Hillsborough to Tryon, September 2, 1768, CO 5/69; Tryon to Hillsborough, January 10 and September 15 and 24, 1769, CO 5/312; Hillsborough to Tryon, July 14, 1769, enclosing additional instructions from king, June 30, 1769, CO 5/241; Tryon to Assembly, January 2, 1771, Charters of Wake and Chatham counties, March 12 and April 1, 1771, Powell, *Correspondence of William Tryon*, 2:557, 630–31, 649–50; Tryon to Hillsborough, April 10, 1770, CO 5/313; Tryon to Hillsborough, March 12, 1771, CO 5/314; Merrens and Paschal, "Map-Maker's View," 273; Powell, "Creatures of Carolina," 163; Jack P. Greene, *Quest for Power*, 341.

17. Mrs. John Burgwin to Mrs. Hugh Waddell, December 22, 1768, Powell, *Correspondence of William Tryon*, 2:274–75; Waightstill Avery's visit, April 4–5, 1769, Avery Diary, Draper Collection, State Historical Society of Wisconsin; Tryon to Hillsborough, March 31, 1769, CO 5/328; Tryon to Horatio Gates, April 24, 1769, Horatio Gates Papers, NYHS; Tryon to Clinton, September 6, 1769, Clinton Papers, WLCL.

18. *Virginia Gazette*, June 15, 1769; Anne Blair to Martha Braxton, August —, 1769, Blair Papers, Earl Gregg Swem Library, College of William and Mary; Tryon to Hillsborough, January 8, 1770, CO 5/313; Tryon to Hillsborough, October 7, 1770, CO 5/314.

19. Tryon to Hillsborough, July 8, 1769, Hillsborough to Tryon, November 4, 1769, CO 5/312; Tryon to Hillsborough, January 8, 1770, CO 5/313.

20. The Townshend Acts are reprinted in Douglas, *English Historical Documents*, 9:701–4.

21. Hillsborough to Tryon, enclosing Massachusetts circular letter of 1768, April 21, 1768, Hillsborough to Tryon, May 14 and July 11, 1768, CO 5/69;

Hillsborough to Tryon, November 15, 1768, enclosing king's speech to Parliament of November 8, 1768, CO 5/311.

22. Assembly journals, December 5, 1768, Saunders, *Colonial Records*, 7:980–82; Proclamation proroguing Assembly, December 5, 1768, CO 5/350; Tryon to Hillsborough, December 15, 1768, CO 5/312; Middlekauff, *Glorious Cause*, 176; Gipson, *British Empire*, 11:178; Jensen, *Founding of a Nation*, 259; Jack P. Greene, *Quest for Power*, 375; Lefler and Newsome, *North Carolina*, 185–86; Lefler and Powell, *Colonial North Carolina*, 252.

23. Hillsborough to Tryon, May 13, 1769, Powell, *Correspondence of William Tryon*, 2:335; Tryon to Hillsborough, September 5, 1769, CO 5/312; Tryon to Clinton, September 6, 1769, Clinton Papers, WLCL.

24. Tryon to Council and Assembly, October 23, 1769, CO 5/314; Council to Tryon, October 30, 1769, Assembly to Tryon, October 30, 1769, *North-Carolina Gazette*, November 10, 1769; Assembly journals, November 2, 1769, Saunders, *Colonial Records*, 8:121–24; Gipson, *British Empire*, 11:187; Jensen, *Founding of a Nation*, 305; Middlekauff, *Glorious Cause*, 183; Jack P. Greene, *Quest for Power*, 376; Lefler and Newsome, *North Carolina*, 187; Lefler and Powell, *Colonial North Carolina*, 253.

25. Tryon to Hillsborough, February 1, 1771, CO 5/314; Tryon to Assembly, November 4, 1769, *North-Carolina Gazette*, November 10, 1769; Gipson, *British Empire*, 11:187; Lefler and Powell, *Colonial North Carolina*, 253.

26. Tryon to Hillsborough, November 22, 1769, CO 5/313; John Pownall (for Hillsborough) to Tryon, April 14, 1770, CO 5/241; Tryon to Hillsborough, February 1, 1771, CO 5/314; Schlesinger, *Colonial Merchants*, 148–49; Lefler and Powell, *Colonial North Carolina*, 253–54; Lefler and Newsome, *North Carolina*, 186; Gipson, *British Empire*, 11:187.

27. Assembly to Tryon, November 6, 1769, Tryon to Hillsborough, January 8, 1770, CO 5/313; Tryon to Assembly, November 6, 1769, *Cape Fear Mercury*, November 24, 1769.

28. Hillsborough to Tryon, May 10, 1770, CO 324/42; Tryon to Hillsborough, July 2, 1770, CO 5/313.

Chapter Five

1. Bassett, "Regulators," 144–64; John C. Miller, *Origins of American Revolution*, 211–13; Gipson, *British Empire*, 11:502–10; Butler, *Coming of the Revolution*, 32–33; Dill, *Tryon*, 128.

2. Clark, *State Records*, 23:664–65, 718.

3. Francis Nash and Thomas Hart to Edmund Fanning, April 17, 1768, Saunders, *Colonial Records*, 7:710–12; Fanning to Tryon, April 23, 1768, CO 5/312; Bassett, "Regulators," 164–67; Gipson, *British Empire*, 11:511–12.

4. Proclamation to Orange Regulators, April 27, 1768, CO 5/350; Tryon to Fanning, April 27, 1768 (two letters), Samuel Spencer to Tryon, enclosing Anson County Articles of Association and Oath of Regulators, April 27, 1768, Tryon to Spencer, May —, 1768, CO 5/312; Proclamation to Anson Regulators, May 17,

1768, Powell, *Correspondence of William Tryon*, 2:105; Gipson, *British Empire*, 11:509. For an argument that the poll tax indeed was regressive and burdensome, see Kay, "Payment of Provincial and Local Taxes," 218–40.

5. Fanning to Tryon, May 3, 1768, Regulators' narrative of events, May 21, 1768, Tryon to Regulators, June 21, 1768, Proclamation of Governor Tryon, July 21, 1768, Petition of Orange County inhabitants, [May 1768], CO 5/112; Tryon to Hillsborough, June 16, 1768, CO 5/311; Herman Husband, "Impartial Relation," in William K. Boyd, *Some Eighteenth Century Tracts*, 267–69; Mark Haddon Jones, "Herman Husband," 128–30; Gipson, *British Empire*, 11:514–15.

6. Tryon's journal of his expedition into the backcountry, July 6–August 12, 1768, Tryon to Regulators, August 13, 1768, CO 5/312; Proclamations of Governor Tryon, August 1, 1768, Powell, *Correspondence of William Tryon*, 2:164–65; Husband, "Impartial Relation," in Boyd, *Some Eighteenth Century Tracts*, 275–76; Bassett, "Regulators," 174–75; Gipson, *British Empire*, 11:516.

7. Tryon to Regulators, August 16, 1768, Regulators to Tryon, August 19, 1768, Presbyterian ministers to Tryon, August 23, 1768, Tryon's journal, August 13–26, 1768, CO 5/312; Chalmers G. Davidson, "Independent Mecklenburg," 122–23; Bassett, "Regulators," 175–78; Gipson, *British Empire*, 11:516.

8. Tryon's journal, September 3–14, 1768, Council of war, September 22–23, 1768, CO 5/312; Troop return, September 22, 1768, Saunders, *Colonial Records*, 7:889; Bassett, "Regulators," 178–79; Gipson, *British Empire*, 11:516–17.

9. Proceedings of Superior Court, September 22–October 1, 1768, Saunders, *Colonial Records*, 7:842–47; Husband, "A Fan for Fanning and a Touch-Stone to Tryon," in Boyd, *Some Eighteenth Century Tracts*, 386–87; Tryon to Hillsborough, December 24, 1768, CO 5/312; Bassett, "Regulators," 180–82; Gipson, *British Empire*, 11:517–18.

10. Tryon's journal, September 24, 1768, the Reverend George Micklejohn's Sermon, September 25, 1768, Tryon to Hillsborough, December 24, 1768, CO 5/312; Proclamation of pardon, October 3, 1768, CO 5/350; Gipson, *British Empire*, 11:519.

11. Tryon to Hillsborough, October 25, 1768, January 10, 1769, Assembly to Tryon, November 12, 1768, Tryon's account of military expenditures, October, 1768, CO 5/312; Tryon to Assembly, November 11, 1768, Council to Tryon, November 10, 1768, CO 5/111; Bassett, "Regulators," 184–85; Gipson, *British Empire*, 11:519–21.

12. Tryon to Hillsborough, December 26, 1768, Hillsborough to Tryon, March 1, 1769, CO 5/312; Proclamation of Governor Tryon, September 9, 1769, Powell, *Correspondence of William Tryon*, 2:361; Petitions of Anson County, Orange County, and Rowan County inhabitants, [October 1769], Saunders, *Colonial Records*, 8:75–84; Gipson, *British Empire*, 11:521–22.

13. Assembly to Tryon, November 12, 1768, CO 5/312; Tryon to Assembly, October 23, 1769, and to Hillsborough, November 30, 1769, CO 5/313; Assembly to Tryon, October 30, 1769, *North-Carolina Gazette*, November 10, 1769; Mark Haddon Jones, "Herman Husband," 149–51.

14. Maurice Moore to Tryon, March 13, 1770, Proclamation of Governor Tryon, April 9, 1770, Tryon to Hillsborough, April 13, 1770, CO 5/313; Richard Henderson to Tryon, September 29, 1770, James Watson et al. to Tryon, Septem-

ber 30, 1770, CO 5/314; Bassett, "Regulators," 190–92; Gipson, *British Empire*, 11:523–24; Mark Haddon Jones, "Herman Husband," 164–71.

15. Tryon to Richard Henderson, October 7, 1770, Thomas McGuire to Tryon, October 18, 1770, Proclamation of governor to justices of the peace, October 18, 1770, Tryon to colonels of Orange and Rowan regiments, October 19, 1770, CO 5/312; Bassett, "Regulators," 192–93; Gipson, *British Empire*, 11:524–25.

16. Proclamation of governor, November 19, 1770, John Butler to Tryon, [December 1770], Powell, *Correspondence of William Tryon*, 2:523, 526; Tryon to John Simpson, to Richard Caswell, and to John Hinton, November 20, 1770, CO 5/314.

17. Tryon to Council and Assembly, December 5, 1770, Council to Tryon, December 10, 1770, Assembly to Tryon, December 10, 1770, CO 5/314; Bassett, "Regulators," 194–95; Gipson, *British Empire*, 11:526; Mark Haddon Jones, "Herman Husband," 172–74.

18. Tryon to Hillsborough, January 31, 1771, CO 5/314; Clark, *State Records*, 23:788–89, 814–19, 833–35, 840–41, 846–49; Bassett, "Regulators," 195–96; Gipson, *British Empire*, 11:528–29.

19. Tryon to Hillsborough, January 31 and April 12, 1771, CO 5/314; Proclamation of governor, February 7, 1771, Powell, *Correspondence of William Tryon*, 2:603–4; Court proceedings, February 2–28, 1771, Saunders, *Colonial Records*, 8:507–10; Powell, *Regulators of North Carolina*, 339–45; Bassett, "Regulators," 196–97; Gipson, *British Empire*, 11:529–30; Mark Haddon Jones, "Herman Husband," 175–76.

20. Tryon to Hillsborough, April 12, 1771, CO 5/314; Court proceedings, March 11–16, 1771, Saunders, *Colonial Records*, 8:528–31; Bassett, "Regulators," 197.

21. Tryon to militia colonels, March 16–April 26, 1771, John Frohock and Alexander Martin to Tryon, March 18, 1771, Tryon to Frohock and Martin, April 5, 1771, CO 5/314; Shy, *Toward Lexington*, 400–401.

22. Tryon to John Harvey, March 19, 1771, to Moses Alexander, March 19, 1771, to Richard Blackledge, April 23, 1771, and to Hillsborough, April 12, 1771, CO 5/314; Tryon to Gage, March 19 and April 26, 1771, Gage to Tryon, April 14, 1771, Gage Papers, WLCL; Account of money disbursed, April 22, 1771, Journal of expedition against the insurgents, April 21–24, 1771, Powell, *Correspondence of William Tryon*, 2:669–71, 716; Bassett, "Regulators," 197–201; Shy, *Toward Lexington*, 400–401.

23. Journal of the expedition, May 3, 6, and 12–13, 1771, Powell, *Correspondence of William Tryon*, 2:716–19; Description of Tryon's army, May 6, 1771, William Smith Papers, NYPL; Tryon to Hugh Waddell, May 10 and 18, 1771, and to Hillsborough, May 18, 1771, CO 5/314.

24. Journal of the expedition, May 14–15, 1771, Powell, *Correspondence of William Tryon*, 2:720–21; Return of the army, May 22, 1771, CO 5/315; *Virginia Gazette*, June 13, 1771; Bassett, "Regulators," 202–3; Gipson, *British Empire*, 11:531, 533.

25. Journal of the expedition, May 16, 1771, Powell, *Correspondence of William Tryon*, 2:721–22; Petition of Orange County inhabitants, May 15, 1771, Tryon to Regulators, May 16, 1771, CO 5/314; *Virginia Gazette*, June 13, 1771.

26. Journal of the expedition, May 16, 1771, Powell, *Correspondence of William Tryon*, 2:721–22; Tryon to Hillsborough, May 18, 1771, CO 5/314; *Virginia Gazette*, June 13, 1771; Bassett, "Regulators," 203–4; Gipson, *British Empire*, 11:533–34.

27. Journal of the expedition, May 17, 1771, Powell, *Correspondence of William Tryon*, 2:722; Bassett, "Regulators," 204.

28. Proclamations of governor, May 17, 21, 24, and 31 and June 11, 1771, CO 5/315; Journal of the expedition, May 21 and 26 and June 1, 4, 7–8, and 13, 1771, William Johnston to Richard Benneham, June 7, 1771, Powell, *Correspondence of William Tryon*, 2:724–30; Tryon to Waddell, May 26, 1771, to Robert Hogg et al., May 27, 1771, and to Hillsborough, August 1, 1771, CO 5/314.

29. Proclamation of governor, June 9, 1771, CO 5/315; Tryon to John Ashe, June 20, 1771, and to Hillsborough, August 1, 1771, CO 5/314; Inhabitants of Craven County and New Bern to Tryon, June 26, 1771, Powell, *Correspondence of William Tryon*, 2:779–80.

30. Gage to Amherst, August 6, 1771, Jeffery Amherst Papers, 078/15, Kent Archives Office; *Massachusetts Spy*, June 27, 1771; *Boston Gazette*, July 29, 1771; *Virginia Gazette*, November 7, 1771; Richard Henry Lee to William Lee, June 19, 1771, Ballagh, *Letters of Richard Henry Lee*, 1:58; Thomas Jones, *History of New York*, 2:6; Helen Hill Miller, *Case for Liberty*, 223–25.

31. *Virginia Gazette*, September 17, 1771; *Essex Gazette*, July 23, 1771. Recent positive assessments of Tryon's North Carolina administration are found in Powell, *Correspondence of William Tryon*, 1:xxxii; Gipson, *British Empire*, 11:509; and Dill, *Tryon*, 160–61. The administrations of all the North Carolina royal governors are conveniently summarized in Lefler and Powell, *Colonial North Carolina*, 113–22, 125–49, 212–49 passim.

32. Earl of Rochford to Tryon, August 2, 1771, CO 5/314; Gage to Barrington, July 3 and August 6, 1771, Gage Papers, WLCL; Barrington to Gage, December 4, 1771, Peckham, *Sources of American Independence*, 1:98; Tryon to Lord Hyde, April 30, 1773, *Manuscripts of Dartmouth*, 2:157.

33. *Journals of Commissioners for Trade*, 13:218–19; Commission of Josiah Martin, December 19, 1770, CO 5/1375; Martin to Hillsborough, March 1, 1771, Hillsborough to Martin, May 4, 1771, CO 5/314; Treasury orders for Tryon's salary, May 8, 1771, PRO, T 53/52; Tryon to Hillsborough, August 31, 1771, CO 5/154; Lord Dunmore to Hillsborough, June 4, 1771, Redington and Roberts, *Home Office Papers*, 3:261–62; Sheridan, "West Indian Antecedents," 267; Stumpf, "Josiah Martin," 72–73.

34. Gage to Tryon, April 14, 1771, Tryon to Gage, April 26, 1771, Gage Papers, WLCL; James Rivington to Sir William Johnson, July 18, 1771, Sullivan et al., *Papers of Sir William Johnson*, 8:51–52; Rhode Island Friends to Tryon, June 13–17, 1771, *Boston Gazette*, July 15, 1771.

Chapter Six

1. Tryon to Council of New York, June 29, 1771, James Hassell to Hillsborough, July 4, 1771, CO 5/314; Tryon to Hillsborough, July 9, 1771, CO 5/1102;

William Smith, *Historical Memoirs 1763 to 1778*, 1:105. Historian Thomas Jones reported a slightly different version of Tryon's arrival, declaring that the new governor "was received with the acclamations of a then grateful and happy people" (*History of New York*, 2:6), and the *Essex Gazette* said "he was welcomed by a Salute of 15 Guns from the Fort, to which he was conducted by the gentlemen of the Council, and others who waited at his Landing" (July 23, 1771).

2. William Smith, *Historical Memoirs 1763 to 1778*, 1:105–6; Dunmore to Hillsborough, July 2, 1771, Redington and Roberts, *Home Office Papers*, 3:272; Tryon to Hillsborough, August 31, 1771, CO 5/154.

3. Tryon to Hillsborough, July 9, 1771, CO 5/1102; William Smith, *Historical Memoirs 1763 to 1778*, 1:107; Henner, "Career of William Tryon," 32.

4. Tryon to Hillsborough, July 9, 1771, CO 5/1102; Martin to Hillsborough, August 15, 1771, CO 5/314; Stumpf, "Josiah Martin," 76.

5. *Old New York and Trinity Church*, 216–17, 221; City of Albany to Tryon, August 12, 1771, Gratz Autograph Collection, HSP; Thomas Hutchinson to Tryon, August 24, 1771, Massachusetts Archives, XXVII, 217; Tryon to Hillsborough, August 30, 1771, enclosing address of students of King's College to Tryon, CO 5/1102; Alexander Colden to Benjamin Franklin, August 6, 1771, Leonard Woods Labaree et al., *Papers of Benjamin Franklin*, 18:197.

6. Cadwallader Colden to Tryon, August 22, 1774, Tryon to Dartmouth, March 29, 1775, Dartmouth to Tryon, May 4, 1775, CO 5/1106; *New York Mercury*, April 4, 1774; Columbia University, *History of Columbia University*, 35–36, 208, and *Officers and Graduates*, 514.

7. William Smith, *Historical Memoirs 1763 to 1778*, 1:107. The letter was to Daniel Burton, secretary of the SPG, March 20, 1769, Tryon Letter Book, 243–47, HL, cited in chapter 2, note 21.

8. Tryon to Dartmouth, July 6, 1773, CO 5/1104; *Old New York and Trinity Church*, 226.

9. Corwin, *Ecclesiastical Records*, 2:1076–79, 6:4233; Richard B. Morris, *John Jay*, 106; Dillon, "Century of Religion," and *New York Triumvirate*, 49–52; Alexander, *Revolutionary Conservative*, 22–24.

10. Tryon to ———, July 16, 1771, Emmett Collection, #3958, NYPL; Tryon to Hillsborough, May 1 and June 4, 1772, CO 5/1103; *Colonial Laws of New York*, 5:335–42, 494–98, 680–87.

11. Tryon to Hillsborough, December 4, 1771, Hillsborough to Tryon, February 5, 1772, CO 5/1103; Redington and Roberts, *Home Office Papers*, 3:425.

12. Tryon to Hillsborough, September 2, 1771, CO 5/1102; Tryon to Privy Council, December 1, 1772, Order of king in Council to Board of Trade, February 21 and April 13, 1774, CO 5/1077.

13. Tryon to Joseph Solano, September 30, 1771, CO 5/1102; Hillsborough to Tryon, January 11, 1772, Solano to Tryon, March 28, 1772, Dartmouth to Tryon, December 8, 1772, CO 5/1103; Tryon to Hillsborough, September 30, 1771, PRO, T 1/516.

14. Gage to Tryon, November 27, 1771, Gage Papers, WLCL; William Smith, *Historical Memoirs 1763 to 1778*, 1:123–24.

15. Gage to Barrington, January 7, 1772, Carter, *Correspondence of Thomas Gage*, 2:596; Tryon to Dartmouth, April 6, 1773, CO 5/1104; Gage to Tryon,

April 30 and May 5, 1772, Gage Papers, WLCL; *Colonial Laws of New York*, 5:271–72.

16. Tryon to Hillsborough, January 16, 1772, CO 5/1103; Tryon to Dartmouth, January 5, 1773, Dartmouth to Tryon, March 3, April 6, and June 3, 1773, CO 5/1104; *Colonial Laws of New York*, 5:342–51; *New York Mercury*, December 7, 1772; Dorothy C. Barck, "Captain Thomas Sowers," 59–64; Wertenbaker, *Father Knickerbocker Rebels*, 30. Although Tryon later sensed some lack of approval for the militia law in London, and thus proceeded at length to explain the necessity for a militia (mostly the danger of New York City lying open to the "insults of an Enemy"), he was assured that the government entirely assented to his actions (Tryon to Dartmouth, June 1, 1773, Dartmouth to Tryon, August 4, 1773, CO 5/1104).

17. Hillsborough to Sir Henry Moore, May 14, 1768, O'Callaghan, *Documents Relative to Colonial New York*, 8:73; Gage to Barrington, February 4 and July 1, 1772, Carter, *Correspondence of Thomas Gage*, 2:598, 611; Tryon to Dartmouth, March 29, 1775, CO 5/1106; Dartmouth to royal governors, April 15, 1775, CO 5/242; William Smith, *Historical Memoirs 1763 to 1778*, 1:237; Henner, "Career of William Tryon," 67–70. See Shy, *Toward Lexington*, 156–63, 286–88, for a general discussion of conflicts over supremacy in command between American Colonial governors and soldiers.

18. William Smith, *Historical Memoirs 1763 to 1778*, 1:107–8; Calhoon, *Loyalists in Revolutionary America*, 99.

19. William Smith, *Historical Memoirs 1763 to 1778*, 1:117–18; Jaunitz-Schürer, *Loyal Whigs and Revolutionaries*, xxi–xxii, 98–99; Upton, *Loyal Whig*, 82.

20. William Smith, *Historical Memoirs 1763 to 1778*, 1:128.

21. Leonard Woods Labaree, *Royal Instructions*, 2:607; Grant and Monro, *Acts of Privy Council*, 4:673–74; Gipson, *British Empire*, 11:315–16.

22. O'Callaghan, *Documentary History*, 4:406–9, 477–78.

23. William Smith, *Historical Memoirs 1763 to 1778*, 1:107–13.

24. Fernow, *New York Council Minutes*, 562.

25. Hillsborough to Tryon, December 4, 1771, CO 5/1102; Tryon to Hillsborough, February 2, 1772, CO 5/1103.

26. Tryon to Hillsborough, April 11, 1772, CO 5/1103.

27. Tryon to John Wentworth, October 2, 1771, CO 5/1102; Wentworth to Tryon, October 19, 1771, January 8, 1772, CO 5/1076; *New Hampshire Provincial, Town, and State Papers*, 7:298; *State of the Evidence*, 10–11; Mark, *Agrarian Conflicts*, 179–80.

28. Tryon to Hillsborough, February 1 and September 1, 1772, Hillsborough to Tryon, April 18, 1772, CO 5/1103; Board of Trade to Privy Council, November 30, 1772, *Manuscripts of Dartmouth*, 2:108; William Smith, *Historical Memoirs 1763 to 1778*, 1:124.

29. Tryon to the Reverend Jedediah Dewey, May 19, 1772, CO 5/1103; Thompson, *Independent Vermont*, 127.

30. Inhabitants of Bennington to Tryon, June 19 and August 25, 1772, Tryon to inhabitants of Bennington, August 11, 1772, Tryon to Hillsborough, September 1

and October 7, 1772, Tryon to Dartmouth, October 22, 1772, CO 5/1103; O'Callaghan, *Documentary History*, 4:786–92; Mark, *Agrarian Conflicts*, 183; Thompson, *Independent Vermont*, 129–34.

31. Tryon to Dartmouth, December 12, 1772, February 8, 1773, Dartmouth to Tryon, March 3, 1773, CO 5/1104; Tryon to Dartmouth, May 5, 1773, *Manuscripts of Dartmouth*, 2:154; Order in Council, April 7, 1773, O'Callaghan, *Documents Relative to Colonial New York*, 8:357–58.

32. Dartmouth to Tryon, April 10, 1773, Tryon to Dartmouth, July 1, 1773, CO 5/1104; Dartmouth to Tryon, February 5, 1774, enclosing additional instructions from the king, February 3, 1774, CO 5/1105.

33. Tryon to Frederick Haldimand, September 1, 1773, Haldimand to Tryon, September 1, 1773, Haldimand Papers, Add. MSS. 21673, ff. 202, 204, BL; Tryon to Dartmouth, September 1, 1773, CO 5/1104.

34. Tryon to Haldimand, September 1 and 9 and October 5, 1773, Haldimand Papers, Add. MSS. 21673, ff. 206, 212, 226, BL; Haldimand to Tryon, September 11, 1773, CO 5/90; Dartmouth to Tryon, October 14, 1773, CO 5/1104; McIlwraith, *Sir Frederick Haldimand*, 89–90.

35. Gipson, *British Empire*, 11:326.

36. Dartmouth to Tryon, August 4, 1773, CO 5/1104; Tryon to Dartmouth, January 2 and April 6, 1774, CO 5/1105; O'Callaghan, *Documentary History*, 4:526–27; Gipson, *British Empire*, 11:326–27.

Chapter Seven

1. Tryon to Clinton, March 3, 1771, Clinton Papers, WLCL; Tryon to Hillsborough, July 4, 1772, CO 5/1103.

2. Tryon to Hillsborough, August 31, 1772, CO 5/1103; *Memoirs of Catherine Schuyler*, chap. 3, in Trevelyan, *American Revolution*, 2:239n; Gerlach, *Philip Schuyler*, 210, 221–22; Lossing, *Life and Times of Philip Schuyler*, 1:262–63; Flexner, *Mohawk Baronet*, 342; McIlwraith, *Sir Frederick Haldimand*, 91.

3. Tryon to Hillsborough, August 21, 1772, enclosing Proceedings at a Congress . . . , July 28, 1772, CO 5/1103; Robert Livingston to James Duane, August 28, 1772, Duane Papers, II, NYHS; Sir William Johnson to Gage, August 6, 1772, Sullivan et al., *Papers of Sir William Johnson*, 8:562; *Memoirs of Catherine Schuyler*, chap. 3, in Trevelyan, *American Revolution*, 2:239n; Philip Schuyler to William Duer, September 21, 1772, in Lossing, *Life and Times of Philip Schuyler*, 1:263–63.

4. Dartmouth to Tryon, November 4, 1772, CO 5/1103; Tryon to Dartmouth, January 5, 1773, CO 5/1104; Grant and Munro, *Acts of Privy Council*, 4:500.

5. Dartmouth to Tryon, March 3, 1773, Tryon to Dartmouth, June 2, 1773, CO 5/1104.

6. Tryon to Dartmouth, June 2, 1773, CO 5/1104.

7. Dartmouth to Tryon, June 2 and August 4, 1773, Tryon to Dartmouth October 3, 1773, CO 5/1104.

8. Tryon to Hillsborough, October 2, 1771, CO 5/1102; H. T. Cramahé to

Tryon, November 11, 1771, CO 5/1076; Tryon to Hillsborough, December 3, 1771, February 3, May 5, September 1, and October 1, 1772, Dartmouth to Tryon, December 8, 1772, CO 5/1103; Tryon to Dartmouth, January 5, July 6, and August 30, 1773, CO 5/1104; Cramahé to Dartmouth, October 1, 1773, CO 42/32; Tryon to Dartmouth, March 31, 1774, CO 5/1105.

9. Tryon to Thomas Hutchinson, November 6, 1771, Hutchinson to Tryon, November 25 and 28, 1771, CO 5/761; Tryon to Hillsborough, October 6, 1772, enclosing correspondence with Hutchinson and Council minutes, September 29, 1772, CO 5/1103; Tryon to Dartmouth, May 5, 1773, CO 5/1104; *Colonial Laws of New York*, 2:756–57; Fernow, *New York Council Minutes*, 496; Gipson, *British Empire*, 11:330–43.

10. Tryon to Dartmouth, May 31 and October 3, 1773, Dartmouth to Tryon, July 5, 1773, CO 5/1104; Tryon to Hutchinson, August 27, 1773, Sedgwick II Papers, MHS; Gipson, *British Empire*, 11:344–45.

11. Tryon to Dartmouth, May 31, 1773, CO 5/1104; John Adams to Abigail Adams, [April–May 1780], Butterfield et al., *Book of Abigail and John*, 256; Adams to Richard Cranch, June 17, 1782, Butterfield, *Adams Papers*, 3:332–33.

12. Tryon to Hillsborough, October 3, 1772, CO 5/1103; William Franklin to Tryon, December 9, 1772, CO 5/1104; Allinson, *Acts of the General Assembly*, 342, 368–73.

13. Tryon to Dartmouth, February 7, 1773, Dartmouth to Tryon, April 10, 1773, CO 5/1104; William Smith, *Historical Memoirs 1763 to 1778*, 1:77–79; Grant and Munro, *Acts of Privy Council*, 4:45–46; Richard B. Morris, *John Jay*, 119–20; Gipson, *British Empire*, 11:356–57.

14. Tryon to Dartmouth, March 4 and April 6, 1773, CO 5/1104; Gerlach, *Philip Schuyler*, 34–35.

15. Tryon to Hillsborough, March 31 and June 4, 1772, Livingston to Hillsborough, February 9, 1772, CO 5/1103.

16. William Smith, *Historical Memoirs 1763 to 1778*, 1:138–39; Gerlach, *Philip Schuyler*, 225.

17. William Smith, *Historical Memoirs 1763 to 1778*, 1:129–30, 132, 154–55; Richard B. Morris, *John Jay*, 132 (n. 4); Dangerfield, *Chancellor Livingston*, 48–49.

18. William Smith, *Historical Memoirs 1763 to 1778*, 1:152–53, 155; Thomas Jones, *History of New York*, 1:232.

19. Tryon to Schuyler, September 15, 1773, Sparks Manuscripts, HL; Smith to Schuyler, July 5, 1773, Philip Schuyler Papers, Box 24, NYPL; Gerlach, *Philip Schuyler*, 228.

20. Montgomery, "Memoirs," Livingston Family Papers, III, 142–43, NYPL; Dangerfield, *Chancellor Livingston*, 50–51.

21. Tryon to Dartmouth, November 3, 1773, CO 5/1104; William Smith, *Historical Memoirs 1763 to 1778*, 1:156; Champagne, *Alexander McDougall*, 46.

22. Tryon to Dartmouth, December 1, 1773, CO 5/1105; William Smith, *Historical Memoirs 1763 to 1778*, 1:157; Leake, *General John Lamb*, 76; Benjamin Woods Labaree, *Boston Tea Party*, 91–97; Mason, *Road to Independence*, 12; Maier, *Old Revolutionaries*, 82–85; Upton, *Loyal Whig*, 87.

23. Force, *American Archives*, series 4, 1:32n; William Smith, *Historical Memoirs 1763 to 1778*, 1:158, 159–61, 254n; Leake, *General John Lamb*, 80–81; Mason, *Road to Independence*, 14–15, 17; Upton, *Loyal Whig*, 88. Champagne (*Alexander McDougall*, 46) asserts that McDougall was only attempting to shock his listeners and did not really mean what he said.

24. Tryon to Dartmouth, January 3, 1774, CO 5/1105; William Smith, *Historical Memoirs 1763 to 1778*, 1:163–66; Becker, *Political Parties*, 108; Mason, *Road to Independence*, 17–18.

25. Tryon to Dartmouth, December 31, 1773, CO 5/1105; William Smith, *Historical Memoirs 1763 to 1778*, 1:166–67; Bargar, "Tryon's House," 295–309.

26. Dartmouth to Tryon, February 5, 1774, CO 5/1105; George III to Dartmouth, February 5, 1774, *Manuscripts of Dartmouth*, 1:438; Tryon's inventory, Bargar, "Tryon's House," 295–309; *Colonial Laws of New York*, 5:614.

27. Dartmouth to Tryon, July 5, 1773, CO 5/241; Tryon to Dartmouth, October 5, 1773, CO 5/1104; Tryon to Dartmouth, June 11, 1774, enclosing report of His Excellency William Tryon . . . , CO 5/1105.

28. Tryon to Hillsborough, October 19, 1772, and to Dartmouth, October 19, 1772, CO 5/1103; Tryon to Ralph Wormeley, May 26, 1773, Wormeley Family Papers, 1939, University of Virginia Library; Tryon to Dartmouth, June 8 and October 6, 1773, CO 5/1104; Tryon to Dartmouth, February 2, March 1, and April 7, 1774, Dartmouth to Tryon, April 6, 1774, CO 5/1105.

29. Osgood, *Common Council of New York*, 8:20–21; *Old New York and Trinity Church*, 244; William Smith, *Historical Memoirs 1763 to 1778*, 1:180–81, 189; Gerlach, *Philip Schuyler*, 234–35; McIlwraith, *Sir Frederick Haldimand*, 91.

30. William Smith, *Historical Memoirs 1763 to 1778*, 1:182.

31. Tryon to Elias Desbrosses, October 4, 1774, Huntington Manuscripts, 9880, Huntington Library.

32. Tryon to Dartmouth, September 30, 1774, *Manuscripts of Dartmouth*, 1:364; Tryon to Desbrosses, October 4, 1774, Huntington Manuscripts, 9880, Huntington Library.

33. Lord North to Dartmouth, August 12, 1774, *Manuscripts of Dartmouth*, 2:221; Tryon to George III, [April 1775], PRO, T 1/484; North to William Eden, September 18, 1775, Letters to Eden, Add. MSS. 46490, BL.

34. North Carolina Assembly to Tryon, [December 1773], Powell, *Correspondence of William Tryon*, 2:857–58; Tryon to Dartmouth, May 24, 1774, CO 5/1105; Tryon to Dartmouth, June 16, 1774, *Manuscripts of Dartmouth*, 2:213–14.

35. Tryon to Desbrosses, October 4, 1774, Huntington Manuscripts, 9880, Huntington Library; Tryon to Dartmouth, March 25, 1775, *Manuscripts of Dartmouth*, 2:277; Tryon to Cadwallader Colden, March 2, 1775, Colden, *Letters and Papers*, 7:267; Tryon to Colden, March 3, 1775, Gratz Autograph Collection, HSP.

36. Tryon to Dartmouth, January 24, 1775, CO 5/1106; Tryon to Dartmouth, April 17, 19, and 21, 1775, *Manuscripts of Dartmouth*, 2:289, 290–91, 292; *Journals of Commissioners for Trade*, 13:413–14, 416, 420–22.

37. Tryon to Dartmouth, April 12, 1775, Dartmouth to Tryon, April 21 and May 4, 1775, CO 5/1106.

38. Colden to Tryon, May 4 and September 7, 1774, *Colden Letter Books*, 2:335–39, 360–61.

39. Colden to Tryon, December 7, 1774, *Colden Letter Books*, 2:375–76; Smith to Tryon, November 25 and December 6, 1774, *Manuscripts of Dartmouth*, 2:236; Dartmouth to Tryon, December 30, 1774, Tryon to Colden, January 2, 1775, Van Schaack Family Papers, Columbia University Libraries; Dartmouth to Tryon, May 23, 1775, CO 5/1106; Bargar, *Lord Dartmouth*, 147–52.

40. Tryon to Colden, June 30, 1774, March 2, 1775, Colden, *Letters and Papers*, 7:226–27, 267–68; Tryon to Dartmouth, January 19, 1775, CO 5/1105.

Chapter Eight

1. Tryon to North, May 3, 1775, and to Dartmouth, May 8, 1775, *Manuscripts of Dartmouth*, 2:300.

2. Tryon to Dartmouth, July 4, 1775, CO 5/1106; *Journal of the Provincial Congress*, 1:54; William Smith, *Historical Memoirs 1763 to 1778*, 1:228c–228d; Thomas Jones, *History of New York*, 1:55–57; Freeman, *George Washington*, 3:467.

3. Tryon to Gage, June 26, 1775, Gage Papers, WLCL; Tryon to Dartmouth, July 4, 1775, CO 5/1106; Force, *American Archives*, series 4, 2:1329.

4. Tryon to Dartmouth, July 4, 1775, CO 5/1106; Tryon to Darmouth, July 6, 1775, *Manuscripts of Dartmouth*, 2:328.

5. Tryon to Dartmouth, July 7, 1775 (two letters), Thomas Pownall (for Dartmouth) to Tryon, September 6, 1775, CO 5/1106.

6. Tryon to Gage, July 8, 1775, Gage Papers, WLCL; George Washington to Schuyler, June 25, 1775, Fitzpatrick, *Writings of George Washington*, 3:302–3, 332; Maier, *Old Revolutionaries*, 86; Gerlach, *Philip Schuyler*, 283–84.

7. Livingston to Jay, February 15, 1776, Jay Papers, Columbia University Libraries; Thomas Jones, *History of New York*, 1:58–59; Dangerfield, *Chancellor Livingston*, 73–74; Gerlach, *Philip Schuyler*, 283–84.

8. George Vandeput to Tryon, July 13, 1775, Tryon to Dartmouth, August 7, 1775, CO 5/1106; William Smith, *Historical Memoirs 1763 to 1778*, 1:237.

9. Tryon to Dartmouth, August 7, 1775, CO 5/1106; Tryon to Gage, August 14, 1775, Gage Papers, WLCL; William Smith, *Historical Memoirs 1763 to 1778*, 1:236–37.

10. William Smith, *Historical Memoirs 1763 to 1778*, 1:234–37.

11. —— to Tryon, August 22, 1775, Clinton Papers, WLCL; Tryon to Vandeput, August 25, 1775, and to Dartmouth, September 5, 1775, CO 5/1106; Mason, *Road to Independence*, 103.

12. Tryon to Dartmouth, September 5, 1775, CO 5/1106; Mason, *Road to Independence*, 105.

13. Tryon to Dartmouth, September 5, 1775, CO 5/1106; Tryon to Dartmouth, January 3, 1776, CO 5/1107.

14. Gage to Tryon, September 10, 1775, Gage Papers, WLCL; William Smith, *Historical Memoirs 1763 to 1778*, 1:241; Moore, *Diary of the Revolution*, 1:138.

15. Tryon to Dartmouth, October 16, 1775, CO 5/1106; William Smith, *Historical Memoirs 1763 to 1778*, 1:242.

16. Tryon to Whitehead Hicks, October 1 and 18, 1775, Hicks to Tryon, October 14, 1775, New York Committee to Hicks, October 17, 1775, Tryon to Dartmouth, October 18 and November 11, 1775, CO 5/1106.

17. Tryon to Dartmouth, November 11, 1775, CO 5/1106; Richard Mansfield to Tryon, November 29, 1775, CO 5/1107; Tryon to William Howe, December 3 and 13, 1775, CO 5/93; Anderson, *Command of the Howe Brothers*, 29, 309.

18. Tryon to Howe, December 13, 1775, Howe to Tryon, January 11, 1776, CO 5/93; Washington to Charles Lee, January 30, 1776, Fitzpatrick, *Writings of George Washington*, 4:293–94; Tryon to Dartmouth, January 3, 1776, CO 5/1107; Stevens, *Howe's Orderly Book*, 314; Tiedemann, "Revolution Foiled," 440; Countryman, *People in Revolution*, 148–49.

19. Tryon to Dartmouth, December 8, 1775, CO 5/1106; Tryon to Carleton, January 31, 1776, CO 5/1107; Howe to Dartmouth, January 16, 1776, CO 5/93; Stevens, *Howe's Orderly Book*, 313; Philip Davidson, *Propaganda*, 254.

20. Willard, *Letters on the American Revolution*, 265–66; John Jay to Committee of Safety of New York, April 7, 1776, Johnston, *Correspondence and Public Papers of John Jay*, 1:51–52; Worthington C. Ford, *Journals of Congress*, 4:273; Stevens, *Facsimiles of Manuscripts*, 24:2024; Justin H. Smith, *Struggle for the Fourteenth Colony*, 2:215–17; Alexander, *Revolutionary Conservative*, 116–17.

21. Force, *American Archives*, series 4, 6:1178–79.

22. James Rivington to Tryon, December 4, 1775, Tryon to Dartmouth, December 6, 1775, CO 5/1107.

23. Smith to Tryon, December 17, 1775, CO 5/1107; Jay to McDougall, December 8, 1775, Richard B. Morris, *John Jay*, 192–93, 204 (n. 6).

24. Smith to Tryon, December 17, 1775, CO 5/1107; Becker, *Political Parties*, 241–42; Mason, *Road to Independence*, 129–33; Countryman, *People in Revolution*, 96.

25. Tryon to Dartmouth, February 8 and 10 and April 6, 1776, CO 5/1107; Clinton to Tryon, February 11, 1776, Clinton Papers, WLCL; Charles Lee to Washington, February 5, 1776, *Lee Papers*, 1:271; Willcox, *Clinton's Narrative*, 24–25; Willcox, *Portrait of a General*, 75.

26. Dartmouth to Tryon, December 23, 1775, CO 5/242; Tryon to Lord George Germain, April 6, 1776 (two letters), CO 5/1107; Lee to Washington, February 19, 1776, *Lee Papers*, 1:308–10.

27. Tryon to Dartmouth, February 7, 1776, CO 5/1107; William Smith, *Historical Memoirs 1763 to 1778*, 1:269–70; Force, *American Archives*, series 4, 5:248–49; Bliven, *Under the Guns*, 199.

28. William Smith, *Historical Memoirs 1763 to 1778*, 1:269; *Holt's Journal*, April 4, 1776; Moore, *Diary of the Revolution*, 1:223–24; Willard, *Letters on the American Revolution*, 303–4; Philip Davidson, *Propaganda*, 83.

29. Tryon to Germain, April 15 and 18, 1776, CO 5/1107; Washington to Committee of Safety of New York, April 17, 1776, Fitzpatrick, *Writings of George Washington*, 3:486–88.

30. Force, *American Archives*, series 4, 6:1084–86, 1120, 1152–83, 1406, 1410–11, series 5, 1:731, 1550; Van Doren, *Secret History*, 12–13; Freeman, *George Washington*, 4:115–21.

31. Tryon to Germain, July 8, 1776, CO 5/1107; *Kemble Papers*, 1:79; Howe to Germain, July 7, 1776, Force, *American Archives*, series 5, 1:105–6; Willcox, *Portrait of a General*, 99n.

32. Thomas Jones, *History of New York*, 2:166n; Oscar Theodore Barck, *New York City*, 49–52.

33. Tryon to Germain, November 26, 1776, CO 5/1107; Inhabitants of New York to Tryon, October 16, 1776, Tryon to inhabitants of New York, October 25, 1776, Force, *American Archives*, series 5, 2:1075–76; Tatum, *Ambrose Serle*, 128–29, 176; Tiedemann, "Patriots by Default"; Klein, "Why Did the British Fail?"; Oscar Theodore Barck, *New York City*, 49–56.

34. Tryon to Germain, July 8, September 24, and November 28, 1776, CO 5/1107; Tryon to Germain, December 24, 1776, Germain to Tryon, January 14, 1777, CO 5/1108; Ranlet, *New York Loyalists*, 147, 149; Tatum, *Ambrose Serle*, 138; Oscar Theodore Barck, *New York City*, 192.

35. Tryon to Germain, August 14, September 15, and November 26 and 28, 1776, CO 5/1107; Tryon to Germain, December 24 and 31, 1776, January 20 and February 11, 1777, CO 5/1108; Tatum, *Ambrose Serle*, 139; Gruber, *Howe Brothers*, 144.

36. Tryon to Germain, September 24, 1776, CO 5/1107; James Thacher, *Military Journal*, 70–71; Tatum, *Ambrose Serle*, 31, 36–37, 40, 52–53, 55, 117, 123, 130.

37. Tryon to Germain, December 24, 1776, February 11 and 12, 1777, CO 5/1108; Gruber, *Howe Brothers*, 149.

38. Tryon to Germain, November 30, 1776, CO 5/1107; Tryon to Germain, December 23, 1776, January 6, 1777, CO 5/1108; Dartmouth to Tryon, December 25, 1781, PRO, T 1/572; Serle to Dartmouth, November 28, 1776, *Manuscripts of Dartmouth*, 2:429.

39. Tryon to Germain, January 7 and June 8, 1777, Germain to Tryon, March 3, 1777, CO 5/1108; Germain to Howe brothers, June 12, 1777, CO 5/177; Tatum, *Ambrose Serle*, 130, 172–73; *Kemble Papers*, 1:108; Gruber, *Howe Brothers*, 138 (n. 23).

Chapter Nine

1. Tryon to Germain, December 31, 1776, CO 5/1108.

2. William Smith, *Historical Memoirs 1778 to 1783*, 95; Conway, "To Subdue America," Clinton quoted, 381.

3. Howe brothers to Germain, November 30, 1776, Germain to Howe brothers, January 14, 1777, CO 5/177; Tryon to Germain, December 2, 1776, CO 5/1108; Germain to Knox, December 31, 1776, *Manuscripts of Knox*, 128; Gruber, *Howe Brothers*, 172–73.

4. Tryon to Germain, January 20, February 11 and 12, and March 28, 1777,

Germain to Tryon, June 11, 1776, CO 5/1107; Germain to Tryon, April 2, 1777, CO 5/1108; Howe to Germain, April 2, 1777, CO 5/94; Barrington to Tryon, September 3, 1777, WO 4/274; Barrington to Howe, September 3, 1777, Carleton Papers, PRO 30/55/6, f. 655; Tatum, *Ambrose Serle,* 186; Gruber, *Howe Brothers,* 193, 199; Hargrove, *General John Burgoyne,* 112–14.

5. Howe to Germain, April 24, 1777, CO 5/179; Lydenberg, *Archibald Robertson,* 126–27; *Kemble Papers,* 1:113–14; Ward, *War of the Revolution,* 2:492.

6. Lydenberg, *Archibald Robertson,* 128–29; Wallace, *Traitorous Hero,* 128–29; Ward, *War of the Revolution,* 2:494.

7. Lydenberg, *Archibald Robertson,* 128–29; Serle to Dartmouth, May 1, 1777, Stevens, *Facsimiles of Manuscripts,* 24:2059.

8. Tryon to Dartmouth, May 2 and June 9, 1777, CO 5/1108; William Smith, *Historical Memoirs 1778 to 1783,* 104.

9. Howe to Germain, May 22, 1777, CO 5/94; Germain to Knox, July 1, 1777, *Manuscripts of Knox,* 132.

10. Tryon to Germain, April 9, 1777, Germain to Tryon, May 19 and June 5, 1777, CO 5/1108; Tryon to Germain, May 5, 1777, *Manuscripts of Dartmouth,* 2:432; Bailyn, *Ordeal of Thomas Hutchinson,* 290.

11. Howe to Clinton, April 16, 1778, Clinton Papers, WLCL.

12. Tryon to Dartmouth, May 5, 1777, *Manuscripts of Dartmouth,* 2:432; Tryon to Darmouth, July 8 and October 3, 1777, CO 5/1108; Tatum, *Ambrose Serle,* 231, 237.

13. *Pennsylvania Gazette,* May 14, 1777; *Pennsylvania Evening Post,* May 22, 1777; *South Carolina Gazette,* July 23, 1777; Philip Davidson, *Propaganda,* 405.

14. Tryon to Clinton, July 1, 8, and 28 and August 4 and 20, 1777, Clinton Papers, WLCL.

15. *Diary of Frederick Mackenzie,* 1:174–75; Willcox, *Clinton's Narrative,* 67–69; *Kemble Papers,* 1:128.

16. Tryon to Germain, October 3, 1777, CO 5/1108; Crary, "Guerrilla Activities of James DeLancey's Cowboys," 14–26, 153–55.

17. Tryon to Clinton, September 20, 1777, Clinton Papers, WLCL; Willcox, *Clinton's Narrative,* 72 (n. 31).

18. Clinton to Tryon, October 2, 1777, Clinton Papers, WLCL; Clinton to Howe, October 9, 1777, CO 5/94; William Hotham to Lord Howe, October 9, 1777, CO 5/127; Willcox, *Clinton's Narrative,* 75; *Kemble Papers,* 1:133–34; Ward, *War of the Revolution,* 2:516–20.

19. Clinton to Howe, October 9, 1777, CO 5/94; Willcox, *Clinton's Narrative,* 77–78.

20. Tryon to Clinton, October 8, 1777, Clinton Papers, WLCL; Willcox, *Clinton's Narrative,* 79–80; Hargrove, *General John Burgoyne,* 185–86.

21. Clinton to Tryon, October 18, 1777, Tryon to Clinton, October 26, 1777, Clinton Papers, WLCL; Willcox, *Clinton's Narrative,* 79–80.

22. Leiby, *Hackensack Valley,* 216; Wertenbaker, *Father Knickerbocker Rebels,* 140.

23. Samuel Holden Parsons to Tryon, November 21, 1777, January 1, 1778, Tryon to Parsons, November 31, 1777, CO 5/1108; *Kemble Papers,* 1:144.

24. Tryon to Germain, December 1, 1777, March 18, 1778, Germain to Tryon, January 7, 1778, Tryon to Howe, December 28, 1777, March 21, 1778, Howe to Tryon, March 5, 1778, CO 5/1108; Tryon to Clinton, February 13, 1778, Clinton Papers, WLCL.

25. Howe to Tryon, March 5, 1778, Tryon to Germain, March 21 and September 6, 1778, Germain to Tryon, June 5, 1778, CO 5/1108; Howe to Barrington, April 13, 1778, Carleton Papers, PRO 30/55/10, f. 1095; Barrington to Howe, May 14, 1778, WO 4/274; Tatum, *Ambrose Serle*, 282–83.

26. Tryon to Germain, March 20, April 15, July 8, and September 5, 1778, Lord Howe to Tryon, April 11, 1778, Tryon to Lord Howe, April 12, 1778, Germain to Tryon, August 5, 1778, CO 5/1108; Tryon to Germain, February 5, March 1, and May 3, 1779, to Marriot Arbuthnot, June 29, 1779, and to Germain, September 5, 1779, CO 5/1109; Germain to royal governors, August 5, 1778, June 17, 1779, CO 5/242; William Smith, *Historical Memoirs 1778 to 1783*, 74; Gruber, *Howe Brothers*, 293.

27. Germain to Tryon, February 19, 1778, CO 5/242; Tryon to Jonathan Trumbull, April 17, 1778, Miscellaneous Bound Papers, MHS; Tryon to Washington, April 17, 1778, CO 5/1108; Trumbull to Tryon, April 21, 1778, Clinton Papers, WLCL.

28. Washington to Tryon, April 26, 1778, Tryon to Germain, May 2, 1778, CO 5/1108; Tryon to Trumbull, May 21, 1778, Trumbull to Tryon, May 25, 1778, Trumbull Papers, VIII, 135, 136, Connecticut State Library; Washington to William Livingston, April 26, 1778, Fitzpatrick, *Writings of George Washington*, 11:311; *New Jersey Gazette*, April 23, 1778; Worthington C. Ford, *Journals of Congress*, 10:374–80, 382; Weldon A. Brown, *Empire or Independence*, 231.

29. Tryon to Clinton, August 9 and 11, 1778, Clinton Papers, WLCL; Tryon to Germain, September 5, 1778, CO 5/1108; Clinton to Germain, September 15, 1778, CO 5/96; Paul Leicester Ford, *Orderly Book*, 37, 40–55; Uhlendorf, *Revolution in America*, 197.

30. Tryon to Clinton, August 18, 19, and 21, 1778, Clinton Papers, WLCL; Tryon to Germain, October 8, 1778, CO 5/1108; Willcox, *Clinton's Narrative*, 102; William Smith, *Historical Memoirs 1778 to 1783*, 8.

31. Tryon to Germain, September 5, 1778, CO 5/1108; William Smith, *Historical Memoirs 1778 to 1783*, 10.

32. Tryon to Germain, October 8, 1778, CO 5/1108; Tryon to Germain, December 24, 1778, CO 5/1109; William Smith, *Historical Memoirs 1778 to 1783*, 14, 17, 29, 33, 38, 40, 59.

33. William Smith, *Historical Memoirs 1778 to 1783*, 41, 75, 109, 120.

34. Tryon to Germain, July 8, September 6, and October 8, 1778, Germain to Tryon, September 2, 1778, CO 5/1108; Tryon to Germain, November 24 and December 24, 1778, CO 5/1109; William Smith, *Historical Memoirs 1778 to 1783*, 40–41.

35. Germain to Tryon, March 3 and April 1, 1779, Tryon to Germain, May 3, 1779, CO 5/1109. Smith edited Tryon's letter of May 3 (William Smith, *Historical Memoirs 1778 to 1783*, 99).

Chapter Ten

1. William Smith, *Historical Memoirs 1778 to 1783*, 40, 69.
2. Tryon to Clinton, February 28, 1779, Clinton to Germain, March 2, 1779, Clinton Papers, WLCL; Tryon to Germain, March 1, 1779, CO 5/1109; William Smith, *Historical Memoirs 1778 to 1783*, 78; Willcox, *Clinton's Narrative*, 117; Lydenberg, *Archibald Robertson*, 188; Cutter, *Life of Israel Putnam*, 349–52.
3. William Smith, *Historical Memoirs 1778 to 1783*, 86, 93, 111.
4. Tryon to Clinton, June 30, 1779, Clinton Papers, WLCL; William Smith, *Historical Memoirs 1778 to 1783*, 120–21; Van Doren, *Secret History*, 236–37; Upton, *Diary and Selected Papers*, 125–26; Tebbenhoff, "Associated Loyalists."
5. Clinton to Tryon, June 27 and 28 and July 3, 1779, Clinton Papers, WLCL; Willcox, *Clinton's Narrative*, 131; Stevens, *Facsimiles of Manuscripts*, 10:1006; William Smith, *Historical Memoirs 1778 to 1783*, 122, 134, 137; Willcox, *Portrait of a General*, 227.
6. George Garth to Tryon, July 5, 1779, Tryon to Clinton, July 20, 1779, Clinton Papers, WLCL; Dexter, *Literary Diary of Ezra Stiles*, 2:351–61; William Smith, *Historical Memoirs 1778 to 1783*, 136; Moore, *Diary of the Revolution*, 2:706–7; Ward, *War of the Revolution*, 2:619.
7. Tryon to Clinton, July 20, 1779, Clinton Papers, WLCL; Willcox, *Clinton's Narrative*, 130–31; Child, *Old New England Town*, 125–54; Ward, *War of the Revolution*, 2:619.
8. Tryon to Clinton, July 12, 14, and 20, 1779, Clinton Papers, WLCL; Trumbull, "Tryon's Invasion of Norwalk"; Ward, *War of the Revolution*, 2:619.
9. Washington to Trumbull, July 12, 1779, Fitzpatrick, *Writings of George Washington*, 15:416; Willcox, *Clinton's Narrative*, 129–33; William Smith, *Historical Memoirs 1778 to 1783*, 138; Johnston, *Storming of Stony Point*, 57.
10. Washington to Marquis de Lafayette, September 12, 1779, Fitzpatrick, *Writings of George Washington*, 16:269; Silas Deane to Simeon Deane, July 27, 1779, *Deane Papers*, 4:23; Burnett, *Letters of Continental Congress*, 4:317–33.
11. Clinton to Germain, July 25, 1779, CO 5/98; J. Pownall to Dartmouth, October 8, 1779, *Manuscripts of Dartmouth*, 1:423; William Smith, *Historical Memoirs 1778 to 1783*, 137.
12. Tryon to Clinton, July 20, 1779, Clinton Papers, WLCL.
13. Germain to Tryon, November 4, 1779, CO 5/1109; Tryon to Clinton, November 7, 1779, Clinton Papers, WLCL; William Smith, *Historical Memoirs 1778 to 1783*, 144, 151, 162, 167, 177.
14. James Pattison to General Silliman, January 20, 1780, *Official Letters of Pattison*, 335; Tryon to Baron Riedesel, December 6, 1779, Emmett Collection, #6437, NYPL; Eelking, *Memoirs, Letters, and Journals of Riedesel*, 2:77, 85–86; William Smith, *Historical Memoirs 1778 to 1783*, 190, 201.
15. Tryon to Germain, February 26, 1780, CO 5/1110; Pattison to Tryon, February 18, 1780, *Official Letters of Pattison*, 370–71; William Smith, *Historical Memoirs 1778 to 1783*, 212–16, 232; Ludlum, *Early American Winters*, 1:111–18; Paul David Nelson, *William Alexander*, 151–53.
16. William Phillips to Tryon, February 10, 1780, Tryon to Phillips, February

12, 1780, Clinton Papers, WLCL; Tryon to Germain, February 26, 1780, CO 5/1110; Pattison to Germain, February 22, 1780, Phillips to Germain, March 25, 1780, CO 5/182; William Smith, *Historical Memoirs 1778 to 1783*, 141, 204, 216, 221–24, 229–31, 249.

17. Tryon to Germain, March 25, 1780, James Robertson to Germain, March 26, 1780, CO 5/1110; William Smith, *Historical Memoirs 1778 to 1783*, 190, 244, 250; Klein, "Experiment That Failed."

18. William Smith, *Historical Memoirs 1778 to 1783*, 201, 248, 250. Robertson's tenure as governor is delineated in Klein and Howard, *Twilight of British Rule*.

19. AZ to Tryon, January 31 and February 5, 6, 19, and 22, 1780, CO 5/1110; William Smith, *Historical Memoirs 1778 to 1783*, 266, 270; Uhlendorf, *Revolution in America*, 353; Leiby, *Hackensack Valley*, 236–37.

20. William Smith, *Historical Memoirs 1778 to 1783*, 271–74; Ward, *War of the Revolution*, 2:621–22.

21. William Smith, *Historical Memoirs 1778 to 1783*, 288; Ward, *War of the Revolution*, 2:621–22.

22. William Smith, *Historical Memoirs 1778 to 1783*, 287; Uhlendorf, *Revolution in America*, 361.

23. William Smith, *Historical Memoirs 1778 to 1783*, 328–29; Lydenberg, *Archibald Robertson*, 240; Uhlendorff, *Revolution in America*, 367.

24. Tryon to Treasury Board, [January 22, 1782], PRO, T 1/572; Treasury authorization for paying Tryon, March 24, 1782, PRO, T 52/70; Tryon's memorial of losses, [January 8, 1783], Tryon's estimate of landed property, [June 18, 1783], PRO, AO 13/132; Act of Attainder in New York, October 22, 1779, Thomas Jones, *History of New York* 2:269–70, 284; Act of Attainder in North Carolina, May 29, 1784, Clark, *State Records*, 19:672, 24:263, 424.

25. Upton, *Diary and Selected Papers*, 1:3, 205, 2:193.

26. Tryon's will, November 21, 1787, Powell, *Correspondence of William Tryon*, 2:889; Upton, *Diary and Selected Papers*, 2:61, 89, 94, 97–98, 121–22, 186.

27. Upton, *Diary and Selected Papers*, 2:89, 98; Powell, *Correspondence of William Tryon*, 1:5 (n. 3).

28. Upton, *Diary and Selected Papers*, 1:33, 228, 2:37, 38, 49, 51, 70, 75, 93, 106.

29. Upton, *Diary and Selected Papers*, 1:4, 28, 2:86.

30. Tryon's certificates for North Carolina claimants, PRO, AO 13/95, 121, 123; William Williams to Tryon, February 24, 1780, Carleton Papers, PRO 30/55/21, f. 2593; Tryon to Montfort Browne, October 4, 1781, Carleton Papers, PRO 30/55/33, f. 3820; Tryon to secretary at war, January 14, 1781, Correspondence of Liverpool, Add. MSS. 38251, f. 94, BL; Tryon to Germain, June 10 and 13, 1781, CO 5/158; Upton, *Diary and Selected Papers*, 2:266.

31. Tryon to Shelburne, February 26, 1782, Lacaita-Shelburne Papers, WLCL; Tryon to Shelburne, April 28, 1782, quoted in Upton, *Loyal Whig*, 131; Tryon to lords of Treasury, January 31, 1786, to George Rose, March 6, 1786, and to Smith, May 10, 1786, William Smith Papers, MG 23, G II 14, Vol. 2, 676–78,

694–96, 743–45, National Archives of Canada; Upton, *Diary and Selected Papers*, 1:li–lii, 47, 76–77, 174, 205–7, 2:37–38, 49, 342, 356, 379, 381, 387, 391, 393, 399, 403, 408, 421, 428, 431, 445, 446.

32. C. Jenkinson to Tryon, November 13, 1781, January 12, 1782, Correspondence of Liverpool, Add. MSS. 38308, ff. 35, 66, BL; William Fawcett to Tryon, June 5, 1783, Richard Fitzpatrick to Tryon, June 7, 1783, Carleton Papers, PRO 30/55/71, ff. 7893, 7919; Tryon to Haldimand, March 31, May 19, and July 29, 1784, Haldimand Papers, Add. MSS. 21735, ff. 393, 459, 510, BL; Tryon to Sir George Yonge, December 8, 1784, September 28, 1787, Sir George Yonge Papers, 809, 810, Huntington Library; Tryon to Yonge, April 11, 1785, Ferdinand T. Dreer Autograph Collection, II, 70, HSP; Cometti, *American Journals of Enys*, 72.

33. Powell, *Correspondence of William Tryon*, 1:xxxvii, 2:891–92.

34. *Gentleman's Magazine and Historical Chronicle*, 58 (1788): 179.

35. See Bailyn, *Ordeal of Thomas Hutchinson*, 380.

Selected Bibliography

Manuscript Collections

British Library, London
    Additions to the Manuscripts:
        Appointment as Governor of North Carolina, 33056
        Correspondence of 1st Lord Liverpool, 38251, 38303
        Sir Frederick Haldimand Papers, 21673, 21732, 21735, 21807
        Letter to Lord Dartmouth, 38650
        Letters to William Eden, 34416, 46490
    Kings Manuscripts
    Stowe Manuscripts
William L. Clements Library, University of Michigan, Ann Arbor
    Sir Henry Clinton Papers
    Thomas Gage Papers
    Lacaita-Shelburne Papers
    Shelburne Papers
College of William and Mary, Earl Gregg Swem Library, Williamsburg
    Blair, Banister, Braxton Papers
    Tucker-Coleman Papers
Columbia University Libraries, Special Collections, New York
    Jay Papers
    Van Schaack Family Papers
Connecticut State Library, Hartford
    Jonathan Trumbull Papers
Harvard University, Houghton Library, Cambridge
    North Carolina Council Journals
    Sparks Manuscripts
    Tryon Letter Book
Historical Society of Pennsylvania, Philadelphia
    Ferdinand T. Dreer Autograph Collection
    Frank M. Etting Collection
    Simon Gratz Autograph Collection
    Penn Papers
    Charles Janeway Stille Papers

Henry E. Huntington Library, San Marino, Calif.
  Huntington Manuscripts
  Sir George Yonge Papers
Kent Archives Office, Maidstone, England
  Amherst Papers
Lambeth Palace Library, London
  Fulham Papers
Library of Congress, Washington
  Facsimile Collection
Massachusetts Archives, State House, Boston
  Thomas Hutchinson Papers
Massachusetts Historical Society, Boston
  Miscellaneous Bound Papers
  James Murray Papers
  J. M. Robbins Papers
  Sedgwick II Papers
Moravian Archives, Winston-Salem, N.C.
  Moravian Records
National Archives of Canada, Ottawa
  Sir Frederick Haldimand Papers
  William Smith Papers
New-York Historical Society, New York
  James Duane Papers
  Horatio Gates Papers
  Robert R. Livingston Papers
New York Public Library, New York
  Bancroft Collection
  Emmett Collection
  Livingston Family Papers
  Personal-Miscellaneous Papers
  Philip Schuyler Papers
  William Smith Papers
New York State Library, Albany
  Broadsides
  Andrew Elliot Papers
Public Record Office, Kew, Surrey, England
  Audit Office Papers
    13/321–36 Declared Accounts
  Carleton Papers
    30/55
  Colonial Office Papers
    5/90–98 Correspondence with Commander in Chief, North America
    5/123–28 Correspondence with Admiralty
    5/154 Private Miscellaneous Correspondence
    5/242 Circular Letters to Colonial Governors
    5/313–14 Correspondence with Governor of North Carolina

5/761–62 Correspondence with Governor of Massachusetts
5/1102–10 Correspondence with Governor of New York
Home Office Papers
  42/1 Original Correspondence
  42/40 Weeded Papers, 1782–1785
Treasury Papers
  1/455–572 In-Letters
War Office Papers
  4/274 Secretary at War to Commander in Chief, North America
Royal Society of Arts, London
  Guard Books
  Letters Received
State Historical Society of Wisconsin, Madison
  Draper Collection
University of Virginia, Alderman Library, Charlottesville
  Wormeley Family Papers
Virginia State Library, Richmond
  Proclamations, 1768–1774

Printed Primary Sources

Allen, Ira. *The Natural and Political History of the State of Vermont.* . . . London: J. W. Myers, 1798.

Allinson, Samuel, ed. *Acts of the General Assembly of the Province of New Jersey, 1702–1776.* Burlington: State of New Jersey, 1776.

Almon, John. *The Remembrancer, or Impartial Repository of Public Events . . . 1775–1784.* 17 vols. London: J. Almon, 1775–1784.

Andrews, Charles M. *Guide to the Materials for American History, to 1783, in the Public Record Office of Great Britain.* 2 vols. Washington: Carnegie Institution, 1912–14.

Annual Register, or a View of the History, Politics, and Literature for the Year 1788. London: J. Dodsley, 1790.

Balderston, Marion, and David Syrett, eds. *The Lost War: Letters from British Officers during the American Revolution.* New York: Horizon Press, 1975.

Ballagh, James Curtis, ed. *The Letters of Richard Henry Lee.* 2 vols. New York: Macmillan, 1911–14.

Bartram, John. *Diary of a Journey through the Carolinas, Georgia, and Florida, from July 1, 1765 to April 10, 1766.* Annotated by Francis Harper. Transactions of the American Philosophical Society, n.s. 33, pt. 1. Philadelphia, 1942.

Bolton, Charles Knowles, ed. *Letters of Hugh Earl Percy from Boston and New York, 1774–1776.* Boston: Charles E. Goodspeed, 1902.

Boyd, William K., ed. *Some Eighteenth Century Tracts Concerning North Carolina.* Raleigh: Edwards and Broughton, 1927.

Brown, Lloyd A., and Howard H. Peckham, eds. *Revolutionary War Journals of Henry Dearborn, 1775–1783.* Chicago: Caxton Club, 1939.

Burnett, Edmund C., ed. *Letters of Members of the Continental Congress.*
8 vols. Washington: Carnegie Institution, 1923.

Butterfield, L. H., ed. *The Adams Papers.* Series 2, *Adams Family Correspondence.* 4 vols. Cambridge: Belknap Press of Harvard University Press, 1963–73.

————. *Diary and Autobiography of John Adams.* 4 vols. Cambridge: Belknap Press of Harvard University Press, 1961.

Butterfield, L. H., Marc Friedlander, and Mary-Jo Kline, eds. *The Book of Abigail and John: Selected Letters of the Adams Family, 1762–1784.* Cambridge: Harvard University Press, 1975.

Calendar of Historical Manuscripts in the Office of the Secretary of State, Albany, N.Y. Vol. 2, *English Manuscripts.* Edited by E. B. O'Callaghan. Albany: Weed, Parsons, 1866.

Calendar of Historical Manuscripts Relating to the War of the Revolution in the Office of the Secretary of State. 2 vols. Albany: Weed, Parsons, 1868.

Calendar of New York Colonial Manuscripts Indorsed Land Papers, 1643–1803. 63 vols. Albany: Weed, Parsons, 1864.

Carter, Clarence Edwin, ed. *The Correspondence of General Thomas Gage with the Secretaries of State, and with the War Office and the Treasury, 1763–1775.* 2 vols. New Haven: Yale University Press, 1931, 1933.

Clark, Walter, ed. *State Records of North Carolina, 1777–1790.* 16 vols. Winston and Goldsboro: State of North Carolina, 1895–1905.

Cobbett, William, and John Wright, eds. *The Parliamentary History of England.* 36 vols. London: Hansard, 1806–20.

[Colden, Cadwallader]. *The Letters and Papers . . . 1711–1775.* Collections of the New-York Historical Society, 1917–23, 1934–35. 9 vols. New York, 1918–24, 1935–36.

Colden Letter Books. Collections of the New-York Historical Society, 1876–77. 2 vols. New York, 1877–78.

Colden Letters on Smith's History, 1759–1760. Collections of the New-York Historical Society, 1868–69. 2 vols. New York, 1869–70.

Collection of Evidence in Vindication of the Territorial Rights and Jurisdiction of the State of New York against the Claims of the Commonwealths of Massachusetts and New Hampshire. . . . Collections of the New-York Historical Society, 1869. New York, 1870.

Colonial Laws of New York from the Year 1664 to the Revolution. 5 vols. Albany: James B. Lyons, 1894–96.

Cometti, Elizabeth, ed. *The American Journals of Lt. John Enys.* Syracuse: Syracuse University Press, 1976.

Commager, Henry Steele, and Richard B. Morris, eds. *The Spirit of 'Seventy-Six: The Story of the American Revolution as Told by Participants.* 2 vols. New York: Bobbs-Merrill, 1958.

Corbitt, D. L., ed. "Historical Notes." *North Carolina Historical Review* 3 (1926): 477–505.

Corwin, Edwin T., ed. *Ecclesiastical Records, State of New York.* 7 vols. Albany: James B. Lyons, 1901–16.

Cunningham, Peter, ed. *The Letters of Horace Walpole, Fourth Earl of Oxford.* 9 vols. Edinburgh: Bentley, 1857–59.

Davies, K. G., ed. *Documents of the American Revolution, 1770–1783.* 21 vols. Shannon: Irish University Press, 1972–81.

The Deane Papers. Collections of the New-York Historical Society, 1886–90. 5 vols. New York, 1887–91.

Dexter, Franklin Bowditch, ed. *The Literary Diary of Ezra Stiles.* 3 vols. New York: Scribner's, 1901.

Diary of Frederick Mackenzie: Giving a Daily Narrative of His Military Service as an Officer of the Regiment of Royal Welch Fusiliers during the Years 1775–1781 in Massachusetts, Rhode Island, and New York. Edited by Allen French. 2 vols. Cambridge: Harvard University Press, 1930.

Douglas, David C., ed. *English Historical Documents.* 12 vols. to date. New York: Oxford University Press, 1955– .

Drake, Francis S., ed. *Tea Leaves: Being a Collection of Letters and Documents Relating to the Shipment of Tea to the American Colonies in the Year 1773, by the East India Tea Company. . . .* Boston: A. O. Crane, 1884.

Eelking, Max von, ed. *Memoirs, Letters, and Journals of Major General Riedesel, during His Residence in America.* Translated by William L. Stone. 2 vols. Albany: J. Munsell, 1868.

Ferguson, E. James, and John Catanzariti, eds. *The Papers of Robert Morris, 1781–1784.* 5 vols. to date. Pittsburgh: University of Pittsburgh Press, 1973– .

Fernow, Berthold, ed. *Calendar of New York Council Minutes, 1668–1783.* Albany: Weed, Parsons, 1902.

Fitzpatrick, John C., ed. *The Writings of George Washington from the Original Manuscripts, 1745–1799.* 39 vols. Washington: Government Printing Office, 1931–44.

Force, Peter, ed. *American Archives: A Documentary History of the Origin and Progress of the North American Colonies.* 9 vols. Washington: Government Printing Office, 1837–53.

Ford, Paul Leicester, ed. *Orderly Book of the "Maryland Loyalist Regiment," June 18th, 1778 to October 12th, 1778. . . .* Brooklyn: Historical Printing Club, 1891.

Ford, Worthington C., ed. *Journals of the Continental Congress, 1774–1789.* 34 vols. Washington: Government Printing Office, 1904–37.

Fries, Adelaide L., Kenneth G. Hamilton, Douglas L. Rights, and Minnie J. Smith, eds. *Records of the Moravians in North Carolina.* 11 vols. Raleigh: North Carolina Historical Commission, 1922–69.

Grant, William, and James Munro, eds. *Acts of the Privy Council of England. (Colonial Series).* 6 vols. Hereford: Privy Council, 1908–11.

Hastings, Hugh, and James A. Holden, eds. *Public Papers of George Clinton, First Governor of New York. . . .* 10 vols. New York and Albany: State of New York, 1899–1914.

Higginbotham, Don, ed. *The Papers of James Iredell.* 2 vols. to date. Raleigh: Division of Archives and History, 1976– .

Hulton, Ann. *Letters of a Loyalist Lady: Being the Letters of Ann Hulton, Sister of Henry Hulton, Commissioner of Customs at Boston, 1767–1776.* Cambridge: Harvard University Press, 1927.

Hutchinson, Peter Orlando, ed. *The Diary and Letters of His Excellency Thomas Hutchinson, Esq.* 2 vols. Boston: Houghton Mifflin, 1884–86.

Jackson, Donald, and Dorothy Twohig, eds. *The Diaries of George Washington.* 6 vols. Charlottesville: University Press of Virginia, 1976–79.

Johnston, Henry P., ed. *The Correspondence and Public Papers of John Jay . . . 1763–1781.* 4 vols. New York: Putnam's, 1890–93.

Jones, Thomas. *History of New York during the Revolutionary War. . . .* Edited by Edward Floyd DeLancey. 2 vols. New York: New-York Historical Society, 1879.

Journal of the Commissioners for Trade and Plantations from April 1704 to May 1782, Preserved in the Public Record Office. 14 vols. London: His Majesty's Stationery Office, 1920–38.

The Journal of the House of Assembly. New Bern, N.C.: James Davis, 1771.

Journal of the Most Remarkable Occurrences in Quebec, from the 14th of November, 1775, to the 7th of May, 1776, by an Officer of the Garrison. Collections of the New-York Historical Society, 1880. New York, 1881.

Journal of the Provincial Congress, Provincial Convention, Committee of Safety of the State of New York. 2 vols. Albany: State of New York, 1842.

Journal of the Votes and Proceedings of the General Assembly of the Colony of New York . . . 1691–1764. 2 vols. New York: H. Gaine, 1764, 1766.

Journals of the House of Lords. 46 vols. London: House of Lords, n.d.

The Kemble Papers. Collections of the New-York Historical Society, 1883–84. 2 vols. New York, 1884–85.

King, Charles R., ed. *The Life and Correspondence of Rufus King.* 6 vols. New York: Putnam's, 1894–1900.

Labaree, Leonard Woods, ed. *Royal Instructions to British Colonial Governors, 1670–1776.* 2 vols. New York: Appleton-Century, 1935.

Labaree, Leonard Woods, William B. Willcox, and Claude Lopez, eds. *The Papers of Benjamin Franklin.* 27 vols. to date. New Haven: Yale University Press, 1959– .

The Lee Papers. Collections of the New-York Historical Society, 1871–74. 4 vols. New York, 1872–75.

Letter Book of John Watts, Merchant and Councillor of New York. Collections of the New-York Historical Society, 1928. New York, 1929.

Letters to General Lewis Morris. Collections of the New-York Historical Society, 1875. New York, 1876.

Letters to Robert Morris. Collections of the New-York Historical Society, 1878. New York, 1879.

Lewis, W. S., and R. S. Brown, eds. *Horace Walpole's Correspondence.* 39 vols. New Haven: Yale University Press, 1937–74.

Lodge, Henry Cabot, ed. *Major Andre's Journal, 1777–1778.* 2 vols. Boston: Bibliophile Society, 1904.

Lydenberg, Harry Miller, ed. *Archibald Robertson, Lieutenant-General Royal Engineers: His Diaries and Sketches in America, 1762–1780.* New York: New York Public Library, 1930.

Manross, William Wilson, comp. *The Fulham Papers in the Lambeth Palace Library: American Colonial Section, Calendar and Indexes.* Oxford: Oxford University Press, 1965.

The Manuscripts of Captain H. V. Knox. Historical Manuscripts Commission. Vol. 6 of *Report on Manuscripts in Various Collections.* Dublin: John Falconer, 1909.

The Manuscripts of the Earl of Dartmouth. 3 vols. Historical Manuscripts Commission. *Eleventh Report*, Appendix 5; *Fourteenth Report*, Appendix 10; *Fifteenth Report*, Appendix 1. London, 1887–96.

Minutes of the Trial and Examination of Certain Persons in the Province of New York, Charged with Being Engaged in a Conspiracy against the Authority of the Congress, and the Liberties of America. London: J. Bew, 1786.

The Montresor Journals. Edited by G. D. Scull. Collections of the New-York Historical Society, 1881. New York, 1882.

Moore, Frank, ed. *Diary of the Revolution.* 2 vols. Hartford: J. B. Burr, 1876.

Morgan, Edmund S., ed. *Prologue to Revolution: Sources and Documents on the Stamp Act Crisis, 1764–1766.* Chapel Hill: University of North Carolina Press, 1959.

Morris, Anne C., ed. *Diary and Letters of Gouverneur Morris.* 2 vols. New York: Scribner's, 1888.

Morris, Richard B., ed. *The American Revolution, 1763–1783: A Bicentennial Collection.* Columbia: University of South Carolina Press, 1970.

———. *John Jay, The Making of a Revolutionary: Unpublished Papers, 1745–1780.* New York: Harper and Row, 1975.

New Hampshire Provincial, Town, and State Papers, Documents, and Records. Edited by Nathaniel Bouton and I. W. Hammond. 40 vols. Concord: Jenks, 1867–1943.

Northamptonshire Notes & Queries, an Illustrated Quarterly Journal . . . 11 (1894): 236.

O'Callaghan, E. B., ed. *Documentary History of the State of New-York.* 4 vols. Albany: Weed, Parsons, 1849–51.

———. *Documents Relative to the Colonial History of the State of New York. . . .* 10 vols. and index vol. Albany: Weed, Parsons, 1856–61.

Official Letters of Major General James Pattison, Commandant of Artillery. Collections of the New-York Historical Society, 1875. New York, 1876.

Old New York and Trinity Church. Collections of the New-York Historical Society, 1870. New York, 1871.

Osgood, Herbert Levi, ed. *Minutes of the Common Council of New York, 1675–1776.* 8 vols. New York: Dodd, Mead, 1905.

Peckham, Howard H., ed. *Sources of American Independence: Selected Manuscripts from the Collections of the William L. Clements Library.* 2 vols. Chicago: University of Chicago Press, 1978.

Pettengill, Ray W., ed. *Letters from America, 1776–1779: Being Letters of Brunswick, Hessian, and Waldeck Officers with the British Armies during the Revolution.* Boston: Houghton Mifflin, 1924.

Powell, William S., ed. *The Correspondence of William Tryon. . . .* 2 vols. Raleigh: Division of Archives and History, 1980–81.

_____. *The Regulators of North Carolina: A Documentary History, 1759–1766.* Raleigh: Department of Archives and History, 1971.

_____. "Tryon's 'Book' on North Carolina." *North Carolina Historical Review* 34 (1957): 406–15.

Redington, Joseph, and Richard Arthur Roberts, eds. *Calendar of Home Office Papers of the Reign of George III, 1760–1775.* 4 vols. London: His Majesty's Stationery Office, 1878–99.

Robson, Eric, ed. *Letters from America, 1773 to 1780: Being the Letters of a Scots Officer, Sir James Murray, to His Home during the War of American Independence.* Manchester: University of Manchester Press, 1951.

Ross, Charles, ed. *Correspondence of Charles, First Marquis Cornwallis.* 3 vols. London: John Murray, 1859.

Saunders, William L., ed. *The Colonial Records of North Carolina.* 10 vols. Raleigh: State of North Carolina, 1886–90.

Scheer, George F., and Hugh F. Rankin, eds. *Rebels and Redcoats.* Cleveland: World Publishing, 1957.

Slade, William, Jr., comp. *Vermont State Papers.* Middlebury: J. W. Copeland, 1823.

Smith, Paul H., ed. *Letters of Delegates to Congress, 1774–1789.* 13 vols. to date. Washington: Library of Congress, 1976– .

Smith, William. *Historical Memoirs from 16 March 1763 to 25 July 1778.* . . . Edited by William H. W. Sabine. 2 vols. New York: Colburn and Tegg, 1956–58.

_____. *Historical Memoirs from 26 August 1778 to 12 November 1783.* . . . Edited by William H. W. Sabine. New York: Arno Press, 1971.

_____. *The History of the Province of New York.* Edited by Michael Kammen. 2 vols. Cambridge: Belknap Press of Harvard University Press, 1972.

Sparks, Jared, ed. *Correspondence of the American Revolution.* 4 vols. Boston: Little, Brown, 1853.

State of the Evidence and Argument in Support of the Territorial Rights and Jurisdiction of New York against the Government of New Hampshire and the Claimants under It, and against the Commonwealth of Massachusetts: by James Duane. Collections of the New-York Historical Society, 1870. New York, 1871.

Stevens, B. F., ed. *Facsimiles of Manuscripts in European Archives Relating to America, 1773–1783.* 25 vols. London: Malby and Sons, 1889–95.

_____. *General Sir William Howe's Orderly Book at Charlestown, Boston, and Halifax, June 17, 1775 to May 26, 1776.* . . . Port Washington, N.Y.: Kennikat Press, 1890. Reprint. New York: Associated Faculty Press, 1970.

Sullivan, James, preparer. *Minutes of the Albany Committee of Correspondence, 1775–1778.* 2 vols. Albany: University of the State of New York, 1923–25.

Sullivan, James, Alexander C. Flick, and M. W. Hamilton, eds. *The Papers of Sir William Johnson.* 13 vols. Albany: University of the State of New York, 1921–25.

Syrett, Harold C., and Jacob E. Cooke, eds. *The Papers of Alexander Hamilton.* 26 vols. New York: Columbia University Press, 1961–79.

Tatum, Edward H., Jr., ed. *The American Journal of Ambrose Serle, Secretary to Lord Howe, 1776–1778*. San Marino, Calif.: The Huntington Library, 1940.

Thacher, James. *A Military Journal during the American Revolutionary War*. Boston: Cottons and Barnard, 1827.

Uhlendorf, Bernhard A., trans. *Revolution in America: Confidential Letters and Journals 1776–1784 of Adjutant General Major Baurmeister of the Hessian Forces*. 1957. Reprint. Westport, Conn.: Greenwood Press, 1973.

Upton, L. F. S., ed. *The Diary and Selected Papers of Chief Justice William Smith, 1784–1793*. 2 vols. Toronto: Champlain Society, 1963–65.

Vaughn, Alden T., ed. *Chronicles of the American Revolution, Originally Compiled by Hezekiah Niles. . . .* New York: Grosset and Dunlap, 1965.

Wharton, Francis, ed. *The Revolutionary Diplomatic Correspondence of the United States*. 6 vols. Washington: Government Printing Office, 1889.

Willard, Margaret Wheeler, ed. *Letters on the American Revolution, 1774–1776*. Boston: Houghton Mifflin, 1925.

Willcox, William B., ed. *The American Rebellion: Sir Henry Clinton's Narrative of His Campaigns, 1775–1782*. New Haven: Yale University Press, 1954.

Wilson, Rufus Rockwell, ed. *Heath's Memoirs of the American War*. New York: A. Wessels, 1904.

Winsor, Justin, ed. *Narrative and Critical History of America*. 8 vols. New York: Houghton Mifflin, 1889.

Newspapers

Boston Gazette
Cape Fear Mercury
Essex Gazette
Holt's Journal
Maryland Gazette
Massachusetts Spy
New York Mercury
North-Carolina Gazette
North-Carolina Magazine: or Universal Intelligencer
Pennsylvania Evening Post
Pennsylvania Gazette
South Carolina Gazette
Virginia Gazette

Secondary Sources

Abbott, Wilbur C. *New York in the American Revolution*. New York: Scribner's, 1929.

Adams, George R. "The Carolina Regulators: A Note on Changing Interpretations." *North Carolina Historical Review* 49 (1972): 345–52.

Alden, John Richard. *The American Revolution*. New York: Harper and Brothers, 1954.
_____. *General Gage in America: Being Principally a History of His Role in the American Revolution*. Baton Rouge: Louisiana State University Press, 1948.
_____. *George Washington: A Biography*. Baton Rouge: Louisiana State University Press, 1984.
_____. *A History of the American Revolution*. New York: Knopf, 1969.
_____. *John Stuart and the Southern Colonial Frontier*. Ann Arbor: University of Michigan Press, 1944.
Alexander, Edward Porter. *A Revolutionary Conservative: James Duane of New York*. New York: Columbia University Press, 1938.
Anderson, Troyer Steele. *The Command of the Howe Brothers During the American Revolution*. Oxford: Oxford University Press, 1936.
Arnett, Ethel Stephens. *From England to North Carolina: Two Special Gifts*. New Bern, N.C.: Owen G. Dunn, 1964.
Arnold, Isaac N. *The Life of Benedict Arnold: His Patriotism and His Treason*. Chicago: A. C. McClurg, 1897.
Bailyn, Bernard. *The Ordeal of Thomas Hutchinson*. Cambridge: Belknap Press of Harvard University Press, 1974.
Bakeless, John. *Turncoats, Traitors, and Heroes*. Philadelphia: J. B. Lippincott, 1959.
Barck, Dorothy C. "Captain Thomas Sowers, Engineer, and the Silver Salver." *New-York Historical Society Quarterly Bulletin* 12 (1928): 59–64.
Barck, Oscar Theodore. *New York City During the War for Independence*. New York: Columbia University Press, 1931.
Bargar, B. D. "Governor Tryon's House in Fort George." *New York History* 35 (1954): 295–309.
_____. *Lord Dartmouth and the American Revolution*. Columbia: University of South Carolina Press, 1965.
Bassett, J. S. "The Regulators in North Carolina." *Annual Report* of the American Historical Association, 1894. Washington: Government Printing Office, 1895.
Becker, Carl L. *The History of Political Parties in the Province of New York, 1760–1776*. Bulletin of the University of Wisconsin, no. 286. Madison, 1907.
Bliven, Bruce, Jr. *Under the Guns: New York, 1775–1776*. New York: Harper and Row, 1972.
Bonomi, Patricia U. *A Factious People: Politics and Society in Colonial New York*. New York: Columbia University Press, 1971.
Boyd, Julian P. "The Sheriff in Colonial North Carolina." *North Carolina Historical Review* 5 (1928): 151–80.
Bradley, A. G. *Lord Dorchester*. New York: Oxford University Press, 1926.
Brandt, Clare. *An American Aristocracy: The Livingstons*. Garden City: Doubleday, 1986.
Bridenbaugh, Carl. *Cities in Revolt: Urban Life in America, 1743–1776*. New York: Knopf, 1968.
Brown, Gerald Saxon. *The American Secretary: The Colonial Policy of Lord*

George Germain, 1775–1778. Ann Arbor: University of Michigan Press, 1963.

Brown, Wallace. *The Good Americans: The Loyalists in the American Revolution*. New York: William Morrow, 1969.

Brown, Weldon A. *Empire or Independence: A Study in the Failure of Reconciliation, 1774–1783*. Baton Rouge: Louisiana State University Press, 1941.

Bush, Martin H. *Revolutionary Enigma: A Re-Appraisal of General Philip Schuyler of New York*. Port Washington, N.Y.: Ira J. Friedman, 1969.

Butler, Lindley S. *North Carolina and the Coming of the Revolution, 1763–1776*. Raleigh: Department of Cultural Resources, 1976.

Calhoon, Robert McCluer. *The Loyalists in Revolutionary America, 1760–1781*. New York: Harcourt Brace Jovanovich, 1965.

Callahan, North. *Royal Raiders: The Tories of the American Revolution*. New York: Bobbs-Merrill, 1963.

Carraway, Gertrude S. *Crown of Life: History of Christ Church, New Bern, N.C., 1815–1940*. New Bern, N.C.: Owen G. Dunn, 1940.

Carrington, Henry B. *Battles of the American Revolution, 1775–1781*. New York: A. S. Barnes, 1876.

Case, James R. *An Account of Tryon's Raid on Danbury in April, 1777, Also the Battle of Ridgefield and the Career of Gen. David Wooster*. Danbury: [Danbury Printing Company], 1927.

Champagne, Roger J. *Alexander McDougall and the American Revolution in New York*. Schenectady: Union College Press, 1976.

Child, Frank Samuel. *An Old New England Town: Sketches of Life, Scenery, Character*. New York: Scribner's, 1895.

Clarke, Desmond. *Arthur Dobbs, Esquire, 1689–1765*. London: The Bodley Head, 1958.

Columbia University. *A History of Columbia University, 1754–1904*. New York: Columbia University Press, 1904.

———. *Officers and Graduates of Columbia University: General Catalogue, 1754–1900*. New York: Columbia University, 1900.

Conkin, Paul. "The Church Establishment in North Carolina, 1765–1776." *North Carolina Historical Review* 32 (1955): 1–30.

Connor, R. D. W. "The Genesis of Higher Education in North Carolina." *North Carolina Historical Review* 28 (1951): 1–14.

———. *North Carolina: Rebuilding an Ancient Commonwealth, 1584–1925*. 2 vols. Chicago: American Historical Society, 1929.

Conway, Stephen. "To Subdue America: British Army Officers and the Conduct of the Revolutionary War." *William and Mary Quarterly*, 3d ser., 43 (1986): 381–407.

Corbett, Julian Stafford. *England in the Seven Years' War: A Study in Combined Strategy*. 2 vols. London: Longmans, Green, 1907.

Countryman, Edward. *A People in Revolution: The American Revolution and Political Society in New York, 1760–1790*. Baltimore: Johns Hopkins University Press, 1981.

Crary, Catherine S. "Guerrilla Activities of James DeLancey's Cowboys in Westchester County: Conventional Warfare or Self-Interested Freebooting?" In *The Loyalist Americans: A Focus on Greater New York*, edited by Robert A. East and Jacob Judd. Tarrytown: Sleepy Hollow Restorations, 1975.

Crittenden, Charles Christopher. "Means of Communication in North Carolina, 1763–1789." *North Carolina Historical Review* 8 (1931): 373–83.

_____. "Overland Travel and Transportation in North Carolina, 1763–1789." *North Carolina Historical Review* 8 (1931): 239–57.

Cross, Arthur Lyon. *The Anglican Episcopate and the American Colonies*. New York: Longmans, Green, 1902.

Crow, Jeffrey J. "Tory Plots and Anglican Loyalty: The Llewlyn Conspiracy of 1777." *North Carolina Historical Review* 55 (1978): 1–17.

Cuneo, John R. *Robert Rogers of the Rangers*. New York: Oxford University Press, 1959.

Cutter, William. *The Life of Israel Putnam, Compiled from the Best Authorities*. New York: Cooledge, 1850.

Dangerfield, George. *Chancellor Robert R. Livingston of New York, 1746–1813*. New York: Harcourt, Brace, 1960.

Davidson, Chalmers G. "Independent Mecklenburg." *North Carolina Historical Review* 46 (1969): 122–29.

Davidson, Philip. *Propaganda and the American Revolution, 1763–1783*. Chapel Hill: University of North Carolina Press, 1941.

Dawson, Henry B. *Battles of the United States by Sea and Land*. 2 vols. New York: Johnson, Fry, 1858.

De Vorsey, Louis, Jr. *The Indian Boundary in the Southern Colonies, 1763–1775*. Chapel Hill: University of North Carolina Press, 1966.

Dickerson, Oliver M. *The Navigation Acts and the American Revolution*. Philadelphia: University of Pennsylvania Press, 1951.

Dill, Alonzo Thomas. *Governor Tryon and His Palace*. Chapel Hill: University of North Carolina Press, 1955.

_____. "Tryon's Palace: A Neglected Niche of North Carolina History." *North Carolina Historical Review* 19 (1942): 119–67.

Dillon, Dorothy Rita. "A Century of Religion in Provincial New York, 1624–1720." Master's thesis, Columbia University, 1940.

_____. *The New York Triumvirate: A Study of the Legal and Political Careers of William Livingston, John Morin Scott, and William Smith, Jr*. New York: Columbia University Press, 1949.

Dunbar, Louise B. "The Royal Governors in the Middle and Southern Colonies on the Eve of the Revolution: A Study in Imperial Personnel." In *The Era of the American Revolution: Studies Inscribed to Evarts Boutell Greene*, edited by Richard B. Morris. New York: Columbia University Press, 1939.

Ekirch, A. Roger. *"Poor Carolina": Politics and Society in Colonial North Carolina, 1729–1776*. Chapel Hill: University of North Carolina Press, 1981.

Elliott, Robert N., Jr. "James Davis and the Beginning of the Newspaper in North Carolina." *North Carolina Historical Review* 42 (1965): 1–20.

Ernst, Joseph. "Andrew Elliot, Forgotten Loyalist of Occupied New York." *New York History* 57 (1976): 285–320.

Fiske, John. *The American Revolution*. 2 vols. Boston: Houghton Mifflin, 1896.

Fleming, Thomas. *The Forgotten Victory: The Battles for New Jersey—1780*. New York: Reader's Digest Press, 1973.

Flexner, James Thomas. *George Washington in the American Revolution (1775–1783)*. Boston: Little, Brown, 1967.

———. *Mohawk Baronet: Sir William Johnson of New York*. New York: Harper and Brothers, 1959.

Flick, Alexander C., *Loyalism in New York During the American Revolution*. New York: Columbia University Press, 1901.

———, ed. *History of the State of New York*. 10 vols. New York: Columbia University Press, 1933–37.

Fortescue, John William. *A History of the British Army*. 13 vols. London: Macmillan, 1902–30.

Freeman, Douglas Southall. *George Washington: A Biography*. 7 vols. New York: Scribner's, 1947–57.

French, Allen. *The First Year of the American Revolution*. Boston: Houghton Mifflin, 1934.

Gerlach, Don R. *Philip Schuyler and the American Revolution in New York, 1733–1777*. Lincoln: University of Nebraska Press, 1964.

———. *Proud Patriot: Philip Schuyler and the War of Independence, 1775–1783*. Syracuse: Syracuse University Press, 1987.

Gipson, Lawrence Henry. *The British Empire Before the American Revolution*. 15 vols. Caldwell, Idaho, and New York: Caxton Printers and Knopf, 1936–70.

———. *The Coming of the Revolution, 1763–1775*. New York: Harper and Row, 1954.

Greene, Evarts Boutell. *The Revolutionary Generation, 1763–1790*. New York: Macmillan, 1943.

Greene, Francis Vinton. *The Revolutionary War and the Military Policy of the United States*. New York: Scribner's, 1911.

Greene, Jack P. "The North Carolina Lower House and the Power to Appoint Public Treasurers, 1711–1775." *North Carolina Historical Review* 40 (1963): 37–53.

———. *The Quest for Power: The Lower Houses of Assembly in the Southern Royal Colonies, 1689–1776*. Chapel Hill: University of North Carolina Press, 1963.

Gruber, Ira. *The Howe Brothers and the American Revolution*. New York: Norton, 1972.

Hall, Charles S. *Life and Letters of Samuel Holden Parsons, Major General in the Continental Army and Chief Judge of the Northwestern Territory, 1737–1789*. New York: Archives of James Pugliese, 1968.

Handlin, Oscar, and Lillian Handlin. *A Restless People: Americans in Rebellion, 1770–1787*. Garden City: Anchor Press, 1982.

Hargrove, Richard J. *General John Burgoyne*. Newark: University of Delaware Press, 1983.

Harrington, Virginia D. *The New York Merchant on the Eve of the Revolution*.

New York: Columbia University Press, 1935.

Haywood, C. Robert. "The Mind of the North Carolina Opponents of the Stamp Act." *North Carolina Historical Review* 29 (1952): 317–43.

Haywood, Marshall DeLancey. *Governor William Tryon and His Administration in the Province of North Carolina, 1765–1771.* Raleigh: E. M. Uzzell, 1903.

Henner, Solomon. "The Career of William Tryon as Governor of the Province of New York, 1771–1780." Ph.D. dissertation, New York University, 1968.

Higginbotham, Don. "James Iredell's Efforts to Preserve the First British Empire." *North Carolina Historical Review* 49 (1972): 127–45.

_____. *The War of American Independence: Military Attitudes, Policies, and Practice, 1763–1789.* New York: Macmillan, 1971.

High, James. "Henry McCulloh: Progenitor of the Stamp Act." *North Carolina Historical Review* 29 (1952): 24–38.

Hoffman, Ross J. S. *The Marquis: A Study of Lord Rockingham, 1730–1782.* New York: Fordham University Press, 1973.

Hudson, Derek, and K. W. Lockhurst. *The Royal Society of Arts, 1754–1954.* London: John Murray, 1954.

Jaunitz-Schürer, Leopold S., Jr. *Loyal Whigs and Revolutionaries: The Making of the Revolution in New York, 1765–1776.* New York: New York University Press, 1980.

Jensen, Merrill. *The Founding of a Nation: A History of the American Revolution, 1763–1776.* New York: Oxford University Press, 1968.

Johnston, Henry P. *The Storming of Stony Point on the Hudson, Midnight, July 15, 1779. . . .* New York: James T. White, 1900.

Jones, H. G. *North Carolina Illustrated, 1524–1984.* Chapel Hill: University of North Carolina Press, 1983.

Jones, Mark Haddon. "Herman Husband: Millenarian, Carolina Regulator, and Whiskey Rebel." Ph.D. dissertation, Northern Illinois University, 1983.

Kammen, Michael. *Colonial New York: A History.* New York: Scribner's, 1975.

Kay, Marvin L. Michael. "The Payment of Provincial and Local Taxes in North Carolina, 1748–1771." *William and Mary Quarterly,* 3d ser., 26 (1969): 218–40.

_____. "Provincial Taxes in North Carolina During the Administrations of Dobbs and Tryon." *North Carolina Historical Review* 42 (1965): 440–53.

Keep, Austin Baxter. *History of the New York Society Library.* New York: DeVinne Press, 1908.

Keys, Alice Mapelsden. *Cadwallader Colden: A Representative Eighteenth Century Official.* New York: AMS Press, 1967.

Klein, Milton M. "An Experiment That Failed: General James Robertson and Civil Government in British New York, 1779–1783." *New York History* 61 (1980): 229–54.

_____. *The Politics of Diversity: Essays in the History of Colonial New York.* Port Washington, N.Y.: Kennikat Press, 1974.

_____. "Why Did the British Fail to Win the Hearts and Minds of New Yorkers?" *New York History* 64 (1983): 357–75.

Klein, Milton M., and Ronald W. Howard, eds. *Twilight of British Rule in Revolutionary America: The New York Letter Book of General James Robertson, 1780–1783*. Cooperstown: New York State Historical Association, 1983.

Kline, Mary-Jo. *Gouverneur Morris and the New Nation, 1775–1788*. New York: Arno Press, 1978.

Knollenberg, Bernhard. *Growth of the American Revolution, 1766–1775*. New York: Macmillan, 1975.

———. *Origin of the American Revolution, 1759–1766*. New York: Macmillan, 1960.

Labaree, Benjamin Woods. *The Boston Tea Party*. New York: Oxford University Press, 1964.

Labaree, Leonard Woods. "William Tryon." In *Dictionary of American Biography*, edited by Allan Johnson and Dumas Malone, 19:25–27. 22 vols. New York: Scribner's, 1928–44.

Lacy, Dan. "Records in the Offices of Registers of Deeds in North Carolina." *North Carolina Historical Review* 14 (1937): 213–19.

Lancaster, Bruce. *From Lexington to Liberty: The Story of the American Revolution*. Garden City: Doubleday, 1955.

Leake, Isaac Q. *Memoir of the Life and Times of General John Lamb. . . .* Albany: J. Munsell, 1857.

Lecky, William Edward Hartpole. *A History of England in the Eighteenth Century*. 8 vols. London: Longmans, Green, 1878–90.

Leder, Lawrence H. *Robert Livingston, 1654–1728, and the Politics of Colonial New York*. Chapel Hill: University of North Carolina Press, 1961.

Lee, Lawrence. "Days of Defiance: Resistance to the Stamp Act in the Lower Cape Fear." *North Carolina Historical Review* 43 (1966): 186–202.

———. *The Lower Cape Fear in Colonial Days*. Chapel Hill: University of North Carolina Press, 1965.

———. "Old Brunswick: The Story of a Colonial Town." *North Carolina Historical Review* 29 (1952): 230–45.

Lefler, Hugh Talmage, and Albert Ray Newsome. *North Carolina: The History of a Southern State*. Chapel Hill: University of North Carolina Press, 1954.

Lefler, Hugh Talmage, and William S. Powell. *Colonial North Carolina: A History*. New York: Scribner's, 1973.

Leiby, Adrian C. *The Revolutionary War in the Hackensack Valley. . . .* New Brunswick: Rutgers University Press, 1962.

Lemmon, Sarah McCulloh. "Genesis of the Protestant Episcopal Diocese of North Carolina, 1701–1823." *North Carolina Historical Review* 28 (1951): 426–62.

Long, Harrold Frances. "Governor William Tryon of North Carolina, 1765–1771." Master's thesis, University of Wisconsin, 1954.

Lossing, Benson J. *The Life and Times of Philip Schuyler*. 2 vols. New York: Sheldon, 1860–73.

Lowell, Edward J. *The Hessians and Other German Auxiliaries of Great Britain in the Revolutionary War*. New York: Harper and Brothers, 1884.

Ludlum, David M. *Early American Winters*. 2 vols. Boston: American Meteorological Association, 1966.

McIlwraith, Jean N. *Sir Frederick Haldimand*. London: Oxford University Press, 1926.

Mackesy, Piers. *The War for America, 1775–1783*. Cambridge: Harvard University Press, 1965.

Maier, Pauline. *From Resistance to Revolution: Colonial Radicals and the Development of American Opposition to Britain, 1765–1776*. New York: Knopf, 1972.

————. *The Old Revolutionaries: Political Lives in the Age of Samuel Adams*. New York: Knopf, 1980.

Mark, Irving. *Agrarian Conflicts in Colonial New York, 1711–1775*. New York: Columbia University Press, 1940.

Mason, Bernard. *The Road to Independence: The Revolutionary Movement in New York, 1773–1777*. Lexington: University of Kentucky Press, 1966.

Merrens, H. Roy. *Colonial North Carolina in the Eighteenth Century: A Study in Historical Geography*. Chapel Hill: University of North Carolina Press, 1964.

Merrens, H. Roy, and Herbert R. Paschal. "A Map-Maker's View of Anson County in 1769." *North Carolina Historical Review* 59 (1982): 271–78.

Middlekauff, Robert. *The Glorious Cause: The American Revolution, 1763–1789*. New York: Oxford University Press, 1982.

Miller, Helen Hill. *The Case for Liberty*. Chapel Hill: University of North Carolina Press, 1965.

Miller, John C. *Origins of the American Revolution*. Boston: Little, Brown, 1943.

————. *Triumph of Freedom, 1775–1783*. Boston: Little, Brown, 1948.

Mintz, Max M. *Gouverneur Morris and the American Revolution*. Norman: University of Oklahoma Press, 1970.

Morant, Philip. *The History and Antiquities of the County of Essex*. 2 vols. London: T. Osborne, 1768.

Morgan, David T., Jr. "Cornelius Harnett: Revolutionary Leader and Delegate to the Continental Congress." *North Carolina Historical Review* 49 (1972): 229–41.

————. "The Great Awakening in North Carolina, 1740–1775: The Baptist Phase." *North Carolina Historical Review* 45 (1968): 264–83.

Morgan, Edmund S., and Helen M. Morgan. *The Stamp Act Crisis: Prologue to Revolution*. Chapel Hill: University of North Carolina Press, 1953.

Nairn, Ian, and Nikolaus Pevsner, *The Buildings of England: Surrey*. Harmondsworth: Penguin Books, 1962.

Nelson, Paul David. *General Horatio Gates: A Biography*. Baton Rouge: Louisiana State University Press, 1976.

————. *William Alexander, Lord Stirling*. University: University of Alabama Press, 1987.

Nelson, William H. *The American Tory*. Oxford: Oxford University Press, 1961.

Neuenschwander, John A. *The Middle Colonies and the Coming of the American Revolution*. Port Washington, N.Y.: Kennikat Press, 1973.

North, Jeremy. *An Eighteenth Century Gentleman and His Books*. New Bern, N.C.: Tryon Palace Commission, 1963.

_____. *The Library of William Tryon, Royal Governor of North Carolina.* New Bern, N.C.: Tryon Palace Commission, 1958.

Pancake, John S. *1777: The Year of the Hangman.* University: University of Alabama Press, 1977.

Parker, Coralie. *The History of Taxation in North Carolina During the Colonial Period, 1663–1776.* New York: Columbia University Press, 1928.

Parramore, Thomas C. "John Alexander, Anglican Missionary." *North Carolina Historical Review* 43 (1966): 305–15.

Paul, Charles L. "Factors in the Economy of Colonial Beaufort." *North Carolina Historical Review* 44 (1967): 111–34.

Pell, John. *Ethan Allen.* Boston: Houghton Mifflin, 1929.

Pevsner, Nikolaus. *The Buildings of England: Northamptonshire.* Harmondsworth: Penguin Books, 1961.

Powell, William S. "Creatures of Carolina from Roanoke Island to Purgatory Mountain." *North Carolina Historical Review* 50 (1973): 155–68.

_____. *North Carolina: A Bicentennial History.* New York: Norton, 1977.

Ranlet, Philip. *The New York Loyalists.* Knoxville: University of Tennessee Press, 1986.

Raper, Charles Lee. *The Church and Private Schools in North Carolina.* Greensboro: Jos. J. Stone, 1898.

_____. *North Carolina: A Study in English Colonial Government.* New York: Macmillan, 1904.

Roberts, Robert B. *New York's Forts in the Revolution.* Rutherford: Fairleigh Dickinson University Press, 1980.

Rossie, Jonathan Gregory. *The Politics of Command in the American Revolution.* Syracuse: Syracuse University Press, 1975.

Sabine, Lorenzo. *Biographical Sketches of Loyalists of the American Revolution.* 2 vols. Boston: Little, Brown, 1864.

Sabine, William H. W. *Murder, 1776, and Washington's Policy of Silence.* New York: Theo. Gaus' Sons, 1973.

Schick, James B. "Regionalism and the Revolutionary Movement in North Carolina, 1765–1776: The Administrations of Governor William Tryon and Governor Josiah Martin." Master's thesis, University of Wisconsin, 1963.

Schlesinger, Arthur Meier. *The Colonial Merchants and the American Revolution, 1763–1776.* New York: Frederick Ungar, 1957.

_____. *Prelude to Independence: The Newspaper War on Britain, 1764–1776.* New York: Knopf, 1958.

Scott, Kenneth. "Counterfeiting in Colonial North Carolina." *North Carolina Historical Review* 34 (1957): 467–82.

Seccombe, Thomas. "William Tryon." In *Dictionary of National Biography,* edited by Leslie Stephen and Sidney Lee, 19:1203–4. 22 vols. London: Oxford University Press, 1921–22.

Sheridan, Richard B. "The West Indian Antecedents of Josiah Martin, Last Royal Governor of North Carolina." *North Carolina Historical Review* 54 (1977): 253–70.

Shy, John. "The American Revolution: The Military Conflict Considered as a Revolutionary War." In *Essays on the American Revolution,* edited by Stephen

G. Kurtz and James H. Hutson. Chapel Hill: University of North Carolina Press, 1973.

————. *Toward Lexington: The Role of the British Army in the Coming of the American Revolution*. Princeton: Princeton University Press, 1965.

Skaggs, Marvin Lucian. *North Carolina Boundary Disputes Involving Her Southern Line*. Chapel Hill: University of North Carolina Press, 1941.

Smelser, Marshall. *The Winning of Independence*. New York: New Viewpoints, 1973.

Smith, Justin H. *Our Struggle for the Fourteenth Colony: Canada and the American Revolution*. 2 vols. New York: Putnam's, 1907.

Smith, Page. *A New Age Begins*. 2 vols. New York: McGraw-Hill, 1976.

Smith, Paul H. *Loyalists and Redcoats: A Study in British Revolutionary Policy*. Chapel Hill: University of North Carolina Press, 1964.

Sosin, Jack M. *Agents and Merchants: British Colonial Policy and the Origins of the American Revolution, 1763–1775*. Lincoln: University of Nebraska Press, 1965.

South, Stanley A. " 'Russellborough': Two Royal Governors' Mansion at Brunswick Town." *North Carolina Historical Review* 44 (1967): 360–72.

Spindel, Donna J. "Law and Disorder: The North Carolina Stamp Act Crisis." *North Carolina Historical Review* 57 (1980): 1–16.

Steacy, Stephen C. "Cadwallader Colden: Statesman and Savant of Colonial New York." 2 vols. Ph.D. dissertation, University of Kansas, 1987.

Stokes, Durward T. "Henry Patillo in North Carolina." *North Carolina Historical Review* 44 (1967): 373–91.

————. "Thomas Hart in North Carolina." *North Carolina Historical Review* 41 (1964): 324–37.

Stokes, Isaac N. Phelps. *The Iconography of Manhattan Island, 1498–1909*. 6 vols. New York: Robert H. Dodd, 1915–28.

Stone, Richard G., Jr. "Governor William Tryon of North Carolina, 1765–1771." Master's thesis, University of North Carolina, 1962.

Stumpf, Vernon O. "Josiah Martin and His Search for Success: The Road to North Carolina." *North Carolina Historical Review* 53 (1976): 55–79.

Tarbox, Increase Niles. *Life of Israel Putnam ("Old Put"), Major-General in the Continental Army*. Boston: Lockwood, Brooks, 1876.

Taylor, H. Braughn. "The Foreign Attachment Law and the Coming of the Revolution in North Carolina." *North Carolina Historical Review* 52 (1975): 20–36.

Tebbenhoff, Edward H. "The Associated Loyalists: An Aspect of Militant Loyalism." *New-York Historical Society Quarterly* 63 (1979): 115–44.

Thomas, Peter D. G. *Lord North*. New York: St. Martin's Press, 1976.

Thompson, Charles Miner. *Independent Vermont*. Boston: Houghton Mifflin, 1942.

Tiedemann, Joseph S. "Patriots by Default: Queens County, New York, and the British Army, 1776–1783." *William and Mary Quarterly*, 3d ser., 43 (1986): 35–63.

————. "A Revolution Foiled: Queens County, New York, 1775–1776." *Journal of American History* 75 (1988): 417–44.

Tilley, Nannie May. "Political Disturbances in Colonial Granville County." *North Carolina Historical Review* 18 (1941): 339–59.

Tingley, Ralph R. "Postal Service in Colonial North Carolina." *The American Philatelist* 62 (1949): 310–12.

Trevelyan, G. O. *The American Revolution.* 4 vols. New York: Longmans, Green, 1917.

Trumbull, Jonathan. "The Conflicting Accounts of Tryon's Invasion of Norwalk." *Magazine of History, with Notes and Queries* 3 (1906): 18–28.

Upton, L. F. S. *The Loyal Whig: William Smith of New York and Quebec.* Toronto: University of Toronto Press, 1969.

Valentine, Alan. *Lord George Germain.* Oxford: Oxford University Press, 1962.

———. *Lord North.* 2 vols. Norman: University of Oklahoma Press, 1967.

Van Doren, Carl. *Benjamin Franklin.* New York: Viking Press, 1938.

———. *Secret History of the American Revolution.* New York: Viking Press, 1941.

Van Schaack, Henry C. *The Life of Peter Van Schaack, LL.D.* New York: Appleton, 1842.

Van Tyne, Claude Halstead. *The Loyalists in the American Revolution.* New York: Macmillan, 1902.

Wallace, Willard M. *Appeal to Arms: A Military History of the American Revolution.* New York: Harper and Brothers, 1951.

———. "Benedict Arnold: Traitorous Patriot." In *George Washington's Generals,* edited by George A. Billias. New York: William Morrow, 1964.

———. *Traitorous Hero: The Life and Fortunes of Benedict Arnold.* New York: Harper and Brothers, 1954.

Ward, Christopher. *The War of the Revolution.* Edited by John Richard Alden. 2 vols. New York: Macmillan, 1952.

Watson, Alan D. "The Appointment of Sheriffs in Colonial North Carolina: A Reexamination." *North Carolina Historical Review* 53 (1976): 385–98.

———. "The Ferry in Colonial North Carolina: A Vital Link in Transportation." *North Carolina Historical Review* 51 (1974): 247–60.

———. "Ordinaries in Colonial Eastern North Carolina." *North Carolina Historical Review* 45 (1968): 67–83.

Weir, Robert M. "North Carolina's Reaction to the Currency Act of 1764." *North Carolina Historical Review* 40 (1963): 183–99.

Wertenbaker, Thomas Jefferson. *Father Knickerbocker Rebels: New York City During the Revolution.* New York: Scribner's, 1948.

Wickwire, Franklin, and Mary Wickwire. *Cornwallis: The American Adventure.* Boston: Houghton Mifflin, 1970.

Willcox, William B. *Portrait of a General: Sir Henry Clinton in the War of Independence.* New York: Knopf, 1962.

Williams, Basil. *The Life of William Pitt, Earl of Chatham.* 2 vols. London: Longmans, Green, 1913.

Williamson, Hugh. *The History of North Carolina.* 2 vols. Philadelphia: Thomas Dobson, 1812.

Worseley, Stephen C. "Catholicism in Antebellum North Carolina." *North Carolina Historical Review* 60 (1983): 399–430.

Index